THE WE[illegible]OK

THE WEDDING BOOK

MIDGE GILLIES

BLOOMSBURY

To Donald and Renee Gillies, with love and in celebration of over fifty years of married life, and to Jim Kelly:

Wine comes in at the mouth
And love comes in at the eye;
That's all we know for truth
Before we grow old and die.
I lift the glass to my mouth,
I look at you, and I sigh.

W. B. Yeats, 'A Drinking Song'

First published in 1997

Bloomsbury Publishing plc
38 Soho Square
London W1V 5DF

A copy of the CIP entry for this book is available from the British Library

ISBN 0 7475 3022 X

10 9 8 7 6 5 4 3 2

Designed by Hugh Adams
Typeset by Hewer Text Composition Services, Edinburgh
Printed in Great Britain by Clays Ltd, St Ives plc

Contents

Preface

Getting married is a full-time occupation and, for a lot of people, a wedding is the biggest and most complicated event they will ever be asked to organize. The aim of this book is to provide ideas, information and shortcuts to help you plan exactly the sort of wedding you want.

It doesn't claim to tell you the right way of doing everything (often there is no *right* way), instead it lays out the main options – together with more unusual alternatives.

The book includes most aspects of wedding etiquette, since although these 'rules' can be difficult to follow in a less traditional wedding, they can also help put people at their ease in an unfamiliar situation.

I've tried to make it the sort of book I would have found useful when I was getting married, but my main aim has been to provide the information for people to pick and mix from different types of wedding so that they end up with – as near as is possible – the celebration they want.

Weddings, as much as marriages, are about compromise, but choice makes compromise easier. Hopefully this book will allow you greater choice in planning your wedding.

PART ONE
FIRST THINGS FIRST

1

Proposal and Engagement

THE PROPOSAL

ON BENDED KNEE

Whether it is intricately planned or spontaneous, something you've been expecting for months, or even years, or completely out of the blue, the moment someone asks you to marry them will be one you remember for the rest of your life – a story to be dusted down and retold to future generations.

Some people favour open-air settings. Actor Arnold Schwarzenegger proposed to his girlfriend Maria Shriver as he rowed her across a lake in Austria. In 1948 politician Tony Benn chose a park bench in Oxford to ask his wife, Caroline, to marry him and later bought the seat as a memento to keep in their garden.

For some couples, though, the idea of getting married seems to evolve rather than take the form of an old-fashioned proposal. In other cases the words 'Will you marry me?' appear too direct. Bruce Willis is said to have casually suggested to his girlfriend and fellow Hollywood star Demi Moore as they sat in the sauna, 'We could get married . . .' President Clinton is reported to have proposed to Hillary Rodham when he picked her up from the airport (their jobs had taken them to different cities) by saying, 'I bought that house you like, so you better marry me because I can't live in it by myself.'

Other proposals have been even less romantic, but just as direct. According to one story, a Scotsman took his intended for a walk in the local graveyard. Pointing at the family plot, he asked her, 'How would you fancy lying there, Jean?'

MODERN ALTERNATIVES

Although 40 per cent of people say they saw it coming (according to a survey by jewellers H. Samuel), many proposers do their best to shock. Rather than go down on bended knee they have broadcast their intentions on the electronic scoreboard at Wembley Stadium or the advertising screen at Piccadilly Circus, or sent Cupid winging round the Internet.

Others have preferred an audience of sympathetic friends. Tim, a 34-year-old Scout leader, proposed to Kate, 31, his girlfriend of ten years, on stage at the end of a gang show in Sheffield and in front of 200 people. Sue, a television announcer, took to the air for her proposal. She waited until the end of the 10.35 p.m. news bulletin to pop the question. Her boyfriend, Mat, was watching at home and fell off his chair in shock, but later accepted.

In other cases the proposal has been a strictly private affair. Tim, a 25-year-old shoe designer from Somerset, had the words, 'Sandra, will you marry me?' tattooed on his bottom for his 22-year-old girlfriend, a teacher, to find. She gave her consent using the same method.

Henry proposed to his girlfriend, Kim, during the eighteen hours the two round-the-world travellers from South London spent clinging to a single lifejacket in shark-infested waters after their ferry sank off Indonesia. 'Nobody can be closer now. We are tied together for life. After this we'll get married,' the 34-year-old said. Kim, who is the same age, managed to mutter 'Okay' through lips swollen by salt water.

Jimmy and Kathleen had a less traumatic but equally watery proposal. While they were snorkelling in Mexico Kathleen found a wooden box nestling near a coral reef. When they brought it to the surface they discovered it contained coins, seashells, old photographs and a tiny box. Jimmy persuaded Kathleen to open the box. Inside she found a diamond ring and a note saying: 'Kathleen, will you marry me? Jimmy.'

A JOB FOR THE BOYS?

Only about 30 per cent of men would say yes if their girlfriend proposed to them, according to research by cosmetics firm Fabergé. Some of the most public proposals by women have later ended in the couple splitting up – although this may be due to the public nature of the proposal rather than the fact that it flouted convention.

Two of the ones that got away:

- Air hostess Sandra proposed to her boyfriend, officeworker Nigel, via a satellite link arranged by Radio 1 when she was on the Empire State Building and he was in Birmingham. He accepted but later changed his mind.
- Sally hired a Cessna light aircraft and then took her boyfriend out for a walk to catch a glimpse of the banner being trailed by the plane which bore the words, 'Peter, will you marry me?' He initially accepted, but they split up a few months later.

But not every female proposal is doomed. Jessica grew tired of waiting for her partner, Mike, to pop the question and so painted a bright red proposal on the side of the van at the milk depot where he worked in North London. Michael made her 'do it properly' by getting down on one knee and then asking his father for permission. They married soon afterwards.

Strict rules about rank meant that Queen Victoria and the present Queen almost certainly had to do the asking. Zsa Zsa Gabor is also reported to have proposed to each of her nine husbands.

LEAP YEAR SPECIALS

Traditionally, 29 February is the one day in 1,461 when women have the chance to propose. The custom was started by Margaret, Queen of Scots who introduced a law to that effect in 1288. If the man refused he was fined £100.

Although the law was revoked, the tradition persists, and leap years always bring a flurry of female proposals. The fine may no longer be enforceable, but one alternative penalty suggests that the man must buy a silk dress for his disappointed suitor.

THE WINNING FORMULA

Research shows that most women would like to be proposed to over dinner and that this is also the setting the majority of men would choose. But most couples probably wouldn't like to think their proposal was a carbon copy of thousands of others.

In the end, timing is probably the most important element – not of the proposal but of the relationship. If the time is right the answer will be yes, and even if the answer is no, countless suitors have found persistence pays off.

ENGAGEMENT

(See also page 93, 'Engagement rings')

The period between deciding you're going to get married and going public with the news should be savoured. Unless you decide to elope, it will be the only time when your wedding plans will involve just the two of you. Use the interlude to thrash out important decisions: the sort of ceremony you want; who you will ask to fill the key roles of bridesmaids and best man or woman; people you will and won't invite; and when you will get married.

The idea of 'becoming engaged' grew out of the contractually binding idea of betrothal. For some people 'getting engaged' today simply marks a separate stage in their relationship – a public acknowledgement of their intention to get married sometime in the future, when they feel ready or when they can afford it. (See page 14, 'Timing') Others miss out the engagement part altogether, either because the announcement that they are getting married means just that and they want to get on with it as quickly as possible, or because the idea of being engaged seems outdated, or even insulting.

You may want to celebrate your decision with a party – some couples even use the event to make the official announcement. This can be a good way of introducing people who will meet again at the wedding and of bringing both families together in a relaxed atmosphere.

Tip You don't have to restrict the guest list to people you plan to invite to the wedding, but casting your net too wide can sometimes raise hopes among friends who won't be asked. If you want a big engagement party, make it clear that your wedding will be a much smaller affair.

BREAKING THE NEWS

(see also Chapter 11, 'Parents, Friends and Family')

Announcing that you are getting married is one of the few times in your life when you will be the bearer of news that is almost certain to put a smile on the face of everyone, from the person you buy your newspaper from to your closest friends and family. But, since it is such a momentous announcement, take care about the order in which you tell people – both friends and family can feel hurt if they don't think they've been informed soon enough.

When you're deciding the order in which to tell people, bear in mind who can keep a secret and who can't, and try to have a bottle of something sparkling to hand to fill the few seconds it may take for the news to sink in. If you suspect your announcement will produce a dramatic reaction, you might want to ensure that you don't make it in a public place, or that the person you are telling isn't operating heavy machinery at the time.

Parents should be told first (unless you have children of your own) and traditionally the bride's parents are the first to know. Only you will be able to judge whether it is a good idea to make the announcement simultaneously to both sets of parents (whether they are still married to each other or not). Bear in mind, though, that parents' speech patterns can switch into stream of consciousness mode when they're presented with such dramatic news. A parent who lets their imagination run away with them may send their counterpart into shock with talk of tabernacle choirs, next-door-neighbours as bridesmaids and a guest list of distant relatives from Canada.

It is no longer seen as essential to ask the bride's father for his permission to marry, but some parents still enjoy being asked (even though their consent may be of only academic interest). If you decide to ask for permission, be prepared for it to be refused. One over-protective father told his son-in-law that he thought the age difference between him and his daughter (seven years) was too great. The groom was reduced to saying politely, but firmly, that he was sorry he felt like that but that they would be getting married anyway. They have been happily married for over thirty years.

Siblings, grandparents and close family usually follow next in the pecking order. Once you start telling friends, try to let them all know as soon as possible and in person. Don't forget to tell other important people, such as your boss, so that they can become used to the idea that you will want some time off.

WAYS TO AVOID GIVING THE GAME AWAY

- Don't leave bridal magazines lying around.
- Don't demonstrate a sudden interest in choral music.
- Don't tell the vicar first – he or she may tell your parents by mistake.
- Don't ask your mother what sort of condition her wedding dress is in.

- Don't get caught studying yourself with a veil-like tea-towel pinned to your head – if your parents don't guess you're planning a wedding they'll be convinced you're set on taking Holy Orders.
- Don't, in December, ask when the Cup Final is.
- Don't inquire how much your sister's wedding cost.

THE DIFFICULT ONES

- **Former partners**: You may have fantasized about telling an ex that you have found someone you want to spend the rest of your life with (who isn't them) but don't fool yourself into believing that you will be able to predict their reaction. Unless communications have broken down completely, it is courteous for them to hear the news from you. If they are likely to feel upset, you could save their pride by telling them through a note or over the phone, rather than in person.
- **Children**: The marriage of a parent can be a bewildering and even threatening time for children – even if the parents are marrying each other. Children need to be told as soon as possible and the reasons for the decision explained. They should be made to feel that the marriage will cement rather than undermine their position in your affections. They should also be offered the opportunity to play an important part in the ceremony.
- **Wedding cynics**: Most people will be delighted at your news, but there may be a few doubters. People who have had a bad experience of marriage – either themselves or through their parents – or those who are ideologically against the institution may at best be lukewarm. Don't take their reaction personally. If you want to defuse any ill-feeling in a flippant way, you could say you're getting married because you like the idea of having a big party. Depending on how well you know the person, you could take the time to explain why you think marriage is a good idea for you.

CASE STUDY

Paul, a 29-year-old accountant, and Clare, 31, from Colchester got married when their daughter Katherine was nearly three. Katherine was used to going to church and Paul and Clare explained to her that there was going to be a very important service in which the three of them would be the centre of attention. Katherine was the only little bridesmaid and she could talk of nothing other than her dress and flowers. Although she was too young to understand the full significance of the service, Paul and Clare believe she realized that the three of them were celebrating something quite special.

GOING PUBLIC

The singer once known as Prince used the Internet to announce his plans to marry bellydancer Mayte Garcia, and as the thirty-minute service progressed a psychedelic image of the couple surrounded by purple patches and manacles unravelled on computer screens. 'Welcome to the dawn, coincidence or fate?' the Internet page announced.

For those still stuck on the sliproad of the Information Superhighway, a formal newspaper announcement is still the most popular choice. The pages of *The Times*, the *Telegraph* and the *Independent* all carry announcements, as do local newspapers. A typical notice might read something like:

Mr A. P. T. Kelly and Miss L. B. Elliott

The engagement is announced between Asa, son of Mr and Mrs Jason Kelly of Brighton, East Sussex, and Lucy, daughter of Mr and Mrs Christopher Elliott of Ealing, West London.

It is up to you if parents include their first names or just initials, and you can also say whether you are their only son or daughter, or the youngest or eldest. If parents have divorced the announcement should say something like:

. . . son of Mr Jason Kelly of Brighton and Mrs Doris Kelly of Exeter.

Or (if the mother has remarried):

. . . son of Mr Jason Kelly of Brighton and Mrs Doris McNaughton of Dublin.

If one parent is dead:

. . . son of the late Mr Jason Kelly.

A less formal wording might be:

Chris and Sue Elliott are delighted to announce the engagement of their daughter Lucy to . . .

Traditionally, the bride's family pays for any announcement.

Although you might cringe at so public a way of letting everyone know you're getting married, announcements can provide the opportunity of stating whether or not you intend to change your name (see page 246, 'What's in a name'):

Paul Denton and Jean Everett are pleased to announce that they are getting married on 27 August 1997 and would like friends and colleagues to know that Jean will be keeping her own surname.

Many publications are eager to carry news of weddings (usually for free, or for a nominal sum). Consider:

- College or school magazines
- Staff newsletters
- Club or association publications

Tip Don't be too precise about where you live as you will be deluged with firms offering wedding services, from photographers to cake-makers.

PRENUPTIAL AGREEMENTS

While some people view the very idea of an agreement as unromantic and indicative of a lack of trust, others find it has a practical side.

Prenuptial agreements can help clarify how each of you feels about marriage and what you expect of it – for example if you want children, when, and how many you will aim to have and who will look after them. Although these agreements are common abroad, lawyers are divided about how much legal weight they would carry in this country.

CASE STUDY

Roger, 39, who has been married twice before and works for a Government defence research centre, and Samantha, 31, who was married briefly once before and works as a computer engineer, live in New Mexico. Their prenup included promises to:

- *Engage in healthy sex three to five times a week.*
- *Buy supreme unleaded fuel (Chevron) and never allow the tank to be less than half full.*
- *Make themselves available for discussions fifteen to thirty minutes each day.*
- *Stay one car's length away from other cars for every 10 m.p.h.*

2

FINDING THE RIGHT TONE

DISCOVERING YOUR WEDDING VISION

Planning a wedding means reaching decisions on a whole range of things to which so far in your life you haven't given a second thought, but now assume awesome significance. Will your bouquet contain gypsophila or gerbera; your dress be A-line or antique; the food be finger buffet or four-course sit-down?

Finding a vision for the day can help you tackle each decision as it crops up. A word or phrase that describes the atmosphere you want can provide a touchstone to turn to when you have difficulty making your mind up. You may want a day that is joyous, elegant, rustic, relaxed, sophisticated, spiritual, colourful or off-beat – or a combination of any of these.

Or a wedding that appears in the movies might capture the style you're aiming for: the high spirits of the celebrations in *Sense and Sensibility*, the effortless elegance of Barbara Stanwyck and Henry Fonda in the screwball comedy *The Lady Eve* or the rural idyll of *Robin Hood, Prince of Thieves*.

Books can also provide inspiration. In Stella Gibbons's *Cold Comfort Farm* even the bull, Big Business, has a celebratory garland of wallflowers and geraniums draped round his neck when the eccentric farming family the Starkadders host a wedding for their youngest daughter. Peonies decorate the table laden with a feast of home-grown foods and wreaths of flowers hang from the rafters at a celebration that is the epitome of the relaxed, rural wedding.

Gustave Flaubert's description of the wedding of Madame Bovary is, by comparison, much more sophisticated. A pastrycook was taken on especially to make the desserts and tarts and his wedding cake drew cries of admiration:

> Finally, at the very top, which depicted a green meadow complete with rocks, lakes composed of jam and little boats made out of nut-shells, was a small cupid balancing himself on a chocolate swing,

the two uprights of which were topped with natural rosebuds by way of finials.

Real-life weddings can also help set a standard to aim for, even if much of the detail will be beyond your reach: the fairy-tale quality of Grace Kelly's Monaco wedding; or the outrageousness of Madonna's cliff-top ceremony; or Christine Brinkley's ski-wear-clad service.

Alternatively, ask yourselves how you have spent your most enjoyable birthdays – did you go for a picnic with close family and friends; spend the night 'clubbing'; or go to a smart restaurant? Think back over the weddings you've been to: what did you like and dislike about each of them?

WHEN VISIONS CLASH

Discovering that you each have quite different views needn't be an insuperable problem. Try to divide the wedding day into different compartments and decide which is best suited to the sort of vision each of you has.

CASE STUDY

Annette had always wanted a church wedding and her parents were keen for her to marry in their local Catholic church which was next to a multi-storey car park in North London. Her fiancé, Paul, had no religious faith and certainly didn't want a city wedding. As he realized how important a Catholic wedding was to Annette and her family he agreed, but as a compromise they married in a country church outside Stroud where he had grown up and where his mother still lived. The reception was held in a hotel set in acres of parkland.

THE ENTHUSIASM GAP

Finding that one of you is not at all interested in the minutiae of the wedding while the other is obsessed with everything from bouquets to bridesmaids' bracelets can lead to conflict.

Don't take it personally if your partner's enthusiasm doesn't match yours but try to find something they can take an interest in. Not only will this lighten the pressure on you, it will also reduce the risk of them feeling excluded. You may start off insisting you don't mind making most of the arrangements but by the time you realize you've taken on too much you could be seething with resentment.

STRESSBUSTER

Often it is the groom whose enthusiasm for bonbonnières and buttonholes starts to wane first. If this is the case, encourage him to take on an aspect of the wedding that he can make his own: finding and hiring the cars, signing up a marquee company, planning the fireworks, choosing the drinks, even commissioning a cake (especially if you're having a less traditional design). Once he's agreed to deal with a specific area, force yourself to stop worrying about it.

TIMING

The average engagement lasts about six months (the longest on record lasted sixty-seven years) but much will depend on practicalities such as saving up for the wedding and giving guests enough notice. Beware too long a run-up which may leave you exhausted before you've even sent out the first invitation.

Other factors to bear in mind:

- The expected arrival of any new babies.
- Any guests travelling from abroad.
- The PMT danger zone.
- Religious festivals during which weddings aren't normally held.
- Work commitments, such as a sales conference, the end of a project, a month that is traditionally very busy.
- Seasonal health considerations, such as hay fever or bronchitis.
- Anniversaries – of either happy or sad occasions.
- Sporting dates – this could be the one year your team reaches the final.

PROS AND CONS OF SEASONS

Spring

Pros: More flowers in season, wild blossoms available and countryside looking fresher.

Cons: Weather and light unpredictable.

Summer

Pros: More flowers in season, greater choice of dresses. Better chance of good weather. Honeymoon at home warmer. Open-top car less of a risk. Anniversary always in summer. School holidays. Children can run around outside.

Cons: Most popular time of year so venues and professionals likely to become booked up early. Flowers, food, guests and couple may show signs of wilting. Greater danger of food poisoning. Bad for hay fever sufferers.

Autumn

Pros: Unusual foliage and flowers available. Church may be decorated for harvest thanksgiving.

Cons: Fewer flowers in season, weather cooler and wetter.

Winter

Pros: More unusual foliage available. Candles in church can produce romantic lighting. Opportunity to make your mark as 'winter bride'. Heavier materials such as damask, moiré and velvet viable, and romantic cloaks and fake fur. Greater scope in menu and less risk of food poisoning.

Cons: Fewer flowers in season. Good weather and natural light limited. Guests may feel cold.

TIME OF DAY

Morning to late afternoon

Pros: Substantial food not expected. More chance for bride and bridegroom to chat to guests. Couple will have time to catch flight for honeymoon. Enough daylight to use hot air balloon.

Cons: Time may drag if you plan an all-day celebration. Fireworks not possible during daylight. In the morning, pollen counts peak between about 10 a.m. and noon.

Afternoon

Pros: Guests will have more time to arrive. Fireworks possible. Bride and bridegroom will be in less of a rush. Less waiting around before reception begins. Pollen peaks at between 6 p.m. and 9 p.m. (earlier in the country), by which time you'll probably be inside (in the city the evening peak is greater than the morning).

Cons: Time will pass very quickly. Guests may expect an evening meal. More time for nerves to build up in the morning. Departure by balloon harder to arrange.

MULTIPLE WEDDINGS

Sharing a wedding with one or several other couples can work out cheaper. You'll only need to decorate the church once, for example, and if you're all from the same family or have friends in common you'll save money on the guestlist.

You need to be sure, though, that you'll enjoy sharing the limelight and that planning a wedding with a friend or relative will bring you closer rather than causing a life-long rift. There's always the chance, too, that a multiple wedding will mean multiple rows between families.

(See page 115, 'A lavish affair')

SUPERSTITIONS

Monday for wealth
Tuesday for health
Wednesday best day of all
Thursday for losses
Friday for crosses
And Saturday, no luck at all.

May has been seen as an unlucky month for weddings for hundreds of years – perhaps because it was the time of the year when the Romans celebrated the festival of the goddesses of chastity and the feast of the dead. Queen Victoria believed so fervently in the saying, 'Marry in May, rue the day' that she forbade her children to hold their weddings then.

Folklore also warns, 'Marry in Lent, live to repent' and some Orthodox Churches still avoid weddings in the run-up to Easter. Vicars also used to frown on Whitsun and Advent weddings but nowadays the timing of church weddings has more to do with trying to avoid congestion than with the ecclesiastical calendar.

THEMED WEDDINGS

PUTTING ON THE STYLE

Adopting an historical or literary theme, or asking guests to come dressed in a particular colour, can help make your wedding memorable.

WACKY WEDDINGS

One couple asked guests to dress up as characters from *Alice in Wonderland* for their register office wedding; another couple marrying in a castle chose a Tudor theme. Horror fans have been known to dress up as vampires, order a cake in the shape of a coffin and honeymoon in Transylvania.

Scarlett O'Hara and Rhett Butler costumes and originals from *Four Weddings and a Funeral* are available to hire from theatrical costumiers Angels & Bermans in London (see also page 87, 'Finding the right fit, and hiring suits').

SECOND TIME ROUND

If you've been married before, a theme will ensure that this wedding is completely different from the last.

INVITATIONS

For most of your guests, the invitation will be their first indication of the sort of wedding they will be attending. A stiff, white card with gold lettering will lead them to expect a formal affair, a naive drawing of a bride and bridegroom or a message to come 'dressed for barn dancing' will set the scene for a much more relaxed occasion.

The wording of the invitation can take several forms, depending on who is hosting the day, the marital status of the parents, and the type of wedding. More and more couples are adapting the traditional words or writing their own.

The names of the guests are usually written by hand (ask a friend with attractive writing to help out) in the top left-hand corner or in the space provided in the text. Remember to include children's names if you are inviting the entire family.

Also remember to include 'RSVP' or 'Please reply to' followed by the address (and telephone number if you think it would help).

Traditionally, the envelopes of formal invitations should be addressed to the wife alone, for example Mrs Robert Smith.

If guests are expected to wear evening dress (which is common at some Jewish and Asian weddings, especially if they are held in hotels) they should be alerted by the inclusion of the words 'Black tie' in the bottom right-hand corner of the invitation. Some guests might prefer to wear ethnic dress, in which case you can say 'Black tie or national dress'.

SAMPLE INVITATIONS

INVITATION FROM THE BRIDE'S PARENTS

1

Mr and Mrs Robert Smith

request the pleasure of your company

at the marriage of their daughter

Zoë Helen

to/with

Mr Richard Paul Dyer

at St Michael's Church, Brantham, Suffolk

on Saturday, 22 June 1996

at 3.00 o'clock

and afterwards at
The White Horse Hotel, Ipswich

or 2

Mr and Mrs Robert Smith
request the pleasure of the company of
———— (guest's name)
at the marriage of their daughter
Zoë Helen
to/with
Mr Richard Paul Dyer, etc.

or 3

Mr and Mrs Robert Smith
would like you to join them
to celebrate the marriage of their daughter, etc.

WIDOWED PARENT AS HOST

Mrs Jean Smith
requests the pleasure of your company . . .
her daughter

REMARRIED MOTHER AS HOST

Mr and Mrs Fergus Styles
request the pleasure of your company . . .
her daughter

REMARRIED FATHER AS HOST

Mr and Mrs Robert Smith

request the pleasure of your company . . .

his daughter

DIVORCED PARENTS AS HOST

Mr Robert Smith and Mrs Claire Todd

request the pleasure of your company

INVITATION FROM THE BRIDE AND BRIDEGROOM

Miss Zoë Helen Smith and Mr Richard Paul Dyer

request the pleasure of your company

at their marriage

at St Michael's Church, Brantham, Suffolk

on Saturday, 22 June 1996

at 3.00 o'clock

and afterwards at

The White Horse Hotel, Ipswich

For alternative wording see parents' invitations above.

RECEPTION ONLY INVITATION

You can use one of the three forms mentioned above: Mr and Mrs Robert Smith request the pleasure of your company . . .; Mr and Mrs Robert Smith request the pleasure of the company of . . .; or Mr and Mrs Robert Smith would like you to join them . . .

Follow this with: 'at an evening reception to celebrate the marriage of their daughter Zoë Helen to Mr Richard Paul Dyer at The White Horse Hotel, Ipswich on Saturday, 22 June 1996 at 7.30 p.m.'

Or: 'at an evening reception to be held at . . . to celebrate the marriage of their daughter. . .'

Or: 'at The White Horse Hotel on . . . to celebrate the marriage of . . .'

It may also avoid any ill-feeling to include an explanation such as: 'Owing to the size of St Michael's Church/Didcot register office it is unfortunately only possible to ask a few guests to the service. We hope you will understand.'

SPECIAL CIRCUMSTANCES

- If the wedding is being hosted by someone other than the couple or their parents – for example, a godparent – their name and the bride's surname are included, e.g. 'Robert Wright requests the pleasure of the company of ——— at the marriage of his niece Victoria Kennett.'
- At double weddings the name of the elder bride appears first.
- Guests can be invited to a celebration after an overseas wedding by using part of the traditional invitation but adding a brief explanation: 'Mr and Mrs John Philips request the pleasure of your company at a reception at . . . following their marriage in Thailand on Wednesday, 8 May 1996.'
- Some invitations, particularly those from Asian families, include the words 'son of ———' after the groom's name.
- An invitation to a blessing can be phrased: 'Mr and Mrs Robert Smith request the pleasure of the company of ——— at the service of blessing, following the marriage of their daughter.'

CANCELLATIONS AND POSTPONEMENTS

It is up to you how much information you supply if you are forced to cancel. If there is enough time, you can write to guests or send out a printed note. A simple: 'Mr and Mrs Robert Smith announce that the marriage of their daughter Zoë Helen to Mr Richard Paul Dyer which was arranged for 22 June 1996 will not now take place/will be postponed (until).' When time is short you should telephone or ask a close friend to do this.

If the arrangements are cancelled because someone has died or is ill, you may prefer to give written notification, but if the reason is a broken engagement or pregnancy you may prefer to tell people in person.

REPLYING TO AN INVITATION

Guests should reply within three days of receipt of the invitation and a formal reply should be written in the third person, positioned in the centre of the page, and should not be signed:

> Mr and Mrs Jack Todd thank Mr and Mrs Robert Smith for their kind invitation to the wedding of their daughter Zoë Helen to Mr Richard Paul Dyer at St Michael's Church, Brantham, Suffolk on Saturday, 22 June 1996 at 3.00 o'clock and afterwards at The White Horse Hotel, Ipswich and have great pleasure in accepting/ but regret they are unable to accept.

Alternatively, many guests prefer to write a less formal letter in which they say how pleased they are about the wedding and how much they are looking forward to meeting the hosts. Parents often enjoy receiving this sort of reply since it may be their first contact with the guest and is much more personal.

BUYING INVITATIONS

There has never been so much choice: as well as formal cards you can personalize your invitation with a cartoon of the two of you; opt for a New Age design; have watermarked cards with gold tassels and an eighteenth-century colour painting of two lovers; choose a colourful beach scene; or print your invitation on a label to attach to a champagne bottle (see Stockists, page 289). Specialist card companies abound, as well as familiar names like Marks & Spencer, W.H. Smith or Paperchase, all of which have a wide selection.

Bear in mind the following when ordering:

- Shop around.
- Ask if prices include post and packaging.
- If ordering by post ask to see a sample beforehand.
- Type out your wording so there are no mistakes.
- Make sure you see a proof and ask a friend to have a good look at it. Pay special attention to place-names.

MAKING YOUR OWN

Designing your own invitations can help you stamp your mark on the day and, as most people have access to a wordprocessor, is not as difficult as it used to be. Several wordprocessing systems have wedding bells designs at the very least, or you may know someone who works in an office with a more sophisticated machine.

- One couple asked a friend to print their invitation on pink, water-marked paper they bought themselves. On the outside he printed a drawing of the church they had made by tracing its outline from a postcard. The invitation was sealed with a belted-Galloway (a cow with a black stripe round its middle common to the area of Scotland where they married) cut out of sticky paper.
- A financial journalist marrying a social worker worded his invitation so that it read like a news story about a successful merger of two companies.
- Another couple sprinkled each wedding invitation with confetti which was sealed in with a laminated covering.

MONEYSAVER

Ask any artistic friends to help you out – perhaps by drawing the building where you'll be getting married, or with sketches of you or a decorative border for the invitation. You might have other friends who like silk-screen printing or photography. High Street printers like Kall-Kwik will help you design something unusual and good stationers and art shops sell unusual papers and marker pens.

SOMETHING WACKY

Jane and Tom, who both work in advertising, used a BT voice mail system, 'Call Minder', to make it easier for guests to reply to their invitation. A telephone number was printed on a plastic card included in the invitation and when guests rang they heard a recording of Jane and Tom speaking in unison with a deliberately schmaltzy version of 'Close to You' playing in the background. Guests were asked to leave a message, and the most interesting replies were read out at the reception.

Tip The correct word is register, not registry, office.

STATIONERY CHECKLIST

Invitations
Map/directions
Order of service sheets (check with the minister before having them printed), include the choir and a few extra for unexpected guests when calculating numbers
Menu cards
Favours (see page 229, 'Bonbonnières and favours')
Seating plan
Cake boxes
Guest book
Matchbox and matchbooks
Napkin rings
Thank-you cards
RSVP

Tip Ask a friend who doesn't know the area to try to follow your written instructions. Leaving out a tiny detail can transform what is meant to be a help into a liability.

GUEST LIST

As most couples are bound by a budget it isn't always possible to invite everyone you want, and most of your friends and colleagues will appreciate that. On the other hand, deciding to exclude someone from the list when everyone else in a group has been invited is effectively drawing a line under your friends and putting them below it.

It might be better in the long run either to invite them or to take them to one side and explain the situation: numbers are extremely tight, you thought it was too far for them to travel, you hadn't known them for as long as your other friends, etc.

The same principle applies if you get to know someone during the run-up to the wedding and decide you would like to invite them at the last minute. Explain that when you were drawing up the guest list you hadn't felt you'd known them well enough, but that now you would hate them to miss the day.

CHILDREN

This can be a very emotive issue. Some friends will be deeply hurt if you don't invite their children and may not even be able to come; others will be overjoyed.

If several of your guests have big families, inviting children will push up the numbers considerably. But if you only have a few friends with children they may feel victimized if you leave their offspring off the guest list. Children also change the nature of the day – you would be unable to hold the reception in a nightclub in London's Soho, for example. On the positive side, though, children are great ice-breakers.

One option is to divide the day into parts (see below) or to explain to parents that you don't think their children would enjoy the sort of celebration you had planned. Some children, for example, would find it impossible to sit quietly in a small wedding room of a register office and registrars have been known to ask noisy children to leave since it is one of the legal requirements of a wedding that the vows exchanged should be heard clearly. (See also page 233, 'Keeping children happy'.)

TRICKY GUESTS

- **Ex-lovers or partners**: One theory is that you should invite them, but that they should decline. This seems a bit of a risk. Instead, discuss with your partner what to do. Some exes have become such good friends that it would seem ridiculous to exclude them. TV and radio personality Kenny Everett, for example, was best man at his wife's second marriage. (See also page 8, 'The difficult ones'.)
- **Separated or divorced guests**: If you're still friends with both sides you should invite them both – but tell them you'll be doing this.

INVITING GUESTS TO DIFFERENT PARTS OF THE DAY

This can work very well as long as guests don't feel they've been put through some grading process. Most people accept that family and very close friends such as the best man or woman and bridesmaids should be invited to an intimate wedding breakfast. But inviting some guests to this and others simply to a disco with no food might cause resentment.

When deciding how to divide the day, bear in mind the following:

- Never invite someone just to the service.
- Inviting some people to an intimate dinner may mean they will be emotionally out of synch with guests who join them for a disco held later in the day. To avoid this you could even hold the different celebrations on different days.
- If you plan a very small family get-together followed by a larger celebration, consider what guests will do between the service and the evening reception. Make sure they have been introduced to other guests who live nearby or know where there is a pub or café.

CHOOSING ATTENDANTS

(See also Chapter 10)

Your best man or woman, ushers, bridesmaids and pageboys will gaze out of your wedding photos for the rest of your life, so make sure you choose them with care. You may decide to ask someone to be your best man or best woman simply because they are your best friend. This is fine so long as you don't expect them to change character for the day and become something they may not be – the world's best public speaker, a born diplomat, or someone with the organizational skills of a sergeant major. On the other hand, many best men or women rise to the occasion and surprise even themselves.

BRIDESMAIDS

You may view bridesmaids as an optional extra, but don't expect the rest of your friends and family to be as relaxed about the subject. For many little girls the chance to dress up in tulle or taffeta and parade in front of admiring guests represents the apogee of their childhood dreams, and they will feel no compunction about demanding that they (and perhaps their best friend) fulfil the role. Parents can be equally unreasonable and see an invitation for their child to be a bridesmaid as an indisputable right.

One aunt of the bride refused to accept that her daughter could not be a bridesmaid and the child turned up at the wedding in an exact replica of the dress worn by the official bridesmaids. At this point the couple decided that she deserved to be given a special role – for persistence if nothing else.

Make sure you have convincing reasons ready as to why applicants for the role of bridesmaid need not apply: you've decided not to have any bridesmaids at all; you want a very low-key wedding; you're trying to keep costs to a minimum; if you ask them someone else will feel left out; there's simply not enough room. 'Serial bridesmaids' can sometimes be put off by reminding them of the superstition: 'Three times the bridesmaid, never the bride.'

When choosing young attendants, bear in mind how other children will react to their elevated position, and how well the chosen ones will behave on the day. Are they prone to tantrums; will they insist on only wearing cotton; will they steal the limelight? If they are teenagers, will they refuse to wash their hair and sulk all day?

ATTENDANTS' OUTFITS

(see also Chapter 6)

Take into account your bridesmaids' colourings, their fashion preferences and the overall look of the wedding. Grown-up bridesmaids might feel more comfortable in a suit, or you could buy the material and ask them to choose a style they would prefer. Little bridesmaids can be just as fashion-conscious and you should ask their parents if there are any materials (such as 'prickly' lace) or styles (anything too tightly fitting) that they won't wear. Remember, too, that children change shape fast and a final fitting near the day is vital.

OTHER FRIENDS

Don't imagine that, just because they're adults, friends won't sulk if they feel they've been left out. One woman was so incensed at not being asked to be a bridesmaid that she pretended to be the bride and rang up the reception, vicar, florist and band to cancel the arrangements.

Bad feeling can be avoided by giving friends a special role in the day, or by asking their advice over important decisions.

SPECIAL ROLES

Witness (you need two and they must be over 18 years old or 16 in Scotland)
In church: reading a lesson, helping with communion, saying (and/or writing) a prayer, leading responses
Singing or performing at the service or reception
Usher (see page 135, 'The role of the ushers')

Driving the car
Giving the bride away (see Chapter 11)
Designing the invitation or other stationery (see page 23, 'Making your own')
Making or icing the cake (see Chapter 13, 'Flowers')
Arranging flowers or making the bridal bouquet

SUGGESTED THANK-YOU PRESENTS

- **For bridesmaids**: Bible or other book, cross or other piece of jewellery, decorative box, jack-in-the-box, hobby horse, picture, puppet, doll's house furniture.
- **For pageboys**: Football or football accessories. (See bridesmaids above for further suggestions.)
- **For men**: Cufflinks, tie, waistcoat, picture, book, picture frame, hip flask, grooming kit, business-card holder, fountain pen.
- **For women**: Earrings, brooch, vase, candlestick, decorative plate. (See men above for further suggestions.)

3
GIFTS

Deciding who buys you what might seem the least of your worries when you've got a wedding to arrange. But you may start to change your mind when the third cut-glass, single-stemmed rose vase arrives from an aunt you didn't know you had.

Some people, and despite your protestations that you have everything you need, may feel cheated if they are not allowed to buy you a gift. Remember, choosing a present is a pleasure and people can be incredibly generous – it's a shame if that generosity is misplaced because someone doesn't know what sort of thing would suit your needs and tastes. Or you may grow to like something which someone has given you, simply because it reminds you of them.

Tip Buying a present with a credit card can offer some protection if it is damaged or proves faulty. Check with your credit card issuer for details.

THE LIST

The concept of drawing up a list of the items you would like to receive is now widely accepted. It can be a practical way of guiding people who don't know you very well or who aren't aware of how well stocked your home is. Most stores will provide you with a printed note or card to slip into invitations which says something like, 'Should you wish to make use of a wedding list one is held at . . .', or you can simply wait for people to ask you or your parents if there is an official list.

Firms such as the Wedding List Company will, usually for a fee, help you to compile a more personal and unusual choice that is not limited to one shop (see Stockists, page 284).

THE HOME-MADE LIST

Use the following pages to help you draw up your own master list which you can keep yourself or ask a relative or friend to take charge of. Simply tick off the items when a guest chooses one or more and write their name or initials next to the entry.

SHOP LISTS

More and more nationwide chains, such as John Lewis, Debenhams, Habitat, Argos and Marks & Spencer, have introduced a gift service. If your guests are far-flung, a chain store might be a good idea so that people can see what they're buying or simply purchase a gift token if they can't make up their mind. The list normally remains open for a few weeks after the wedding.

The shop will usually deliver gifts free of charge or wedding guests can pick them up themselves. Some shops offer interest-free credit to allow you to buy anything left on the list.

STRESSBUSTER

Wandering round compiling your 'bride's list' should be a pleasurable experience – you've been let loose in a sweet shop and someone else is picking up the bill – so don't rush it. Try to complete the list together and use it as a romantic interlude in which to plan your future home.

POINTS TO BEAR IN MIND

- Choose gifts in a wide range of prices.
- Consider colour schemes in your home.
- Remember you will have to live with any whimsical choices, like an orange fun-fur footstool.
- If a particular gift is aimed at one of you, include something suitable for the other.
- Include a few extravagant items you would never buy for yourself.
- Ask about delivery and make sure this won't take place while you're on honeymoon.

Tip An unusual design may stay in stock for one season only which could make adding to a dinner set, for example, problematic in future years. If you're worried about this, check to find out where the manufacturer is based.

THINGS YOU CAN NEVER HAVE TOO MANY OF

You may decide against a list, but it's a good idea to have a standby mini-list for persistent friends and relatives who want suggestions.

- White towels.
- White sheets – state size and type.
- Alcohol – specify wine or spirits.
- Drinking glasses – wine or tumblers.
- Garden plants.
- Gift tokens from your favourite shop.

CASH

At some African weddings it is traditional for guests to slip money under the tablecloth in front of the bride and bridegroom at the reception. It is seen as rude to check how much you have amassed until after the guests have left, but some couples find the suspense too great to bear and take a surreptitious look. At Greek wedding receptions money is pinned to the bride and groom during the dancing (see page 238, 'Dancing').

Asking for money can be awkward, but in a lot of cases cash is the only thing that's really wanted. A financial gift can be made more personal if it is linked to a specific item. This is how one couple phrased their request (which they included on a piece of paper slipped in with the invitation):

> As Jane and Tony both bought their own flats some time ago they are fortunate enough to have most things they need for their home together and have decided against a wedding list. They hope no one will feel obliged to buy them a present, but if anyone still wants to mark the occasion they might want to help them save up for rugs and carpets for their new flat.

TAX TIPS

In Britain, the following wedding gifts are free from inheritance tax:

- Each parent can give £5,000.
- Each grandparent (or great-grandparent) £2,500.
- Anyone else £1,000.
- The bride and bridegroom can give each other £2,500 before they are married (in addition to annual gift allowances).

SOMETHING DIFFERENT

Even if you have everything you could wish for, you may still recognize that your guests will want to give you a present. One solution is to choose a theme, or give people certain guidelines so that they have the scope to spend as much or as little money as they like. These 'rules' can also lead to more imaginative choices.

Sue and Gerry stipulated that all gifts must be second-hand. This gave people the chance to trawl through junk shops and jumble sales for something inexpensive but unusual; to choose a personal possession of their own; or to buy an antique if they preferred.

Another couple asked people to plant a tree for them – a long-lasting gift which also offers a wide price range – and one bride and bridegroom requested that guests should buy them old 75-r.p.m. records.

EPHEMERAL GIFTS

A gift that is as fleeting as the wedding day, but which creates an experience to remember for the rest of your life, can make an unusual alternative:

- Balloon ride.
- Weekend in a top hotel.
- Theatre season ticket.
- Residential cookery course for both of you (perhaps as part of your honeymoon or a wedding anniversary).

- Donation to a charity.
- Bet (see case study below).

The company Red Letter Days specializes in unusual gifts (see Stockists, page 284).

WACKY WEDDING LIST

Alice and Terry, who married in Dublin, decided that a wedding list of bets would make a change. Terry drew up a wish list (mostly connected with sporting events) which guests could choose from and punters were allowed to suggest their own bet. The couple received any profits from the flutters – although winnings were modest. The largest bet was £300 on Chelsea reaching the top six of the Premier Football League and the most successful was for the couple's firstborn to be a boy. Alice and Terry had twins but the first to arrive was male.

THE SHOWER

In America girlfriends of the bride throw parties where they shower her with gifts. The parties, and the gifts, usually follow a theme: kitchen shower (guests bring cooking utensils); a pink shower in which all presents are of that colour; a pantry shower (all the gifts are edible); a round-the-clock shower (a certain time is written on the invitation and an appropriate present should be brought – 9 a.m. and the gift might be a set of egg cups, or 6 p.m. and the present might be a cocktail shaker).

THANK-YOUS

In the long run it is less painful (and more courteous) to write thank-you notes as you receive your gifts. That way you will have time to produce something more personal and it will be less daunting than the prospect of writing fifty letters when you return from your honeymoon. People will be anxious to know that you have received their present and many guests will feel aggrieved if they have to wait months for an acknowledgement.

Try to share out the letter-writing duties between you. Swap guests so that you each write to the other's family and friends. It can be less demanding to write to someone you don't know well and they will appreciate the contact.

If you find letter-writing difficult you could send out a note or card – but try to include a few significant lines about the gift.

STRESSBUSTER

One couple who kept putting off writing their thank-you letters had a photo of them being showered with confetti printed on to cards which they sent out to guests with personal, handwritten messages inside.

Tip Use a notebook to keep a list of presents you receive which aren't on your official list.

GIFT LISTS

HOMEMAKER LIST

	Size	Colour	Style/Make	Quantity	From
Linen					
Bath-mat set					
Bedspread					
Blankets					
Duvet					
Duvet cover					
Eiderdown					
Pillow-cases					
Pillows					
Sheets					
Table-cloths					
Tea-towels					
Towels					
Valance					
China					
Butter dish					
Cereal bowls					

	Size	Colour	Style/Make	Quantity	From
Coffee cups and saucers					
Coffee pot					
Cream jug					
Dessert dishes and bowls					
Dinner plates					
Dinner service:					
25-cm/10-in plates					
22.5-cm/9-in plates					
20-cm/8-in plates					
15-cm/6-in plates					
Egg cups					
Egg storer					
Everyday china set					
Milk jug					
Mugs					
Oval dishes					
Oven-to-table ware					
Sauce-boat					
Soup bowls					
Soup tureen					
Sugar bowl					
Tea/Coffee service					
Tea cups and saucers					
Tea plates					
Teapot					
Vegetable dishes					

Cutlery

Canteen of cutlery
Fish knives and forks
Pastry forks
Serving spoons
Steak knives
Teaspoons

Glassware

Brandy goblets
Champagne glasses
Crystal vase

	Size	Colour	Style/Make	Quantity	From
Decanters					
Liqueur glasses					
Red wine glasses					
Tumblers					
Water glasses					
Water jug					
White wine glasses					
General					
Alarm clock					
Bedside lamp					
Bathroom scales					
Books					
Bookends					
Bucket					
Clothes-horse					
Coffee table					
Cushions					
Candlesticks					
Coasters					
Fruit bowl					
Hat/coat stand					
Linen basket					
Luggage					
Mirror					
Mug tree					
Photo frame					
Pictures					
Plant pots					
Roof rack					
Tea-maker					
Tray					
Vases					
Wine-cooler					
Wine rack					
Kitchenware					
Baking tins					
Bread bin					
Bread board					
Bread knife					

	Size	Colour	Style/Make	Quantity	From
Can opener					
Casserole set					
Cheese board					
Cheese grater					
Chopping board					
Coffee grinder					
Colander					
Deep-fryer					
Electric carving knife					
Flan dish					
Fondue set					
Food processor					
Frying pan					
Garlic press					
Hot plate					
Ironing board					
Juicer					
Kitchen knives					
Kitchen scales					
Kitchen scissors					
Kitchen tool set					
Knife-sharpener					
Ladle					
Measuring jug					
Mixer					
Mixing bowls					
Napkins					
Omelette pan					
Pastry brushes					
Pedal/swing bin					
Place mats					
Pressure-cooker					
Ramekins					
Salad bowl/servers					
Salt and pepper mills					
Sandwich-maker					
Saucepan set					

	Size	Colour	Style/Make	Quantity	From
Slow cooker					
Soufflé dish					
Spaghetti jar					
Spice rack					
Storage tins/jars					
Toaster					
Trays					
Trolley					
Vegetable rack					
Wok					

Electrical

Answering machine					
Built-in hob					
Built-in oven					
Clock radio					
Coffee-maker:					
filter					
espresso					
cappuccino					
Computer					
Cooker					
Dishwasher					
Electric blanket					
Electric toothbrush					
Freezer					
Fridge					
Hairdryer					
Handheld vacuum cleaner					
Iron					
Microwave					
Personal stereo					
Phone					
Radio/cassette recorder					
Satellite system					
Tool box					
Tumble dryer					
Television					
Vacuum cleaner					

	Size	Colour	Style/Make	Quantity	From
Video recorder					
Washing machine					

Garden

Barbecue
Broom
Dustbin
Fork
Garden furniture
Gloves
Greenhouse
Hanging basket
Hoe
Hose pipe
Kneeling pad
Ladders
Lawnmower
Shed
Spade
Rainwater tub
Rake
Rotary line
Terracotta pots
Watering can
Wheelbarrow

ESTABLISHED HOUSEHOLDS

Barometer
Bird table
Bread-making machine
Climbing frame
Cookery book-rest
Fan
Fish kettle
Food mill
Footstool
Grapefruit knife
Griddle

Hammock
Meat mallet
Melon scoop
Mincer
Nutcrackers
Orange-squeezer
Pasta-making machine
Pestle and mortar
Roses or other plants
Shoe-scraper
Sun dial
Swing
Thermometer
Tongs
Towelling robes
Tree-house

FOR COUPLES WHO HAVE EVERYTHING

Body part cast (two sets of lips, for example – see Stockists, page 285)
Bust
Garden gnome
Ionizer
Personalized number plate (contact DVLA)
A star named after them (see Stockists, page 285)
Statue
Tree-house
Trampoline
Wall-hanging
Wind vane

EPICUREAN LIST

Bain-marie
Individual bread tins
Brioche mould
Chinese bamboo steaming basket
Cocktail shaker
Couscoussière
Crêpe pan

	Size	Colour	Style/Make	Quantity	From
Dariole moulds					
Grape scissors					
Jelly mould					
Mezzaluna (double-handed knife with curved blade for chopping)					
Oyster knife					
Paella pan					

GROUP PRESENTS

Authentic cappuccino machine (the full works)					
Butcher's block					
Chair					
Compact disc player					
Gazebo					
Hamper					

4

Choosing the Ceremony and Making Preliminary Preparations

See page 193, 'The Ceremony', for details of the ceremony itself.

THE CHOICE

There has never before been so much choice of where to marry – from a cave in South Wales to a country church, Caribbean island or Scottish beach. Changes to the law in England and Wales mean you no longer have to marry in a register office if you want a civil wedding but can choose from well over a thousand places, such as stately homes and castles, that are licensed to carry out weddings. Under the Act of Parliament which approved the new wedding venues, you can now also marry in any register office in England and Wales, not just the one nearest where you live.

This chapter concentrates specifically on choosing and preparing for the wedding ceremony in the Anglican and Catholic faiths, and the civil ceremony. See Chapter 17 for an account of ceremonies in other faiths.

THE FOUR MOST POPULAR CHOICES

- **Register office**: The fastest and cheapest way to get married. Although register office weddings only last about twenty minutes, the best registrars try to make the ceremony as dignified as possible. Not all register offices resemble a doctor's waiting room. Coventry's is a timber-framed medieval building, and Dudley register office, in the West Midlands, is set in parkland and features carved oak panelling.

- **Approved buildings**: Essentially the same ceremony as a register office but in more interesting surroundings and usually more expensive. There's time to linger and to make the ceremony more personal, for example by decorating the room and including longer pieces of music. If you hold the reception there you won't have to worry about losing guests on the way to the hotel. Many venues have a member of staff dedicated to organizing weddings.
- **Churches**: Wedding ceremonies don't vary greatly from faith to faith – it is usually the minister who makes the difference. A church wedding is more expensive than a civil ceremony, and different ministers have different views on marrying divorced people (see page 55, 'Church ceremonies for divorced people').
- **Abroad**: Several travel companies offer special packages which can help cut costs as your honeymoon is part of the deal. Marrying overseas can also solve rows over the guest list (see Stockists, page 279).

SORTING OUT THE RED TAPE

DOCUMENTS

Whether you are getting married in a church, a register office or another authorized building, you will need to show the superintendent registrar or the minister the following documents when 'giving notice' (see page 45, 'Civil Weddings'):

- If you have been married before, a degree absolute of divorce carrying the court's original stamp.
- A death certificate if your former spouse has died.
- In England, Wales and Northern Ireland the minimum age of marriage is 16, but proof of parental consent is necessary if either of you is under 18 (see also page 46, 'Marrying in Scotland', and page 47, 'Marrying in the Republic of Ireland').
- A birth certificate, passport or other form of identity is usually requested (photocopies aren't normally accepted).

CIVIL WEDDINGS IN ENGLAND AND WALES

- **Preliminaries**: Contact the superintendent registrar of the district where you will be getting married to book an official for your wedding, whether it will be in a register office or one of the new venues. You will find the telephone number in your local telephone directory under 'Registration of Births, Deaths and Marriages'.

  You can make a provisional booking twelve months before the ceremony, but you should confirm it within three months of the marriage date. Like churches, some register offices are much in demand. You will often have to wait four months, for example, for a Saturday wedding at Kensington and Chelsea register office, which is a favourite choice for celebrities and society weddings.
- **Notice of marriage**: You must give notice of marriage at the register office for the district where you live. There are two ways of doing this, but each must be done in person and is only valid for three months:

By certificate

- Allow twenty-two clear days before your wedding day.
- Both of you must have lived in England or Wales for at least seven days before you give notice.
- You must give notice in the district(s) where you each live. If you both live in the same district one of you can give notice for both of you, but it must be done in person.
- Twenty-one days after giving notice you must collect your Certificate of No Impediment, a legal document which means the wedding can go ahead. This must be given to the superintendent registrar of the district where the wedding will take place.

By licence (sometimes known as 'special licence')

- This is more expensive but takes only three working days, rather than twenty-two.
- One of you must have lived in a registration district for at least fifteen days before giving notice.

- Your partner only needs to be a resident of, or to be physically present in, England or Wales, on the day notice is given.

- The marriage can take place one clear day after notice is given (excluding a Sunday, Christmas Day or Good Friday). Under this method you could give notice on a Tuesday and be married on a Thursday.

APPROVED BUILDINGS – THE CHOICE

You can choose from the sublime – the Gothic splendour of Lord Byron's home at Newstead Abbey in Nottinghamshire or the thirteenth-century grandeur of Powis Castle in Wales – to the ridiculous: London Zoo, Coronation Street or a James Bond-themed nightclub. Sporting venues such as football stadiums and Sandown Park Racecourse offer a special atmosphere for fans and, usually, purpose-built catering facilities.

Points to bear in mind

- **Timing**: Some venues hold ceremonies on days when a register office is closed. Others close because of the nature of their primary business: sports venues for sporting events, schools during term time.
- **The ogle factor**: If you're getting married in a tourist venue, will you become one of the attractions?
- **The ceremony**: Will it take place in a room that's obviously part of the main building, or in a broom cupboard round the back?
- **Parking**: City attractions are sometimes short on facilities, country sites often have more room.
- **Afterwards**: Where can you take photos (on the pitch at a football ground, or by a lake at a stately home, for example); will you be able to erect a marquee and if so what will stop members of the public wandering in; will you be charged if a guest accidentally drives over a bed of roses?

MARRYING IN SCOTLAND

BEN NEVIS OR MARY QUEEN OF SCOTS' BIRTHPLACE?

Getting married north of the border has always been more straightforward (hence the popularity of Gretna Green for English couples who wanted to marry fast and with few questions asked). Ministers authorized to carry out weddings can perform the service almost anywhere, although civil weddings must take place in a register office.

The only proviso is that you must be able to provide an address where the wedding took place so that it can appear on the certificate: if you're cruising down Loch Ness the boat will have to be moored at a given point; if you're in a hot air balloon it must be tethered, and if you're in a submarine you must be near enough to an identifiable point on shore. If you're at all unsure whether your choice will be legal, the registrar will advise you.

THE FORMALITIES

Notice must be given to the registrar about four weeks before the marriage (allow six weeks if either of you has been married before), but need not be done in person. The minimum period is fifteen days before the wedding, but there is no guarantee the paperwork will be completed in time.

Anyone over 16 can marry without parental consent and you don't have to live in Scotland. Couples in England and Wales can carry out some of the formalities through their local register office but it's more straightforward to deal directly with the Scottish registrar.

At least one of you must visit the registrar's office beforehand to collect the marriage schedule (in the case of a religious marriage), or to finalize the details if the marriage is to be a civil one. The documents required are similar to those needed in England and Wales (see page 43, 'Documents'). The paperwork is the same for both religious and civil weddings.

The registrar will produce the wedding schedule for signature at the civil wedding, but a couple marrying in a religious ceremony must collect their schedule in person not more than seven days before the wedding. It should then be given to the person officiating at the wedding. The schedule is signed immediately after the ceremony by the couple, the person performing the ceremony and two witnesses. It is returned to the registrar within three days so that it can be registered.

Anyone not based in Scotland wishing to marry there should contact their local superintendent registrar.

MARRYING IN NORTHERN IRELAND

Northern Ireland was not included in the legislation which introduced new wedding venues, and couples have less choice about where they marry. A wedding must take place either in the register office of the district where one of them lives, or must be conducted by a religious celebrant.

- **Registrar's licence**: If both of you live in the same registrar's district, one must have lived there for at least fifteen days and the other for at least seven immediately before notice is given to the registrar.

  If you live in different districts, notice must be given to the registrar of each district and each of you must have lived in the respective district for fifteen days immediately before giving notice.

  The registrar will issue the licence seven clear days after notice is given.
- **Registrar's certificate**: If you both live in the same area you must have resided there for at least seven days immediately before giving notice. If you live in different areas you must have lived there for at least seven days. The certificate will be issued after twenty-one clear days.

MARRYING IN THE REPUBLIC OF IRELAND

Whether you're marrying in a register office or a church (of whatever denomination) you must give three months' notice (known as 'notification') to the registrar for the district in which the marriage will take place. This can be done by completing a pre-printed form which must be signed by both of you. The minimum age at which you can marry is now 18.

After completing notification you should contact the minister arranging your wedding or the registrar (if you plan a civil wedding).

RESIDENCY REQUIREMENTS FOR A CIVIL WEDDING

- **By licence**: One person must establish residency of fifteen days in the district where the marriage will take place and serve notice on the sixteenth day. The other person can serve notice to their local registrar if they live elsewhere in Ireland. The marriage can then take place eight days later.
- **Without licence**: One or both people must establish residency in the district where the marriage will take place for seven days before serving notice. The marriage can take place twenty-one days later.
- If both people already live in the area where the marriage will take place they can be married eight days after serving notice.

DIVORCE

Legislation to allow divorced people to marry in Ireland came into effect on 1 August 1996 and the procedures are expected to be modified slightly over the first few years.

When serving notice (see above), the divorced person must produce a copy of the decree absolute and – if you or your ex-spouse were born outside Ireland – a birth certificate. You also have to fill in a questionnaire about you and your former wife or husband. The questions are not of a confidential nature but cover areas such as employment and where you lived. This is then forwarded to the registrar general who will take about five weeks to make sure it is all in order.

CHURCH WEDDINGS

THE CHURCH OF ENGLAND AND THE CHURCH IN WALES

Calling the banns

The idea of calling (also known as 'reading' or 'publishing') the banns dates back to pre-Christian times. Its original purpose, in the days when communications were poor, was to announce the wedding so that if anyone suspected the couple were related they could say so.

Banns are called for Church of England and Church in Wales weddings and fulfil the role of giving notice (see page 41, 'Civil weddings'). The minister usually also registers the marriage so you shouldn't need to involve the superintendent registrar.

Depending on which service they prefer, the minister will say something like: 'I publish the banns of marriage between N of — and N of —. If any of you know cause, or just impediment, why these two persons should not be joined together in holy matrimony, ye are to declare it. This is the first (second/third) time of asking.'

Usually the banns are read after the second lesson of the Sunday service (either in the morning or the evening). They are called on three (usually consecutive) Sundays before the wedding in the church or churches where you each worship (and in the church where you are getting married, if different). Banns are effective for three months after they have been read. You don't have to be there when they're read, and some people think it is bad luck to hear your own banns called. Others enjoy the thrill.

A small fee is payable to cover the reading of the banns and for the certificate which the minister completes as proof that they have been read.

Alternative to banns

Banns are not called if you marry under a common licence, which is issued by the bishop of the diocese or his representative. This means you can get married in a parish where one or both of you has lived for at least fifteen days before the licence is issued. At least one of you must be baptized to obtain this form of licence.

A common licence is necessary if one of you comes from a country where the laws regarding marriage are different (for example the age of consent), even if you normally live in England or Wales. This enables the diocesan registrar to ensure that the legal requirements of that country have been met.

RELIGIOUS WEDDINGS OUTSIDE THE CHURCH OF ENGLAND OR CHURCH IN WALES

If you're getting married in a religious building other than Church of England premises you still have to give notice (see 'Civil weddings' page 44) to the register office of the district where you live. You may also need to book a registrar for the day, depending on whether or not your minister is qualified to perform the ceremony.

THE SERVICE

Who can officiate at a church wedding?

The choice of celebrant depends on the resident minister. They may well agree to allow another ordained person to take the service – perhaps a family friend or parent, or a minister who has helped you through a particularly difficult time. Even if they don't act as the main celebrant, there is normally scope for them to take part in at least part of the service.

Similarly, if you are marrying from two different denominations ministers are usually willing to share the service by dividing the duties: reading passages from scripture, saying prayers or giving an address. You should decide in advance who will be doing what, which prayers will be said and whether or not there will be a Communion or Mass.

Church of England and Church in Wales ministers are usually able to register the marriage. If you're marrying in another church you may need to book a registrar for the day, depending on whether or not the minister is qualified to register the marriage.

Which church?

Some churches become booked up very early in the year and in the height of the wedding season brides can be seen circling the church in shiny cars like aeroplanes waiting for clearance to land at a busy airport. Other churches are lucky to see one wedding a year, and not necessarily because they are in unattractive settings.

A church which serves a transient population such as students may celebrate few weddings because couples prefer to marry in their parents' parish. Another church might serve housing estates where single people are rare, or it might be situated in an area of high unemployment where a church wedding is seen as a luxury. (The latter could just as easily be in a beautiful rural setting as in a bleak inner city area.)

If you have a choice of where you want to marry, you might decide on a church where yours will be the only wedding that day. Everyone, including the minister, will be more relaxed if they know there isn't the danger of the wrong bride ending up in the wedding photos. If there hasn't been a wedding there for some time you could have a crowd of well-wishers to greet you at the door.

Traditionally, couples marry in the church attached to the bride's parish. Sometimes, though, it can be difficult to tell which church you belong to and are entitled to get married in. The attitude to where you can get married will vary from minister to minister: you might stumble across one who wants to do everything by the book, or you could find one who is very relaxed about the 'rules'.

How long you have lived in a parish is only one factor a Church of England minister may consider when deciding whether or not you may marry in a particular church. He or she may also be influenced by whether it is your main residence and how long you spend there. Giving a friend or relative's address in the area or leaving a suitcase in the minister's hall does not constitute residence.

A minister may agree to take a booking for a wedding on the understanding that you will be living in the parish by the time the banns are called. But the banns can only be called if your planned move goes ahead.

You can marry in the church where one of you regularly worships, even if you don't live in the parish, if you are registered on the electoral roll of that church. To qualify for this you must have attended the church regularly for six months and be baptized in the Church of England.

You don't have to be christened to have a church wedding, nor will the church refuse you if you've been living together or you're expecting a baby or already have children.

Getting to know your minister

Different ministers take a different approach to the run-up to the wedding. For some, meeting the bride and bridegroom is merely an opportunity to discuss formalities – when you hold the rehearsal, which hymns you will choose, whether the church's car parking will be sufficient for your needs and who normally decorates the church.

Others like to spend more time on marriage preparation. This may be restricted to just the three of you, or you might be asked to take part in classes with couples from other parishes which can involve group discussions and role playing. Or you might simply be given a booklet or video on marriage.

The minister will try to make you concentrate on what marriage means to each of you and whether there are any large discrepancies in your expectations. Some ministers use a questionnaire to help you pinpoint any potential areas of conflict, and you may be surprised by the difference in answers that you and your partner give. Even a simple question like, 'Where will you spend Christmas when you marry?' can be quite telling.

Initially, you may begrudge time spent talking about your relationship when you've got bridesmaids' dresses and caterers to worry about, but some couples find it helps to put organizational worries into perspective.

THE CHURCH OF ENGLAND SERVICE

There are three versions of the wedding service to choose from:

- **The Book of Common Prayer**: The most traditional form of wording, and the woman has to promise to obey her husband. The order of service is usually: vows; prayers; reading and sermon.
- **Alternative Services, First Series**: Wording includes lots of 'wilts', 'thous' and 'giveths', but the promise to obey is optional. The order is similar to the Book of Common Prayer.
- **The Alternative Service Book**: Modern wording and the option to obey or not. The order is usually: reading and sermon; vows; prayers and blessing.

Communion

It is up to you whether you decide to celebrate Communion. If you do, it will usually be included in the service after you have exchanged vows. In most cases, it will extend the length of the service from about twenty-five minutes to forty.

Church of England ministers usually allow Christians of other denominations who habitually take Communion in their own church and are in good standing with it to celebrate the Eucharist. Since this can cause some confusion it can be helpful to add a few lines to the order of service, such as: 'Christians from other Churches are welcome to celebrate Communion, or to receive a blessing if they prefer.' You might also ask the minister to reiterate this point during the service. Strictly speaking, Catholics should not take communion at other churches.

Non-Christian faiths

If one of you is a devout member of a non-Christian faith, getting married in a Church of England ceremony may present problems. The minister must be assured that your faith does not prevent you from adhering to the vows and sentiments of the Christian ceremony. If in any doubt, they may leave the decision up to the local bishop.

Sorting out the red tape

It is possible to arrange a church wedding within six weeks, but to be on the safe side you should contact your church as soon as you have set the date, especially if it is at busy time of year (such as during the summer months, or on a Bank Holiday weekend).

What to do if the church is not in your parish

If you have a special reason for wanting to marry in a church other than one in your parish, you must apply for a 'special licence' from the Archbishop of Canterbury. This isn't automatically granted, and you must have a good argument – such as one of you was confirmed there and your family still attends it, or you want to get married in your old school or college chapel. The fact that the church would look good in the photos is not sufficient reason.

Write to the Registrar of the Faculty Office, 1 The Sanctuary, London SW1P 3JT. To be married by either common or special licence at least one of you must be baptized. A fee is payable for the licence.

ROMAN CATHOLIC WEDDINGS

The procedure for getting married in a Catholic church is very similar to that for an Anglican church – except perhaps that there is slightly more paperwork involved. The minister, for example, has to fill in forms showing that you are free to marry and other forms if one of you is not baptized. Try to visit your local minister six or nine months before you intend to get married. If you would like to marry in a church which is not local to you there should be no objection, but don't assume that the minister will automatically agree to this.

Most minister are authorized to solemnize marriage but you will need a certificate or licence from the register office (see page 44, 'Civil weddings'). You will normally be asked to take part in some sort of marriage preparation classes or meeting with the minister and, perhaps, other couples.

Mixed marriages

Marriages between Catholics and people from other faiths are common these days. Whichever church you decide to marry in, you should go to see your local minister. If you want a Catholic wedding you will need a dispensation to marry from the parish priest – in very rare circumstances he may think you are not in the right frame of mind to marry, in which case he will ask the bishop to decide.

It is a widely held myth that non-Catholics must promise to bring up any children in the Catholic faith. In fact, if you are not Catholic the Church does not demand any promises of you or that you convert to Rome. The onus is on the Catholic side of the couple, but even then the Church recognizes that some sort of compromise is often necessary in a marriage of different denominations.

If you are Catholic the priest will want reassurance that: 1) you will preserve your faith; and 2) you will 'do all in your power' to have any children baptized and brought up as Catholics. However, the Church recognizes that 'all in my power' means without putting the marriage at risk.

Most ministers are happy for ministers from other faiths to take part in the service, usually by saying a prayer or a reading.

Marrying in Rome

Some devout couples like to marry in Rome because of its special meaning for their faith. On a more practical level, a wedding in Rome is usually an intimate and, therefore, a less expensive option. Most couples celebrate with a party on their return home.

Your local minister will advise about arranging such a service, which is usually held in one of the English-speaking colleges, such as the Irish college, St John's Laterans.

The service

You will have to decide whether you have the longer, full Nuptial Mass which may be difficult for non-Catholics to follow and can sometimes be divisive, or a service without Mass.

The general rule is that non-Catholics may not celebrate Communion in a Catholic church, although there are some rare circumstances in which this is allowed – for example if a non-Catholic does not have access to a minister of their own Church (perhaps if the wedding is taking place in Rome). The minister must obtain permission from his local bishop before administrating the Communion to non-Catholics and the whole issue of the Eucharist should be discussed by the couple and the minister at the very beginning of marriage preparation.

If non-Catholics will be allowed to take Communion, the minister should make this clear to the congregation.

There is plenty of scope for friends and family to take part in the service: by reading from the Bible or saying or writing the prayers, or acting as altar servers. As with other Churches, different ministers have slightly different ways of conducting the service. Some, for example, follow the old tradition of asking the bridegroom to place the ring on his bride's thumb first, followed by three other fingers, saying: 'In the name of the Father, the Son and the Holy Ghost.'

CHURCH CEREMONIES FOR DIVORCED PEOPLE

The Church of England

The marriage of a divorced person whose ex-partner is still alive is not sanctioned by the Church of England. But since a minister is also a registrar, they may decide to use their civil authority to conduct such a marriage.

However, the refusal of a minister to marry a divorcee is final and, because of the restrictions on where you can marry (see page 50, 'Which church?', and page 53, 'What to do if the church is not in your parish'), a couple cannot simply seek out a minister who is sympathetic to their wishes. The minister may also refuse to allow their church to be used for the marriage of a divorced person.

The alternative is a service of prayer and dedication (also called a blessing) which takes place after a civil marriage. Although the service can be every bit as solemn and spiritual as a full wedding service, and may include Communion, there are a few differences (although some ministers will overlook these points so that the dedication is almost identical to a traditional church wedding):

- Since it is not, strictly speaking, a marriage service, banns are not called and there is no entry in the church's marriage register.
- The husband and wife enter together 'without ceremony' and sit together at the front of the church.
- Because the marriage has already taken place, rings may not be exchanged. If you are already wearing rings and the service includes reference to them as symbols of 'unending love and faithfulness', you can extend your hands towards the minister at this point in the ceremony.

If your minister agrees, you can also ask them to perform a version of the dedication service (abridged or full) in other settings. One couple, for example, had their marriage blessed on the football pitch before their team kicked off.

The Catholic Church

If you are divorced, you will be unable to marry in a Catholic church unless you have obtained an annulment. The latter may be granted for a range of reasons, but is usually a long and often painful procedure. It can mean tracing witnesses to give statements at a Church tribunal and can take from eighteen months to seven years.

Officially, ministers are not permitted to offer a blessing to a couple if one of them is divorced, but a few are willing to do this.

Free or Nonconformist Churches

The Methodist, Baptist and United Reformed Churches have a much more relaxed view of marriage for divorced people. The decision is normally up to individual ministers, and the Methodist and United Reformed Churches in particular carry out a high proportion of marriages in which at least one person is divorced.

MARRYING ABROAD

See also page 164, 'Cakes that travel'; 'Getting married abroad', page 76; Stockists, page 279.

Choosing a foreign wedding is a bit like choosing a foreign holiday. Using a well-known and reputable firm can reduce the chance of disaster, but at the same time you run the risk of feeling you are on a package tour. 'Doing your own thing' can lead to a very personal experience but you may encounter hidden pitfalls and expenses.

Be prepared for a mixed reaction from family and friends. Some guests will jump at the chance of accompanying you to the Caribbean (and you may be able to secure a cut-rate price for them), others will not be able to afford the trip or will be disappointed that you haven't chosen a traditional wedding.

One bride planned a wedding in the Seychelles because she wanted a ceremony as different as possible from an earlier church wedding (to someone else) which had been called off at the last moment. But she eventually abandoned the idea because her grandmother (to whom she was very close) did not feel physically up to the long flight and hot weather.

Weddings in exotic situations also have a very different feel to them, especially if they take place in a holiday complex. They can be extremely relaxed, but one couple complained that their ceremony took place so near to the hotel swimming pool that the wedding video was ruined by the raucous sound of children larking around in the water. Prepare, too, to be sharing a hotel with several other couples waiting to get married on the beach or in the hotel garden.

SECOND TIME ROUND

A wedding abroad is often chosen by couples who want something completely different from a previous wedding.

IS IT LEGAL?

In most cases your marriage will be valid if carried out in accordance with local laws and so long as it falls within the requirements for marriage in this country – for example you're not under age or already married. If you are worried, check with the Lord Chancellor's Department Trevelyan House, 30 Great Peter Street, London SW1P 6DW (0171 210 8500) or consult a lawyer.

WHAT YOU NEED

Your travel firm should be able to make sure you have all the relevant documents, but if you're arranging your own wedding it's best to double-check with the embassy in your home country. Ask how long you have to be in the country, what age you must be, if you need to have any medical tests and how easy it is to obtain extra marriage certificates.

Most countries will want to see the following documents. Take the original and photocopies. Some tour operators ask for the information six weeks ahead of your holiday:

- Valid passport.
- Birth certificate.

- Your original decree absolute, if either of you is divorced.
- If you are widowed, your earlier marriage certificate and your spouse's death certificate.
- Proof of your parents' consent if you are under age.
- Deedpoll proof of change of name.
- Some countries demand a sworn affidavit as proof of your single status.

SPECIAL REQUIREMENTS

- **Bali**: Four passport-sized photos of the two of you (the bridegroom on the right-hand side of the bride, or left as you look at the photo).
- **Malaysia**: Four passport-sized photos of each of you.
- **Mauritius**: If the bride has been divorced for less than ten months at the time of the wedding she has to obtain a medical certificate locally to confirm she is not pregnant.
- **USA**: Rules vary tremendously – from county to county as well as from state to state – and some local authorities will ask you to take a blood test. The reference centre of the American embassy will give you the name and address of the county clerk responsible for the area where you plan to marry so that you can check the requirements. Tel. 0171 499 9000.

WACKY WEDDINGS WORLDWIDE

See Stockists, page 279.

1. **Gracelands wedding chapel**, Las Vegas. Elvis impersonator will customize your vows: 'I, Sue, take you, Jeff, to be my wedded husband, to always love you tender, and never return you to sender.'
2. **Walt Disney World**, Orlando. Arrive in Cinderella's glass coach, have your rings carried to the altar in a slipper, and ask Minnie and Mickey Mouse to greet guests.
3. **Viking weddings**, Denmark. Jelling Viking Fraternity provides special costumes, food and choir. Contact Danish Tourist Board.

4. **Hot-air balloon wedding**, Masai Mara game park, Kenya.
5. **Igloo weddings**, Jukkasjarvi Ice Hotel. Available between January and April, ceremonies take place in the Ice Chapel and the wedding night is spent in a log cabin or snow bed.
6. **Underwater**, Army Slates Amoray Dive Resort in Key Largo, Florida. Must be qualified scuba divers. Price includes veil and tuxedo T-shirt. See Virgin Holidays.
7. **Cable car**, Rufikopfbahn, Lech, Austria. Holds thirty people and is licensed for drinks. Contact Austrian National Tourist Office.
8. **Drive-in chapel**, Little White Chapel, Las Vegas. Follow in the footsteps of Joan Collins, Mickey Rooney and guitarist Slash of Guns n' Roses.
9. **Ski slopes** – either on-piste or at the resort in USA, Austria, or Canada. Contact Virgin Snow or Crystal Ski Weddings.
10. **Park of Love**, Lima, Peru. Every Saturday evening about forty couples are married here with views of the Pacific.

THE DIY CEREMONY

If you simply want to confirm your commitment to one another in public, and perhaps acknowledge the part played by your family and friends in nurturing your relationship, you may want to draw up your own ceremony. This could take place anywhere – a clifftop or walled garden, at sea, in a stately home (it needn't have a special licence) or in your own home. You may decide to write your own vows (see page 209, 'Humanist weddings', for an example).

The one drawback in pledging your troth without signing an official piece of paper is that you won't enjoy some of the legal benefits of marriage. You may be able to get round some of these problems (for example by making a will) but it is best to take professional legal advice.

POSSIBLE PITFALLS FOR UNMARRIED COUPLES

- **Money**: Make sure you have up-to-date wills and agreements drawn up by a solicitor spelling out how property and other assets will be divided if the relationship doesn't work out. Consider making gifts during your lifetime to avoid inheritance tax.

- **Pensions and other benefits**: It may be a struggle to obtain pension rights for your partner. Consider an insurance policy to ease the burden after one of you dies, and put forward your partner's name for pension rights.
- **Death**: In extreme cases you may be excluded from funeral arrangements or even denied the right to know cause of death.
- **Children**: Unmarried fathers have fewer rights over access to children if the partnership breaks up.

A MARRIAGE OF CONVENIENCE

Some couples decide to get married purely to avoid some of the pitfalls mentioned above, even though they don't believe in marriage as an institution. This can be done quietly and with the minimum of fuss. Apart from the paperwork, all you really need is two witnesses – and they can be complete strangers. One couple simply marched into a police station on the Isle of Wight and said they needed two witnesses – a police officer and a traffic warden obliged.

HUMANIST WEDDINGS

Humanists do not hold any religious views but believe in the good within human beings. They view everyone as equal, regardless of their sex, culture, age or race, and believe that solutions for the future are to be found within ourselves rather than through a supernatural force.

A Humanist wedding is not legally binding and couples who want their marriage to be recognized by law usually have a register office ceremony beforehand. Often the civil wedding is kept as low-key as possible – the couple turn up in everyday clothes with witnesses but no guests. Occasionally it is possible to hold a Humanist ceremony in a religious building (usually a Unitarian or non-denominational university chapel) if the minister is willing. In such cases a register office wedding is not necessary.

The British Humanist Association is happy to help gay and lesbian couples to create their own wedding ceremony. Couples unable to marry in a church because one of them is divorced have also found the Humanist wedding a meaningful alternative.

DEVISING YOUR CEREMONY

For a fee, the British Humanist Association will provide celebrants to help you plan your wedding (see page 274 for helpline and address). Usually the celebrant will meet you at least once before the ceremony to discuss the structure of the wedding. They will talk about your relationship and how you want that reflected in the ceremony; the meeting also gives you the chance to decide whether the celebrant is the right person for the ceremony you had in mind.

You can leave the format of the ceremony entirely up to the celebrant, write it all yourself or contribute parts of it. Celebrants will also suggest music, readings or poetry (see page 209, 'Humanist weddings'). Because of their beliefs, celebrants will not normally include anything religious within the ceremony although some are happy to leave room for a guest to say a prayer.

The ceremony can take place almost anywhere, from a deconsecrated chapel (see 'Venues', page 278), clifftop or wood, to your front room or a hotel. There is also a great deal of flexibility in how the ceremony is structured. The guests can sit either side of an aisle down which the bride will walk on her father's arm, or the couple might arrive together. If you already have a child, the wedding can be incorporated into their naming ceremony.

GAY AND LESBIAN WEDDINGS

The law, as it stands at the moment, does not offer single-sex couples the same rights as heterosexuals, but things are changing – slowly. In San Francisco officials are allowed to conduct symbolic weddings that 'solemnize the existence of a domestic partnership' but carry no legal weight, and Hawaii has approved gay marriages, but this is being reviewed by the Supreme Court.

Gay and lesbian couples in Scandinavia can register their partnership with the state and claim some, though not all, of the rights accorded to married couples. The rules, though, only apply if one half of the couple is from that country. The Dutch Parliament has also voted in favour of legalizing same-sex marriages.

Homosexual weddings remain a highly contentious issue within the Christian Church. The Lesbian and Gay Christian Movement puts couples in touch with a minister who will arrange for a blessing for their relationship and provide a certificate to commemorate the event (see 'Useful Addresses', page 274).

Many couples have devised their own commitment ceremonies (see page 209, 'Humanist weddings'), but gay couples remain legally vulnerable in the same way as unmarried heterosexual couples and should take legal advice.

PART TWO

THE LOOK

5

AND THE BRIDE WORE . . .

THE DRESS

The tradition of wearing white at weddings started in the eighteenth century, but only the wealthy could afford such an impractical colour – everyone else had to make do with their Sunday best. Although people referred to white weddings, the bright white associated with today's bride is a relatively new invention made possible through modern dyeing methods. Even Queen Victoria's wedding dress was nearer a Cornish ice-cream colour than pure white.

Today many brides are prepared to invest a sizeable chunk of their budget on a dress which, while only worn for a day, will play an important part in creating memories for years to come. Others prefer to save their money for an exotic honeymoon or a down-payment on a flat or house. It is traditional for the bride to keep her dress a secret from at least the bridegroom, if not everyone, and the cost can mean the bridegroom is usually kept in the dark about the price of the outfit too.

DECIDING ON A STYLE

(see also page 17, 'Themed weddings', and page 74, 'Something blue – alternatives to white')

There are no rules about what you should wear to a particular type of wedding. Brides have appeared in extravagant, 'meringue' dresses at a register office and in sober tailored suits in church. If it's not your first wedding you needn't feel constrained to wear a colour other than white or to choose something fitted rather than frivolous. Your only consideration should be to wear something you feel happy in.

Some people grow up knowing exactly what they want to wear on their wedding day, others only realize when they catch sight of a dress on a hanger or a picture in a magazine. Whether you decide to buy your dress, or have it made, it is a good idea – and a lot of fun – to try on as many different outfits as possible. You might be surprised at what suits you, or, if you're not, you'll at least go away happy in the knowledge that your original choice of style was the right one.

Clippings from magazines, even if it's a sleeve from one dress and a neckline from another, can help you build up a photofit of the look you want. Bridal fairs, usually held in the run-up to Christmas or in the spring, can also provide inspiration from the catwalk or a chance to chat to dress designers.

Bear in mind what kind of wedding you're having. If a vigorous session on the dance-floor is important, an off-the-shoulder shawl neckline will cramp your style. Low necklines are frowned upon in some religious services, so ask the person officiating for guidelines well in advance.

Tip A detachable train will give you more manoeuvrability at the reception.

MAKING THE MOST OF WHAT YOU'VE GOT

Few people are entirely happy with the way they look, but the most positive way of dealing with what you see as an imperfection is to show off your strong points: if you think your hips are a bit too well padded, choose a style that accentuates your tiny waist, or if you're worried about your tummy, draw attention to your elegant collarbone instead.

Take heart from the fact that there is a myriad of styles and fabrics to pick and mix from, and that dress shops are used to making minor adjustments. Remember that this will probably be the best-fitting outfit you'll ever wear and your figure will look its best as a result.

HOW TO CHEAT

See also page 170, 'Bouquet – shape and size'.

- **If you're very tall**: Long, tightly fitted dresses can give a bean-pole effect. Lose inches by wearing something that creates a horizontal line. Avoid high heels and towering headdresses.
- **Adding height**: A full skirt often looks better, whilst an ankle-length dress may make you appear shorter. But a voluminous skirt or dress with large bows can be overpowering. Features at the top of the outfit – a halter or even a polo neck – will draw the eye upwards and give the appearance of height. Too much detail, such as a cluster of rosebuds on the top of the bodice, will create a horizontal line to 'cut you in

two'. Wearing your hair up (especially with a veil) can add inches, and a short train can also make you seem taller.

- **Wide hips**: Put a full skirt over them. A bodice that ends below the waist will stress the hips. Features around the neck will draw attention away from your bottom half.
- **Large bust**: Look for styles that allow you to wear a bra, and avoid tops with little support. If you feel very self-conscious, cover up with a second layer, such as a high-collared coat or jacket in a lightweight material. Alternatively, flaunt what you've got with a boned bodice or bra to create a dramatic cleavage (don't go over the top if you're having a religious wedding).
- **Flat chest**: Add bulk with heavily beaded fabric, pearls or lace. A sweetheart neckline can boost the bust, and padded and boned bodice (or uplifting underwear) will also give you lift. Draw the eye away from the chest with other details such as a plunging back or horizontal line such as a large collar. Avoid a plain bodice or plunging neckline.
- **Tummies**: Long, clean lines and a lack of fussy details help. A full skirt and a bodice tapering down to a V at the front adds length and will flatten a stomach. A boned bodice and long, flat front panel will also hold you in. Dark-coloured bodices (for example, a midnight-blue velvet top for a winter wedding) can be slimming.
- **Arms**: Skinny or flabby arms can be covered with a light fabric such as lace or organza. Choose from short or three-quarter length, or make a feature of a full-length sleeve – a pointed Maid Marian-style design, for example.
- **Neck**: Uncluttered effects such as a scoop or V-shaped neckline will lengthen your throat.
- **Manufacturing curves**: Most parts of the dress can be padded (see 'Flat chest' above) and a full dress will give the impression of volume.

NON-EUROPEAN CULTURES

White is the exception rather than the norm outside European cultures. Muslim and Hindu brides wear gorgeous silks of red, pink and orange – in Islam white is often associated with widowhood. Chinese brides normally wear deep reds.

If you want to include African influences in your wedding, you can either wear traditional costume or incorporate African colours into a European-style dress. Designers like House of Ronke (see Stockists, page 282) blend imported hand-beaded and hand-embroidered materials and traditional African colours such as orange and gold into white dresses and outfits for the entire bridal group – including the African costume of waistcoat, hat and poncho-style shawl for the bridegroom.

Some black brides opt for the brilliant oranges, blues, yellows and greens of Ghanaian Kente cloth, and use the same pattern as a border for their invitations or table settings. Others wear a traditional head-wrap rather than a veil.

A WINTER WEDDING

Being the centre of attention can banish the cold, but if you're worried that you may turn blue, opt for heavier materials like Duchesse satin, or velvet. Lined sleeves will also help and you can now buy thermal underwear that is made to look more like delicate lace than boiler lagging.

A sweeping cloak with voluminous hood, knee-high white boots, fake-fur trimmings and muff, and delicate, crystal crown can transform you into a Snow Queen (see Stockists, page 283).

Consider an outfit that will create a new look for the reception, perhaps a detachable bodice that you can take off in the evening to reveal a pretty silk top.

SOMETHING OLD

ANTIQUES

Wearing an old wedding dress or veil, or spicing up a new outfit with an antique piece of lace which will drape more naturally than modern materials, is one way of ensuring you avoid looking like a mass-produced bride. If your dress has a special resonance for your family, the effect will be even more potent.

Nineteenth-century lace flounces, collars, scarves, borders, bridal fans, parasols and handkerchiefs can be picked up at auctions, but examine them for signs of wear and tear and consider whether they will stand up to cleaning.

Modern detergents can be too strong for nineteenth-century lace and may either damage it or tamper with its natural light-fawn hue. Old veils should be washed using tepid water with a very small amount of non-allergenic washing-up liquid available in some chemists. Don't agitate the veil in the water and let it dry naturally, draped over a towel. In the case of very old material it is safer to call in an expert (see Useful Addresses, page 273). Often this will still work out cheaper than buying something new.

If you're looking for inspiration, most local history museums have at least one wedding dress, and some costume museums include substantial collections which, if not on display, can often be viewed privately. Interesting collections include: The Museum of London (which houses Queen Victoria's wedding dress); Kensington Palace Museum (which includes recent royal gowns); Cheltenham Art Gallery and Museums (occasionally displayed in the Pittville Pump Room Museum in Cheltenham); The Museum of Costume, in Bath; Elmbridge Museum, in Weybridge, Surrey; and Chertsey Museum in Chertsey, Surrey.

MONEYSAVER

Look out for wedding dresses displayed in the shop windows of charity shops. Some branches (mainly the ones which specialize in bridalwear – see Stockists, page 281) also sell brand new items or hire-out dresses (often in small and large sizes).

Charity shops sometimes benefit from closing-down sales when businesses donate stock. Suppliers also give shops brand-new wedding accessories such as shoes, veils, head-dresses, tights, outfits for the mothers of the bride, artificial bouquets and underwear – simply because they are discontinued lines.

SOMETHING NEW

BUYING A DRESS

Start looking for your dress six to nine months before the wedding and try to go to a variety of outlets, such as a large department store, a shop that's part of a chain (see below) and a smaller boutique, to give you some idea of the range of prices and styles.

Visiting some of the larger bridal collections of department stores is like being let loose in a giant dressing-up box, but don't be surprised if some of the dresses aren't in your size and you have to suffer the indignity of being held in with elastic bands stretched over the back buttons. Many shops become so busy that you have to make an appointment and even then you may be forced to queue for the changing room. Wear loose clothing (avoid black underwear and tights which will look strange with most bridal dresses) so that you can change quickly and don't get over-heated.

It also helps to take a good friend with you, but make sure this is someone you trust to tell the truth (diplomatically) and who knows what suits you. Ask them to note down the name of the designs you like (and their prices) and even to draw a sketch of details – such as a sleeve or front panel – which appeal. Avoid taking friends who try to make you buy something that only they would look stunning in.

MONEYSAVER

Sales are normally held in January and July, but make sure you've done your homework beforehand and are buying a dress you really like rather than solely for the price-tag.

STRESSBUSTER

Consider taking your mother along with you (especially if she's paying) and make a special day of it. Try to shop mid-week and build the day round a relaxing lunch or other treat. If you've got the time, visit bridal departments just before Christmas, or during the week, when you are more likely to have the assistant to yourself and won't feel self-conscious about parading up and down in a frou-frou skirt.

Chain stores

- **Berkertex Brides**: The dresses are aimed at brides in their mid-twenties who want to be able to choose from a range that includes dresses that are slightly more adventurous than the traditional wedding gown. Bridesmaids' dresses can be bought or hired. The group also includes Short Stories (see below) and Warren York (a range of headdresses).
- **Brides International**: Part of the same group as Berkertex Brides. The dresses are slightly more traditional, less expensive, and aimed at the younger bride. Some brides' and bridesmaids' dresses can be hired.
- **Short Stories**: Primarily aimed at the second-time around bride, and

overseas or register office weddings. Includes less fussy gowns, shorter dresses, suits and trouser suits.

- **Pronuptia Youngs**: hires out and sells a wide range of outfits. Also has seventy men's outfitters (which are mostly hire) and includes less traditional designs such as frock-coats.

HAVING A DRESS MADE

The ideal dressmaker should be a bit like the ideal doctor: a professional you trust implicitly and with whom you can be completely frank; someone who is aware of any physical weaknesses and can discuss the best way of treating them without making you feel like Quasimodo. Your sister, mother, aunt or friend might normally fit this description exactly, but your wedding may not be the time to put them to the test. Telling a professional who is paid to listen to your wedding bulletins that you've decided on a train rather than a mini-skirt after all is a lot less painful than breaking the news to a close friend or relative who has lived and breathed your wedding for the last six months and may well be making your gown for little or no financial reward.

Before you ask a friend or member of your family to make your dress or any other outfit for the wedding party, bear in mind:

- The other tasks you have asked them to undertake.
- How well they stand up to criticism of their work.
- Any other commitments they have which might prevent them from finishing the dress on time.
- How fat away you live from one another.
- Whether they understand, and are sympathetic to, the sort of 'look' you are aiming for.
- Will they be flattered to be asked, or will they see it as a huge chore or an immense worry?
- They may make the best scatter-cushions in the world, but how finely honed are their bodice-boning skills?

Where to go for help

Whoever is making the outfit might consider going along to one of the workshops offered by the major sewing schools (see Stockists, page

283). Many provide intensive one-day sessions in techniques such as: working with veiling, silks and lace; ways of concealing zips and fastenings; and piping. Others offer courses on bridal beading, covering shoes, and making veils, headdresses and tiaras. Book well in advance and check that the course is within your capabilities.

Some department stores, such as John Lewis in London's Oxford Street, have a dressmaking adviser on hand to answer specific queries such as which thread to use with which material, and the correct tension of your sewing machine for a particular fabric (especially important with heavy materials such as velvet). Although other shops may not have anything quite so formal, you should usually be able to find an assistant who can give you advice.

- Remember to take very accurate measurements and to make all fitting adjustments to the pattern tissue before cutting out the fabric.
- Always make up a toile of the bodice (a version in calico or sheeting) so that three-dimensional adjustments can be made before you cut your material.
- Bridal fabrics can mark easily, so use sharp, fine needles and pins, and pin the seam allowances to avoid leaving marks in the fabric.
- Take care when transferring markings from tissue to fabric – use tailor's tacks rather than carbon paper in case the colours show through.
- Always test your stitches, interfacings and ironing on a swatch beforehand.
- Spread a clean sheet or dust-sheet on the floor to keep the dress clean.
- Make sure your sewing machine is free of oil or dust that might damage the material.

Laces, ribbons, brocade and sequined and beaded material can be found in the fabric department of large department stores or from mail-order specialists (see Stockists, page 283).

Finding a professional

Choosing a dressmaker means entrusting a stranger with your dreams. You don't *have* to like the person, but it makes the whole process a lot more pleasurable if you do. After the first fitting your dressmaker may fall into the role of unofficial counsellor, having been through the wedding process countless times. A visit to the dressmaker should be a calming experience and a chance to escape from decisions about marquees and vol-au-vents.

Look at photos of other wedding dresses they have made. If yours is a dressmaker who has concentrated on traditional styles, they may feel uncomfortable with a commission to make a sequin and fake fur creation. Other dressmakers, though, will relish the chance to be a bit more creative. You should be able to tell quite quickly if a dressmaker will be keen to offer suggestions – which could be a plus or minus depending on your own approach.

Ask to see a sample of their work and take a good look at finishing in areas such as zips, hems and buttonholes. Speak to other customers to see whether the dressmaker met their deadline and stayed within budget. Personal recommendations count for a lot, especially in a small town where a good reputation is usually well earned.

If you don't know of a dressmaker, pattern producer Butterick will provide a list of professionals in your area (see Useful Addresses, page 273).

MONEYSAVER

Remember that a dressmaker who has to travel a long way will charge more.

Making sure the price is right

- Check whether the dressmaker charges an hourly rate or a set price for the job, and whether fittings are included in the quote.
- If they ask how much you intend to spend, avoid the question – instead describe exactly what you want and ask for a quote. Decide beforehand on your budget and don't be trapped into making any on-the-spot decisions.
- Weigh up how much a similar outfit would cost in a shop (if you were able to find it) and the pros and cons of having it made: whether it would fit as snugly and whether there would be scope to adopt the design to your taste.
- Your dressmaker should give you a detailed drawing of the dress. Make sure it covers the back as well as the front.

SOMETHING BORROWED

CASE STUDY

Joanna, a 26-year-old lawyer from Suffolk, had always had a secret hankering to wear the dress her mother got married in during the 1960s. Every time her grandmother, who kept the dress in a cupboard in her house, suggested cutting it up, Joanna protested that someone might want to wear it one day.

She made half-hearted attempts at trying on wedding dresses in shops but knew that what she really wanted was hanging up in a cupboard in her grandmother's house. Her mother was convinced the dress would be too dusty, damaged or stained to wear, but Joanna insisted in trying it on. A neighbour let out the darts under the bust by about a centimetre and Joanna had the dress dry-cleaned.

Wearing her mother's dress gave Joanna a sense of continuity – especially as many of the guests at her wedding had attended the same celebration for her parents more than thirty years before.

SOMETHING BLUE – ALTERNATIVES TO WHITE

For some brides white seems inappropriate or simply doesn't suit them. But if you're used to wearing outrageous clothes a white dress is probably the most surprising thing you could wear and your wedding might be the one day in your life when you'll enjoy setting aside your red Doc Martens and gold lamé mini-skirt. And not everyone wants to look like Paula Yates, who wore a tightly fitting scarlet Jasper Conran dress with a long train and matching red veil, when she married Bob Geldof. He chose top hat, tails and medals.

SUPERSTITIONS SURROUNDING COLOURS

Married in white, you have chosen all right,
Married in black, you will wish yourself back,

Married in red, you will wish yourself dead,
Married in green, ashamed to be seen,
Married in blue, you will always be true,
Married in pearl, you will live in a whirl,
Married in yellow, ashamed of your fellow,
Married in brown, you will live out of town,
Married in pink, your fortunes will sink.

'Married in blue, you will always be true' resulted in the tradition whereby the bride wears something blue on her wedding day, irrespective of the colour of her dress – a blue garter or handkerchief, for example, or a sapphire engagement ring or earrings.

SECOND TIME AROUND AND OLDER BRIDES

You can, of course, wear whatever you want on your wedding day and your choice should be guided by what is going to make you feel wonderful rather than what other people think or what you are *supposed* to wear. Many older brides want something less frivolous than, for example, a ballerina-type tulle skirt and tightly-fitting bodice, but don't want to forfeit romance in their search for sophistication.

One option is to look to the past for inspiration. Victorian- and Edwardian-style dresses – either originals or copies – can be both romantic and more forgiving on the figure than modern styles. Or you may feel more comfortable in a suit – either skirt or trousers, and jacket. But don't feel you have to stick to mute colours or sober, tailored cuts.

SECOND TIME AROUND

Sarah, 33, didn't want to wear a white dress for her second wedding, which was in a London register office. She went shopping with her fiancé's sister and eventually found an outfit in Harrods produced by an American designer which suited her blonde hair and willowy figure. It was made of a pale pink cotton with a very light floral pattern on top and white brocade and pearls at the cuffs and in the centre panel. The fitted skirt came to a few inches above the ankle and the jacket was mid-thigh length.

She managed to find a clutch handbag in a similar shade of pink and Superglued pearls to it to match the outfit. Her court shoes were also pink and her bouquet contained pink lilies, lemon roses, red berries and lots of greenery. She wore her grandmother's pearl choker. Sarah, whose husband's family are French, liked the fact that the outfit had a Louis XIV feel to it.

GETTING MARRIED ABROAD

Just because you've chosen an exotic island for your wedding doesn't mean you have to forgo flounces and frills. Brides have worn outfits ranging from lightweight sun-dresses (see page 208, 'Getting married abroad') to full-length silk gowns. Then, of course, there was Pamela Anderson's white bikini.

When you're choosing your outfit, bear in mind local customs and humidity. If you get married in a Muslim country such as Egypt, for example, you are likely to cause offence and get stared at if you wander around with a plunging neckline or even bare shoulders. This advice is equally pertinent for honeymoons (see Chapter 19).

TRANSPORTING YOUR DREAM GOWN

- Carry your outfit as hand luggage (that way you and your dress will arrive at the same destination). If the airline won't allow this, use their fragile goods service. (Berkertex Brides provides free boxes with all dresses, or will sell you one.)
- Put your underwear, shoes, headdress and bouquet (if you're taking an artificial one) into the same container as the dress, or use tissue to 'pack out' the box or case. This way there will be less room for the dress to move around and become creased. Alternatively, zip it into a hanging dress bag (available from haberdashers).
- Bear in mind which materials will travel well. Some silks have a natural crease in them, while satin looks better completely smooth.
- Hang your dress in your bathroom so that the steam will help any creases to fall out, or ask staff if it can be kept somewhere safe.

THE VEIL

Brides have long been seen as a target for evil spirits (see page 136, 'The role of the bridesmaids and pageboys') and a veil was traditionally used as a disguise to outwit supernatural forces. In many parts of the world the veil also carries undertones of submission.

But, like many wedding traditions, choosing to wear a veil is as much about what it means to you personally as the custom's precise origins. Some women find throwing back their veil a fitting and moving way of symbolizing a transition from a single life to a partnership. Others simply don't feel a bride until they try on their veil.

Wearing a veil can make you walk and stand differently. You may love the mystery of peeping out at your guests from behind it, or you may feel restricted and awkward. There are plenty of alternatives if a veil doesn't suit either you or your outfit (see page 79, 'Other gear – hats, head-dresses, bonnets and tiaras').

THE JEWISH TRADITION OF BEDEKEN

Many Jewish weddings still include the custom of bedeken in which the bridegroom lowers the veil over his bride's face before the service begins. This usually takes place in a private room in which a few close relatives may also be present and offers the couple a moment of quiet reflection.

The tradition stems from a desire to avoid Jacob's mistake in marrying the wrong woman. He had been promised the hand of Rachel in return for seven years' labour but the morning after his wedding awoke to discover that his heavily veiled bride was in fact Rachel's sister, Leah. Some couples still observe bedeken whether or not the bride wears a veil.

WHAT SORT OF VEIL?

The style and material you choose for your veil will depend on your dress and how you plan to wear your hair. Veils normally come in four lengths: bouffant (brushing the shoulders); cascade or hand (falling halfway down your back); church length (stretching about a foot beyond the floor); or cathedral length (trailing behind you by some six feet).

- **Cost**: Silk (which will hang more naturally), lace, organza or additions such as pearls, embroidered motifs, diamanté that will glisten in the light, or sequins will push up the price. Nylon or polyester netting will give the veil more stiffness and some people would argue that only the discerning eye can tell the difference.

- **Length**: A very long veil can look elegant and make you appear taller, but avoid it if you think you'll worry about tripping over it or will feel drowned by it. Bear in mind how the veil will complement the shape of your dress. A shorter veil, for example, would look perfect with a three-quarter-length Grace Kelly-type dress, but might introduce a harsh line into a very long, flowing gown.
- **Colour**: Sepia suits an antique-style dress, and black can look stunning – especially if you are dark-skinned and decide to wear a white dress.
- **DIY**: Patterns are available to help you make your own veil, and, since netting is comparatively cheap, some brides are happy simply to buy a length of material and cut it to the required shape, securing it with a headdress or comb sewn on to the fabric.

HOW TO WEAR A VEIL

(see also page 195, 'At the altar', and page 83, 'At the reception')

If you're buying a veil, ask the shop to show you how to secure it and experiment with the position until you feel comfortable. Usually the veil is held in place by a comb. White grips found in most haberdashery departments of large stores will provide extra security.

1. Hold the comb upside down in front of you.
2. Push it firmly into your hair.
3. Turn the comb back on itself and up into your hair, taking the veil behind you.

Veils can also be secured with headdresses, tiaras or crowns, worn on top of the head, on the crown or at the very back. A Juliette cap – a small dome-like hat worn at the back of your head with the veil sprouting from it – will expose more of your hair.

CARING FOR YOUR VEIL

Nylon veils won't need ironing and should simply be draped from a coathanger, but if your veil is silk, use a very cool temperature and be careful not to put the nose of the iron through the netting. If the veil has beading or other attachments, lay that side face down on a towel to protect it.

OTHER HEADGEAR – HATS, HEADDRESSES, BONNETS AND TIARAS

- **Bareheaded**: A liberating way to start your new life, especially striking with short hair.
- **Flowers**: Flowers and foliage can be threaded into long hair or secured to a shorter style with combs. Other alternatives include a full garland of fresh flowers or an Alice-band effect across the front of your head (consider artificial flowers if you suffer from hay fever).
- **Crowns and tiaras**: There's a whole range of headgear to choose from: a Ruritanian jewel-encrusted crown, delicate pearl tiara or simple metal crown to make you look like a medieval princess. Bear in mind the weight (and how tiring you will find this), whether you will worry about it slipping, and the extra inches a headdress will add.
- **Themed**: Consider a bonnet for a Jane Austen-style Regency dress, or a top hat with a riding-style jacket and skirt.
- **Hats**: Tall women can carry off hats with wide brims, shorter brides might prefer small brims or brims that are turned up – in both cases use stronger make-up to draw out the eyes. A large hatpin from a haberdashery department will help keep your hat in place (although you risk damaging it), or ask for an elastic band to be fitted under the back of the hat. A custom-made hat should give a better fit. Remember that milliners will be particularly busy in the run-up to Ascot and Henley Regatta (in June).

ACCESSORIES

FRAGRANCES

The perfume you choose for your wedding will remind you of that day for the rest of your life. It may already hold good memories for you – perhaps you were wearing it when you first met your partner or when he proposed.

An eau de toilette is the lightest fragrance you could choose, followed by an eau de parfum. Tell your partner not to be heavy-handed with his fragrance so that the two of you aren't competing. Unless you have the chance to shower, don't apply a different perfume later in the day. Bear in mind that you might be carrying strong-smelling flowers, so try to choose a fragrance that won't clash.

Build up 'layers' of your own fragrance when you're getting ready. If your favourite brand of eau de toilette is part of a complementary set, consider buying the soap, bath gel or oil and body lotion that comes with it. If this is not available, or seems excessive, look for products with a similar note – for example citrus, oriental or floral.

After your bath pat yourself dry and then apply some body lotion before dusting yourself with powder to absorb it. Dab eau de toilette behind your ears and knees, in the crook of your elbows and down your cleavage – or spray a cloud in front of you and walk through it to ensure even distribution. Your skin should be perfectly dry before dressing as perfume can leave nasty stains, especially on silk.

UNDERWEAR

A lot of women have never quite got round to being properly measured for a bra but since wedding dresses are often closely fitting, at least from the waist up, it is especially important to have underwear that's the right size.

New materials such as Tencel and Lycra mean underwear is tempting rather than torturous. Basques and bodyshapers are ideal for wedding dresses as there is less chance of them showing through your clothes (especially if they're seamless). A balconette or underwired bra will help you achieve a cleavage, while knickers with special front panels will keep a tummy under control. If you're not wearing tights or stockings with suspenders, try hold-ups with pretty laced tops.

Bear in mind the shape of your dress – will you need a strapless or backless bra? – and take your underwear along to your dress fittings. Don't forget to plan ahead for your going-away outfit, too. One newly-wed had bought a sexy white basque for her wedding night but discovered her going-away dress had very thin straps which revealed her underwear. She was forced to remove the straps from her basque and hope that it stayed in place until she and her husband got to their hotel.

SHOES

Tiny feet used to be so admired on Chinese women that, until the 1920s, the bridegroom's mother would pick up the hem of the bride's dress to examine her feet. If they were more than about 4 inches long she would throw down the skirt in disgust.

Hollywood film star Julie Roberts left no doubts about size when she went barefooted to marry singer Lyle Lovett, but unless your wedding is on a Caribbean beach, the chances are you'll opt for shoes. Comfort should play a big part in your choice as you will spend a lot of the day on your feet, and much of the night dancing. Try to wear your shoes in – both for comfort's sake and so that you feel poised in them. Remember to take them along to your final dress fitting.

Edwardian ankle-boots look good with historical dresses, and slingbacks suit 1950s-style dresses. You might want to dye your shoes to match your outfit or have them covered in the same material (see Stockists, page 288).

PUTTING ON THE STYLE

Having your shoes specially made for you is expensive, but you'll be sure of a perfect fit and can bask in the knowledge that your footwear is unique. As well as the comfort factor, they'll look particularly stunning if your dress isn't full-length.

BITS AND PIECES

- Gloves and mittens come in most lengths and materials.
- Parasols can suit an Edwardian outfit.
- Fans and shawls can be cumbersome.
- Fur muff (see page 15, 'Winter').

TATTOOS

Having the name of your first boyfriend tattooed on your shoulder may not seem such a good idea now and can be removed at a laser clinic (see Stockists, page 289).

Or a tattoo may seem the perfect way to remember the day:

- One couple decided to have matching designs on the inside of their wrists to mark their wedding – he had a beehive and she a bee.
- Another couple had Celtic rings engraved on the middle finger of their left hands so that their 'wedding rings' could never be removed.

- A groom had two interlocking wedding bands tattooed on his back with his name engraved inside one and his fiancée's on the other. His bride discovered them on their wedding night.

Self-adhesive alternatives will last only for the duration of your honeymoon and come in a wide range of designs and colours (including those that glow in the dark) such as: little red devils, nubile nymphs, cherubs, pouncing tigers, cuddly bunnies and bleeding hearts. You can find them in the fashion section of department stores, gift shops and some stationers.

WHAT TO DO WITH YOUR DRESS AFTERWARDS

One woman had her dress mounted in a glass case and put on display at the top of the stairs. Victorians would wear theirs when they were presented at Court, and Queen Victoria wore sections of her wedding lace mounted on new material at the christenings of her many grandchildren. Another tradition is to use part of the wedding dress to line the firstborn's cot.

Many dressmakers insist that creating a wedding dress with a view to adapting it afterwards means you will end up either with a half-baked version of the dress you really wanted or a cocktail dress, ballgown or other piece of clothing that will never quite manage to throw off its associations with a wedding. Some brides find it's just too much of an emotional wrench to have their dress tampered with.

- **Preserving for posterity**: Have the dress cleaned as soon as possible (see Stockists, page 282). Remove it from the drycleaner's plastic, wrap in acid-free, white tissue paper (put extra tissue along the fold-lines) and store in an acid-free box somewhere dry. You could also have the dress hermetically sealed.
- **Selling**: Several firms will give you a reasonable price for your dress (see Stockists, page 283).
- **Adapting**: Dyeing the material will instantly transform the dress – and shoes: see Stockists, page 282).

Tip Have pieces of fabric made to shield the underarm area from perspiration stains.

AT THE RECEPTION

- **Veils**: It is up to you when you remove the veil. You might decide to keep it on until the first dance as a symbol that the more exuberant part of the day has started.
- **Going away**: Some people like to change about forty minutes before leaving so that guests have a chance to see their outfit, others prefer to make a dramatic entrance and immediately sweep off to their honeymoon. Smart suits and dresses make a practical option if you think you will be able to wear them at work or at least at other weddings and special occasions. You might prefer to wear something entirely frivolous, or an outfit that's as seductive as your wedding dress was demure.

CHECKLIST

FOR THE SERVICE

Dress or suit
Shoes
Tights, stockings and suspender belt, hold-ups (two pairs of each)
Underwear: knickers, bra, basque, petticoats, garter
Gloves
Earrings
Necklace
Rings
Veil
Headdress/hat/tiara
Handbag
Handkerchief
Something old
Something new
Something borrowed
Something blue
A sixpence in the shoe (final line of the traditional rhyme)

GOING AWAY

Shoes
Underwear
Dress/suit
Handbag
Jacket, shawl, cloak or coat

6

Bridegroom and Male Guests

BRIDEGROOM

Traditionally, the bridegroom's outfit has tended to be completely overshadowed by what the bride is wearing – and a lot of men are more than happy to take second place in the fashion stakes. Even within the confines of the traditional wedding suits, though, there are several ways in which you can become more than simply an accessory to the bride without drawing too much attention to yourself. Or you might just keep something up your sleeve for the grand finale – your going-away outfit.

If, like one (auburn-haired) bridegroom, who wore a red tartan suit of drainpipe trousers and frock-coat, you want to stamp your own personality on what you're wearing, it's best to consult the bride first. Otherwise you run the risk of clashing in colour and tone, and it is only fair to let her know that she may not be the only one turning heads on the day (this may even come as a relief to her).

TRADITIONAL CHOICE OF SUITS

Rules on what you can wear have become blurred at all but the most royal occasions.

- **Morning suit**: Usually worn for weddings between 11 a.m. and 3 p.m. For the jacket choose between black herringbone and charcoal or pale grey. Navy herringbone is also becoming more popular. Trousers are usually grey pin-striped (and sometimes blue) or plain light grey, and can be worn with any colour combination of jacket and waistcoat. This type of suit has the advantage of flattering most shapes and sizes.
- **Dinner jacket**: For later weddings (perhaps at a hotel), or if the

ceremony will be followed by a very formal reception, you might choose a dinner jacket (tuxedo) and black tie. (The word includes matching trousers.) It is also a popular choice at many Jewish and Asian weddings (see page 217, 'wedding clothes'). Variations on the black jacket include a shawl collar (a long lapel with no peak), and it can be single- or double-breasted. The bow-tie doesn't have to be black and, like the waistcoat, can be as extravagant as you like. You might also choose a cummerbund, but don't wear it with a waistcoat.

- **White tuxedos**: A variation on the black jacket, this is especially popular in the summer or at weddings in hot climates. It is normally worn with a bow-tie and cummerbund and black trousers.
- **Highland dress**: Either Highland morning or evening dress is acceptable for a day wedding. If you are not wearing a waistcoat you don't need a dress belt. Traditionally, non-Scots are only allowed to wear Stewart or Gordon tartan. Large store chains like Moss Bros hire out kilts (the Scottish shops have a wider selection of tartans) and Moss Bros will even make one to order. Lords Formal Wear hires out kilts in the tartan worn by Mel Gibson in *Braveheart* (complete with plaid – the length of material you throw over your shoulder). Moss Bros hires out all the accessories: the distinctive Scottish jacket or doublet, sporran, laced brogues, stockings, jabot (the frill on the front of a doublet), cuff and skean-dhu (the small dagger carried in the stocking). The kilt should fall about an inch above the knee. (See Stockists, page 286).
- **Lounge suits**: A popular option and one that you can wear afterwards.

ACCESSORIES

The following can be bought or hired:

- **Shirt**: For morning suits choose between a classic white shirt and tie and wing-collar shirt and cravat. For black tie, shirts are usually plain or wing-collared with a pleated front.
- **Tie**: Consider teaming with a matching handkerchief in your top pocket. You might also want to show off with a tie-pin. Even if you have managed the art of securing a bow-tie you may not want to test your nerves on the wedding morning. Make sure no metal parts are showing on a ready-made bow-tie.
- **Waistcoat**: The range extends from a simple beige, double-breasted style to an extravagant creation such as those produced by Favourbrook (makers of the handpainted Angel waistcoat for Simon Callow's character in *Four Weddings and a Funeral*). If your waistcoat does not have a back,

make sure the tension on the elastic isn't too tight, and that you've chosen the right size, otherwise it won't sit properly. You should also leave the bottom button undone, for reasons of etiquette as well as comfort.

- **Hat**: Wearing a hat is becoming less popular. If you do wear a hat, make sure it sits flat on the front of the forehead when you're standing up straight. Take it off when you enter the church and hold it by the brim in your left hand – together with gloves if you're wearing them – so that your right is free for greeting people. The hat should be left on the pew during the ceremony and then put on again for the photos. The most common mistake is to wear a hat too far back on the head. Normally hats are black or grey.
- **Gloves**: These are rarely worn but should be grey with a morning suit.
- **Shoes**: Black lace-up shoes such as Oxfords are ideal with most suits. Avoid suede shoes. If you're wearing new shoes, score the soles to prevent slipping, and remove price labels (if you're getting married in church you'll be spending some time on your knees).
- **Socks**: Fred Flintstone designs can spoil the overall effect. Stick to black.
- **Cummerbund**: Originally used to store opera tickets – a good way of remembering that the pleats should face upwards. Don't wear with a waistcoat.
- **Skean-dhu**: If you're right-handed, this small dagger is carried in the stocking on your right leg (and vice versa). Tradition says that if you draw a skean-dhu you should always draw blood, so try to avoid showing the blade to any guests as you may feel compelled to give yourself a nick to avoid any large-scale bloodshed.

PUTTING ON THE STYLE

At weddings taking place in the City of London or in high society the tradition is to wear black hats.

FINDING THE RIGHT FIT, AND HIRING SUITS

One of the most common mistakes made by men wearing formal clothes is that their trousers are too long. If you hire or buy from a reputable men's outfitters, you stand a better chance of wearing something that fits properly.

The temptation is to wear a shirt with a large collar so as not to feel restricted, but this will mean the shirt is too big and won't hang properly.

You should be able to fit no more than one or two fingers between your neck and the collar. If you feel you have a rather fat neck, you are probably better off avoiding a wing-collar which can make you look squat. If you don't enjoy the crispness of a brand-new white shirt, you can always hire a shirt which will feel less stiff.

If you're getting married away from home but will be using a chain of outfitters, you can always pop into their local branch to be measured and ask the shop to send your details to the outlet nearest your wedding venue.

For anyone who can't make it to the shop himself the measurements they will need include: chest, waist, inner leg, sleeve length, collar size and height. You should book your hire clothes about three months before the wedding – less if you're using a large store such as Moss Bros in Covent Garden which has more stock in store. Some times of the year are busier than others – June is hectic in an upmarket London store, for example, because of Ascot. Also allow more time if you're not a standard size.

Tip Remember to iron out the folds in a brand-new shirt.

STRESSBUSTER

Visit the shop with your ushers, best man and, if possible, your father and your partner's father. That way you will make sure that whatever you are all wearing is coordinated, and there will less chance of mix-ups if you hire from one shop.

MAKING THE MOST OF WHAT YOU'VE GOT

The range of suits available for the bridegroom provides plenty of scope for you to show off your assets, and even hide a few sensitive areas. You may, for example, find yourself standing at the altar next to a bride whose hairdo and tiara or floral headdress make her look as if she's grown several inches since you last met.

- **Height**: Look taller by creating vertical lines (for example in pin-striped trousers) and avoid anything that cuts you in two – turn-ups, blazer and trousers. Details at the top of your body such as a chunky or unusual tie, peaked lapels or a Nehru jacket help to draw the eyes upwards. Waistcoats will elongate your body, and good sturdy shoes like Oxfords will give you height without the need for lifts.

- **Weight**: If you think you're a bit on the heavy side, the dark jacket and pin-stripes of the morning suit will have a slimming effect.
- **Breadth**: Peaked lapels and a cravat will give you extra width.

PUTTING ON THE STYLE

Frock-coats – long coats with lapels which became popular in Victorian times – are available in a range of colours and materials from stockists such as Favourbrook. If you want to swagger around you could even hire an evening cane from Moss Bros or a fob chain from Lords Formal Wear. (See Stockists, page 286)

Other alternatives to the traditional suit include tartan trousers, a Nehru jacket and one of the many lavish waistcoats available. A designer suit in white makes a change, and lightweight suits or jackets are popular for weddings in hot climates (you won't need a tie with a grand-dad shirt).

CASE STUDY

Seth, a 36-year-old artist, wanted an outfit that would surprise, but not shock his in-laws; pander to his interest in history; and be wildly romantic. He visited theatrical costumers Angels and Bermans about nine times with his brother Derek (who was also best man), before hiring three Regency suits for them and his fiancé's brother. A full Elizabethan costume came a close second.

On the day of his wedding at a register office in Marlborough the three of them paraded through the town. Derek had grown sideburns specially and Seth's orange tail-coat made a startling contrast to his curly ginger hair. The trio also wore purple trousers and waistcoats, top hats and white shirts with big bows.

Seth and his fiancée, Emma, a 28-year-old editorial assistant who also had a passion for history, had kept their choice of costume a secret from each other. By chance, Emma had also opted for a Regency look.

GROOMING TIPS

- **Shaving**: Shave after or during your bath as the steam will soften your skin and beard and make for a closer shave. Always shave the jawline and cheeks first, followed by the neck and upper and lower lips and chin. Shave in the direction of growth.

- **Nails**: Make sure they're clean and trim.
- **Hair**: Have a good cut six weeks to a month beforehand and a tidy-up a fortnight before.

GOING AWAY

What you wear when you leave the wedding depends, up to a point, on how you're leaving. If it's by hot-air balloon, or if you will have a long drive in an open-topped car followed by a ferry crossing, you'll want something practical. If you're taking a taxi to a nearby hotel you can make your choice knowing that you won't be wearing the outfit for long.

You may choose something that you'll be able to wear for work, or something that will be smart enough for big occasions for years to come.

OTHER MALE GUESTS

MEMBERS OF THE WEDDING PARTY: BEST MAN, USHERS, FATHERS OF THE BRIDE AND GROOM

Male members of the bridal party usually wear a similar suit, although they can choose slightly different accessories (the bridegroom might wear a distinctive waistcoat). If you all decide to wear a similar tie or waistcoat you could extend this uniform to other team members such as the friend driving you to the church or family member in charge of the video. One bridegroom who was getting married in the traditional morning suit presented his best man and ushers with a horizontally striped, knitted silk tie in amber and black – the colours of Barnet FC, the football team he had followed since he was a boy.

Who pays for the attendants' outfits is a rather grey area. The best man normally pays for his clothes, although the bridegroom may buy him a special tie or waistcoat as a gift. It has been customary for the bride to pay for the ushers' outfits but, like most traditions, this is open to interpretation. The attendants may want to pay for their own clothes if they know that the couple are financially stretched (or vice versa).

PAGEBOYS

The range of clothes available for the pageboy is even wider than for the adult attendants, but bear in mind their personality. One boy may love showing off – in which case he'll enjoy being dressed up as a morris man to fit in with your Olde England theme. Another will make you pay for what he sees as the indignity of being made to wander around in a floral hat with bells on his trousers.

If you think your pageboy is too old for a sailor suit but would enjoy wearing grown-up clothes, you can normally hire an outfit similar to those worn by the male adults. Moss Bros caters for children from the age of five onwards and recommends an initial fitting three months before the day, and that final measurements are taken two weeks before.

Usually the bride pays for the pageboys' and bridesmaids' outfits, but parents sometimes offer to (see page 139, 'Meeting the cost').

MONEYSAVER

Hiring special clothes is expensive and buying them can seem like a waste since they will soon be outgrown. One option is to buy or hire a special waistcoat and team it up with ordinary black trousers (or jeans if the wedding isn't too formal) and a white shirt.

CHECKLIST

Draw up a list to include the following items, with columns for colour, size, budget, actual cost, date to be picked up or bought. Repeat the list for best man, ushers, and fathers of bride and bridegroom, omitting the going-away outfit.

Jacket/Coat
Shirt
Cufflinks
Tie/Cravat/Bow-tie
Waistcoat
Trousers/Kilt
Shoes
Socks
Hat
Gloves

Cummerbund
Accessories
Going-away outfit

7

Rings

Legally, you don't need a ring to get married, but for most people a wedding would not be complete without the presence of at least one ring, if not the exchange of two. The practice of giving a ring as a sign of betrothal dates back to Ancient Egypt when it was believed that a delicate nerve ran directly from the heart to the third finger of the right hand. Although the wedding ring is still worn on this finger in many countries, it is thought that the switch to the left hand was made in Britain at the time of the Reformation. During the seventeenth century the wedding ring was sometimes worn on the thumb.

Mary Tudor helped to set the trend for plain wedding bands in 1554 by saying she wanted to be married 'like other maidens'. By the time of the Commonwealth (1649–60) the wedding ring tradition was so well established that the Puritans' attempt to ban it because of its heathen origins failed. The sentimental Victorians established the trend of wearing the ring continuously, giving birth to the superstition that to remove it meant putting the marriage at risk.

ENGAGEMENT RINGS

Promises to marry have been sealed by a wide range of love tokens, from a Coca-Cola can ring to wildly expensive pieces of jewellery in settings prepared by master craftsmen. Early Jewish rings were often made in the shape of a house to symbolize the marital home, and Irish Claddah rings feature two hands holding a heart.

Barbara Hutton, the American Woolworths heiress who had seven husbands (including Cary Grant) and was known in her day as the original 'poor little rich girl', chose a black pearl from Cartier as one of her most distinctive engagement rings. Jackie Kennedy's second husband, Aristotle Onassis, gave her the 40-carat Lesotho III diamond said to be worth around £400,000, which itself came from a stone thought to be one of the largest diamonds ever found.

Although it is still more common for men to present an engagement ring when they propose, many couples choose the ring together. Others simply dispense with the idea of any engagement ring, and some couples, especially those who are already living together, incorporate the idea of the wedding band and the engagement ring into one piece – usually a gold band studded with gems.

The sort of ring you decide on should depend on your budget, lifestyle and character. Generally, diamonds, rubies and emeralds are the most expensive (and the most hard-wearing), although of course this depends on size and quality.

MONEYSAVER

If you have your heart set on a ruby but find you can't afford one, a good jeweller will be able to suggest a cheaper alternative of a similar colour. You may even end up preferring your second choice, especially if it is an unusual stone from a smaller mine.

The sort of job you do is also important: if you work on a farm it is probably not practical to choose a large, raised setting, but if that's the sort of ring you want you might decide just to wear it outside work. Or if you want a more unusual ring like a delicate, papier-mâché creation, it will have a greater chance of survival if you reserve it for special occasions. Traditionally you shouldn't wear your engagement ring until your engagement has been officially announced.

Bear in mind the sort of wedding ring you'll be wearing, too. Ideally they should be of the same carat (see below), otherwise the harder ring may, over several years, wear away at the other ring. You should also take into account the shape and style of each ring and whether they will complement one another. If your engagement ring has a heart-shaped setting, for example, you might want a wedding ring with a slight chink in it so that they fit snugly together.

DIAMONDS

The ancient Greeks thought that diamonds were splinters of stars fallen to earth, and as early as the fifteenth century they were seen as a girl's best friend among wealthy families where they became a symbol of marital fidelity because of their resistance to fire and steel.

Queen Elizabeth II has a platinum engagement ring set with eleven diamonds, a central solitaire and five smaller stones on each shoulder supporting the main stone. Prince Philip designed the ring, which was made up of stones from a tiara belonging to his mother, Princess Andrew of Greece.

Diamond solitaire rings are still among the most popular engagement rings. Other popular styles include: the round brilliant; oval; the marquise (long and pointed); heart-shaped; emerald (rectangular); pear-shaped; and square (also known as the princess). The diamond industry would like you to spend a month's salary on your engagement ring, but it is, of course, entirely up to you.

Look for the 'Four Cs' – cut, clarity, colour and carat – when choosing a diamond.

- **Cut**: A diamond that is cut well will sparkle.
- **Clarity**: The clarity of the stone is determined by the degree to which it is free from inclusions – natural imperfections such as spots, bubbles or lines (a flawless diamond is very rare).
- **Colour**: The most valuable diamonds are colourless, although diamonds with a pink, blue or canary-yellow hue are also highly valued.
- **Carat**: This is the weight of a diamond. There are 100 points in a carat, so a diamond of 50 points weighs half a carat.

BIRTHSTONES

Gemstones associated with birthdays are popular choices for an engagement ring. Traditionally, each month has a stone associated with it and that stone has a meaning of its own.

January: garnet (constancy, truth) – red
February: amethyst (sincerity) – purple
March: aquamarine (courage) – pale blue-green
April: diamond (innocence, light) – white, pink, blue or yellow
May: emerald (happiness, success in love) – green
June: pearl (beauty) – white or black
July: ruby (love, chastity) – red
August: peridot (joy) – green
September: sapphire (wisdom) – blue
October: opal (hope) – white, red or turquoise with multi-coloured flecks
November: topaz (fidelity) – yellow, brown or pink
December: turquoise (success) – blue

WEDDING RINGS

CHOOSING A STYLE

Wedding rings, symbolizing the unity of marriage, have been fashioned out of a wide range of materials, depending on the circumstances. The end of a church door key was used on one occasion, a leather ring cut out of a glove on another. Rush wedding rings were also common in rural weddings, and actor Richard Gere and model Cindy Crawford were reported to have married in such a hurry that they had to make do with a twist of silver chocolate foil.

Gold is the obvious choice for most people – perhaps because they want the same type of ring as their mother wore. Silver and platinum are both growing in popularity. Platinum wasn't widely used in Europe until the Art Deco and Art Nouveau periods when its strength made it ideal for delicate jewellery, but it has gained ground recently because of its distinctive colour which never tarnishes, its strength which makes it ideal for supporting precious stones in delicate settings, and its non-allergenic properties.

The most popular form of wedding ring is the band, which is usually one of four models: the francesina (round and fine); the traditional band; the mantovana (with a wide band); and the flat band (smooth or engraved). More substantial designs usually suit larger hands.

A particularly romantic traditional wedding ring consists of two intertwined bands, often in contrasting yellow and white gold.

RINGS AND OTHER THINGS FOR MEN

Some grooms are adamant that they are simply not a ring person, but if you want to give him something to mark your engagement or even the wedding, there are plenty of alternatives. A watch; cufflinks; bank note or business-card holder; picture frame; engraved wooden box or letter rack for his desk; cigarette box or lighter; shaving set: all will provide a daily reminder of your wedding.

If you like the idea of your husband wearing a wedding ring, you could try winning him round with a signet ring as an engagement present. There are also plenty of modern rings such as the wide 'cigar' design or rings with a hammered effect or maxim engraved on the outside which are far enough away from the traditional wedding band to entice someone new to ring-wearing.

HALLMARKS

British hallmarks have offered protection to consumers for over 600 years. Originally designed for gold and silver, they were extended to cover platinum in 1975.

The main purpose of the hallmark is to tell you exactly what you're getting for your money. Since pure gold, silver and platinum are too soft to be used by themselves, they are mixed with other metals to toughen them up. A hallmarked ring will have been tested at one of the official Assay Offices to make sure that the metals used meet certain standards. The carat is the amount of gold contained in the ring: a 9-carat ring is hallmarked with the number 375 showing that it is 37.5 per cent pure gold (nine parts gold to fifteen parts alloy). The higher the carat, the greater the amount of gold in the ring.

A typical hallmark will include:

- **The sponsor's mark**: A symbol (normally the initials) of the designer or company who made the ring.
- **The standard or quality mark**: This is a number which represents carat quality and shows how much gold (symbolized in the UK by a crown), silver (a lion or Britannia) or platinum (an orb) is contained in the piece of jewellery by weight in parts per 1,000:

Gold

916.6 shows a ring is 91.6 per cent pure gold – or 22-carat
750 shows a ring is 75 per cent pure gold – or 18-carat
585 shows a ring is 58.5 per cent pure gold – or 14-carat
375 shows a ring is 37.5 per cent pure gold – or 9-carat

Silver

958.4 denotes Britannia silver (shown by Britannia), which is 95.8 per cent silver.
925 denotes Sterling silver (shown by a lion), which is 92.5 per cent silver.

Platinum

Platinum has only one standard – 950 parts in each 1,000.

- **The Assay Office mark**: This shows which office tested the piece. There are now only four British Assay Offices, each of which has its own symbol: Birmingham (an anchor); Edinburgh (a castle); London (a leopard); and Sheffield (a rose). Dublin is shown by Hibernia (a seated woman leaning on a harp).
- **The date letter**: The letter tells you which year the item was made in. After January 1975 the British Assay Offices started to use the same date letter. See Further Reading (page 271) for information on understanding older hallmarks.

WHERE TO FIND A WEDDING OR ENGAGEMENT RING

- **Jewellers**: A long-established family firm or county jewellers is likely to have a reputation they are keen to hang on to and this should be reflected in the quality of their service. High street chains offer the security of a large name but may not always sell more unusual items.
- **Designers**: If you're looking for something a bit different, visit one of the many shops which now operate as galleries by displaying work from a range of designers (many offer mail order). A cluster of this type of shop has sprung up around Beauchamp Place in London, and the Fine Jewellery Room at Harrods also has a wide selection. The Goldsmiths' Fair in London, which is usually held in October, is another way of seeing a range of work in silver and gold. Commissioning a work especially for you is not necessarily more expensive than buying something ready-made.
- **Jewellery centres**: Birmingham has a long-established Jewellery Quarter where you can see craftsmen and women at work. Since rings are still made in the area, you can pick up bargains simply because you are cutting out the retailer. Hatton Garden in London has a range of jewellery shops, although quality can vary from shop to shop.
- **Auctions or antiques fairs**: Take along a magnifying glass to examine the ring beforehand, and set yourself an upper price limit.
- **Heirlooms**: Wearing a family ring can upset other members of the family, so make sure you consult everyone first. Ideally, it should be suggested to you, rather than the other way round.

MONEYSAVER

If you have enough nerve, you can sometimes reduce the asking price by haggling or offering cash.

WEAR AND CARE OF YOUR RING

CHOOSING THE RIGHT SIZE

Many people find their fingers can change dramatically in size from day to day, depending on temperature and, in the case of women, hormones and even some forms of contraceptive pill. It is therefore important to have your fingers measured at a time when you know they are a fairly average size – not after a day spent trailing round overheated shops or just before your period (if you suffer from water retention), or when you've been standing in the cold. Ideally, your ring should not feel too loose but you should be able to rotate it gently.

If you find that your fingers change shape as you grow older, the ring can be stretched to give you more room, or made smaller through various techniques such as adding another layer inside. Many women remove their ring during pregnancy, and you should definitely do this if you feel it becoming tight. One option is to wear it on a chain round your neck.

CARE

Wrap rings separately in a soft cloth to protect them from scratching, or keep them in a presentation box. Since it is normally up to the bridegroom to buy the rings, he usually looks after them in the run-up to the wedding. If you're worried about security you can ask the jeweller to keep them for you until the last moment.

A wedding band shouldn't need much cleaning – if you wear it in the bath or shower this will often be enough. Otherwise tap it clean with a soft brush such as a toothbrush dipped in a small amount of soapy water made up of mild liquid detergent, and rinse well.

Diamonds, which should be stored separately because they can damage other stones, can also be cleaned using the toothbrush method and patted dry with a soft, lint-free cloth. Alternatively, you can have the ring cleaned professionally.

SECURITY

Make sure your rings are properly insured against theft, loss of a stone or damage. It is usually possible simply to add them to household insurance if you list them separately. Obtain a dated valuation when you buy the ring and keep it, together with the receipt, in a safe place. Another precaution is to take photographs of your rings so that they are easily identifiable if lost or stolen.

THE GREAT REMOVAL DEBATE

Whether or not you take off your rings from time to time is not solely a matter of superstition. Some jewellers advise wearing your wedding ring at all times, simply because that way you are unlikely one day to leave it in a washroom somewhere in the Australian outback.

If you can trust yourself always to remember to put your ring back on, there are some times when it make sense to put it to one side.

- **At home**: Some abrasive household cleaners will damage the surface of rings. Hardened pastry can also be very difficult to remove from behind precious stones.
- **At play**: Chlorine and salt water can also damage some rings.
- **Make-up**: Perfume, hairspray and suntan lotions can harm gold.

ON THE DAY

Transfer your engagement ring to your right hand before the service and afterwards slip it on top of your wedding ring, which traditionally should be worn nearest the heart.

Tip If your finger becomes swollen during the service, your partner should twist the ring slightly to help it over your knuckle.

8

Health and Beauty

The chances are that your partner likes you the way you are and is likely to be startled if confronted by a highly made-up, mannequin version of the person he's used to. Very bright colours, too, can detract from your dress and will quickly look dated in your wedding photos.

The most effective make-up is subtle and natural-looking, but despite this, there are still several bridal hazards worth bearing in mind.

BEAUTY

WHY IT'S DIFFERENT FOR BRIDES

- **The Shining**: Photography has a nasty way of producing a shiny face. Apply a translucent make-up base to prevent oil building up, and consider other products such as the Body Shop's TeaZone which will help give your skin a matt appearance. Avoid eye-shadows, lipsticks and bronzing powders with too much shimmer, and touch up your make-up with matt face powder just before the photos are taken.
- **The Tearjerker**: Waterproof mascara will guard against panda smudges. If you want to curl your eyelashes, do so before applying mascara, and remember to pack eye make-up remover suitable for water-proof mascara in your honeymoon bag.
- **The Epic**: Bear in mind that you want your make-up to stay in place all day (and probably much of the night). Give your face powder and lipstick to someone responsible so that you can touch it up when necessary (see page 101, 'A helping hand').
- **Colour**: Very strong shades on your lips and eyes may drain your face of colour if you're wearing a light-coloured outfit.

A HELPING HAND

Many beauty schools, salons and cosmetic houses will provide a make-up artist on the day (see Stockists, page 286) who will also attend to mothers and bridesmaids. This can be very expensive, though, especially when travelling costs and the price of a rehearsal are taken into account.

Take a swatch of material from your dress to the consultation and discuss any flowers you have in mind for your bouquet or your hair. You could also bring along beauty products that you feel particularly comfortable with so that they can be incorporated into the make-over. Remember, though, that the consultation is likely to take place in the middle of a shop floor, so you might want to pick a quiet time of the shopping day, or a store that isn't round the corner from work.

MONEYSAVER

A halfway house is to have a make-over which will give you the chance to discuss your preferences and specific problems and jot down any colours you like. You can then ask a friend to apply the make-up on the day. This way you have the best of both worlds – a professional consultation and a make-up artist with whom you feel relaxed.

TRICKS OF THE TRADE

Whether it's eye shadow or foundation, the key to natural-looking make-up is to blend, blend and blend again. This helps to avoid a mask-like effect and will ensure your make-up stays in place longer.

Choose somewhere with good natural light such as by a window, and make sure everything you need is arranged on a tray beforehand. Moisturize your skin well and leave plenty of time for it to be absorbed. Ideally, you should apply your make-up last and then step into whatever you are wearing.

STRESSBUSTER

Make sure you practise applying your make-up. The colours may look dramatically different against the backdrop of your dress or outfit.

Tip Invest in a good set of make-up brushes.

LUSCIOUS LIPS

You're going to be doing a lot of kissing and smiling on your wedding day, so it's important your lips are in good shape. Lipscuff from the Body Shop is effective for sloughing away dead skin, but don't overdo it or you will end up with a rather frayed smile. Keep your lips moisturized with a good lip balm.

On the day, leave applying your lipstick until the very last moment. Define your lips with a lipstick pencil which matches your own lip colour to stop the lipstick 'bleeding', or use No Wander from the Body Shop which forms a barrier around your mouth. Apply the lipstick with a brush, blot your lips with a tissue and dust powder over it to seal, apply more lipstick and blot again. You could also seal your lipstick with a product like Lipcote, or consider a long-lasting lipstick such as one from Clinique's range.

HANDSOME HANDS

From the moment the ring is slipped on your finger to the cake-cutting at the reception, your hands will be on display. Even if you've been rather hard on your hands in the past, the run-up to most weddings should provide ample time for a full rehabilitation. Get in the habit of wearing gloves if it's cold outside, and when you're washing up.

Soaking your hands once a week in warm almond oil will help replace some of the moisture lost through cold weather, central heating and frequent washing. While still wet, push back the cuticles with a towel or cotton bud. Vaseline Intensive Care hand-cream is an effective and cheap way of repairing the ravages of modern life and nail-biting. Pay particular attention to the base of the nail, and if applying it, or a similar cream, at night, wear a pair of cotton gloves for extra absorption.

Unless you're used to very long nails, keep them short and rounded. A whitener such as Revlon's nail pencil will give the appearance of long, healthy nails, while very strong colours can look dated and clash with the flowers in your bouquet (you can let your imagination run wild on your toe-nails).

AFTER THE SERVICE

If you want a slightly different look in the evening, swap to darker, more intense shades of lip and eye colours and blusher, but don't attempt anything too ambitious.

ZAPPING THAT ZIT AND OTHER TROUBLE-SHOOTING HINTS

- **Blemishes**: If you can feel a spot erupting forty-eight hours before your wedding day, reach for a product like Clinique's Anti-Blemish Spot Treatment which contains salicylic acid to dry out and soothe the area. Only squeeze if you're sure the spot is at the end of its life – tackling it too early will inflame the area – and use a tissue. Apply ice the night before and an hour or so before you're ready to put on your make-up. If you've got the time, take your spot to a professional dermatologist (ask your doctor or a beauty salon).
- **Colour**: Brides are traditionally expected to blush, but if you are prone to turn crimson, a green corrective layer (such as the Body Shop's Prebase, or Boots' No 7 Rosy Tone Colour Control or No 17's Colour Corrective Fluid) beneath your foundation on the parts of your face that cause most problems will tone down the redness. Similarly, lilac will lift your complexion if you look a little pale. Apricot will also bring a glow to black or Asian skin tones.
- **Dark circles and puffy eyes**: Use a creamy concealer under your eyes. Apply after foundation to avoid using too much. If your eyes look puffy, a splash of iced water will get your circulation moving, and you could try the old standby of chilled cucumber under the eyes. Clinique's Turnaround cream will also give a boost to tired skin.

BACKS AND SHOULDERS

Don't forget the rest of your body, especially if your dress or going-away outfit will reveal your back and shoulders. This part of the body has a lot of natural moisture but tends to get hidden away under clothes and can be prone to blackheads and other blemishes.

Make sure you exfoliate with a body scrub or loofah and moisturize with a light lotion. Exposing your back to the sun can improve its condition, but be wary of suntan marks which can appear with the slightest exposure to the outdoors (alternating swimming costumes helps). If you want a golden look, consider a fake tanning lotion, or dust your décolletage with bronzing powder.

OLDER BRIDES

Less really is more for older brides. Using heavy foundation will highlight any lines and give a caked effect. Exfoliation is even more important.

The one exception to this rule is the eyebrows, which sometimes become sparser as you get older, and you may want to give them extra definition with an eyeliner pencil. You should also be careful about avoiding 'lipstick bleed' (see page 103, 'Luscious Lips').

YOUR KIT FOR COPING

Ask someone like your mother or a close friend to pack a bag of beauty essentials. This may make them feel like a branch of Boots, but it will give you a lot of comfort to know that help is at hand – even though you probably won't need it.

- Tissues
- Make-up remover (decant a small amount into a miniature container)
- Foundation
- Face powder
- Lipstick and lip-liner pencil
- Water atomizer
- Hairspray (regular rather than firm hold)
- Headache remedy
- Hairpins
- Fragrance
- Breath freshener

BEAUTY TREATMENTS

- **Eyelash tinting**: One week before – earlier if it's your first time.
- **Facial**: At least a week before because it may bring out spots.
- **Eyebrow shaping**: A few days before, or longer if you're anxious about the results (once you've got the basic shape you can keep the eyebrows tidy yourself). If you're doing it yourself, only pluck from below the browline. As a guide for the shape of your eyebrow lay a pencil from the side of your nose to the outer corner of your eye – your brow should finish just above the end nearest your eye. If you find you've been a bit over-enthusiastic, use powder eyeshadow (grey if your hair is dark, brown if it's

light) to cover up the damage. An eyebrow gel will tame unruly hairs.

- **Leg waxing**: One week before, so you have maximum benefit for your honeymoon.
- **Bleaching and depilatories**: A few days before, to give your skin a chance to calm down.
- **Manicure**: The day before if it's being done professionally, but start pampering your nails six weeks to three months before the wedding day.

Tip Don't try any new product too near your wedding day as it may lead to an allergic reaction.

KEEPING COOL

If you're getting married in a humid country, or you're not used to wearing foundation, try something like Clinique's Workout Make-up which won't feel too heavy. The Body Shop's Cooling Leg can be used on feet and arms as well as legs.

A squirt of mineral water from something like Evian's atomizer can help cool you down and also pep up tired-looking hair. Try it on your neck if you're wearing your hair up, on your wrists, backs of your legs and any exposed part of your body. But keep it away from make-up that's not water-proof. Ice-cubes held to your temples before you put on your make-up will also lower your temperature.

HAIR

Your wedding is the very worst time to experience a bad hair day. To avoid any disasters, visit your hairdresser well in advance to discuss the look you are aiming for. Don't be too ambitious or choose a style that will make you look drastically different or which you will worry may collapse just as you are saying your vows. If you want an idea of what you'll look like without going for the chop, try computer imaging (available at some salons or by mail order) in which various styles and colours are superimposed on your picture.

If you're getting married away from home but want to have a professional to style your hair on the day, do a bit of research before you book in with a salon. It's vital to have a trial run and to be absolutely honest about the results. If you're not the most assertive of people, take a friend who can make it clear what you're after.

Don't despair if the only available hairdresser's is an old-fashioned salon where the staff think a diffuser is something you use to unblock drains. More traditional hairdressers are usually expert at putting hair up, and you can always purchase accessories such as pearl-headed pins yourself.

DOING IT YOURSELF

- Practise your whole routine (including wearing your veil and headdress) and time how long it takes. If you're having problems, ask your hairdresser to show you where you're going wrong, even if it's only with blow-drying.
- If your dress is difficult to put on, leave the finishing touches to your hair until you're fully dressed.
- Don't wash your hair on the day if you plan to wear it up – it will be too smooth to work with.
- Clip your fringe in place before you dry it if you want a smooth look.
- Wearing your hair up can sometimes look severe. Tease out a few strands using curling tongs to twist them into tendrils, or leave a loose fringe.
- Allow your hair to cool down before using heated rollers.
- Add volume by scrunch-drying, back-combing or blow-drying using a styling mousse, or think about hair extensions.

HAIR COUNTDOWN

- **As soon as possible**: Book an appointment with your hairdresser to discuss what you're aiming for. If you're getting married away from home, start looking for a hairdresser you feel comfortable with.
- **Three months to go**: Begin a course of special conditioning treatments, especially if your hair is long.
- **Six weeks before**: Take a picture of your outfit and anything you will wear on your head (headdress, veil, tiara, etc.) and have a trial run.
- **Three to four weeks**: Have your hair cut to allow it time to relax into the desired shape and to allow you to get used to it.
- **Two to three weeks**: Have a perm or any major colourings. Avoid swimming, or make sure your hair is covered up.
- **One to two weeks**: A semi-permanent or vegetable colour will give your hair an extra shine. A kerotene treatment, which you can have as near the wedding day as possible, will put moisture back into your hair.

HEALTH

LOSING WEIGHT

Don't feel you have to lose weight, but if you're looking for an excuse to shed some pounds, a wedding date is a good goal to aim for. Most brides find that as the excitement mounts, food is the last thing on their minds.

FITNESS TIPS

- Keep a bottle of water on your desk at work and swig at it through the day. This will stave off hunger pains and help flush out impurities in your system.
- Eat more fruit and vegetables.
- Take up regular exercise with a friend.
- Cut down on sugary foods – you'll soon lose the craving.
- Consider joining a slimming club if you need moral support.

BEATING PERIOD BLUES

If you are already on the Pill you can avoid having a period on your wedding day by missing out the usual break between each course of tablets – but make sure you discuss this with your doctor first as instructions differ between brands.

It is not usually advisable, however, to go on the Pill simply to avoid your period. Your body may take a while to get used to this form of contraceptive (depending on which type of Pill you take) and you could even be unlucky enough to suffer break-through bleeding that lasts longer than your usual period. If, however, you were planning to start taking the Pill after your wedding, you might want to begin the course two to three months in advance to allow your body to adjust to it and give yourself the option to postpone your period.

FIGHTING PREMENSTRUAL TENSION

- **Diet**: Adopt a detox diet without grains, wheat, oats, barley and rye but with plenty of fresh fruit and vegetables. Ideally, start three to four months before your wedding. This will help bloating, but as a temporary measure, try a diuretic. Cut down on alcohol, salt and caffeine. (See Useful Addresses, page 272.)
- **Lifestyle**: Get enough sleep and regular exercise.
- **Therapies**: Some people find acupuncture or a course of B6 vitamins or evening primrose oil helps.
- **Planning**: Bear in mind when your periods will start when fixing the wedding date, hen party, a dinner party for both sets of parents and your final dress fitting.

CONTRACEPTION

- **Planning a baby soon**: Consider barrier methods such as condoms or diaphragm, or ask for advice about natural methods of contraception. See overleaf for health advice and remember that it can take up to twelve months to conceive. (See also Useful Addresses, page 272.)
- **A baby in the first few years of your marriage**: Ask for advice about contraceptive pills, intrauterine devices (IUD) and injections (fertility can take up to a year or more to return to normal). If you're on the Pill, wait for a natural period before trying to conceive as this will make it easier to work out when the baby is due.
- **A child within the first ten years, or not at all**: Implants give protection for five years. If you don't want children or already have a family, consider a vasectomy or – if you're certain you don't want children – sterilization.

Tip If you plan to go anywhere exotic for your honeymoon, pack condoms as the Pill can be affected by sickness or severe diarrhoea, making extra protection advisable for seven days afterwards (see instructions on packet).

GETTING IN SHAPE FOR CONCEPTION

- **German measles (rubella)**: Before you start to try to conceive, ask for a blood test to see whether you are immune to measles, which can damage your baby, and if you're not covered ask for a jab.
- **Inherited diseases**: If you know of any conditions, like sickle cell anaemia or thalassaemia, that run in either family, take advice from a doctor before stopping contraception.
- **Medicine**: Ask the pharmacist's advice when buying over-the-counter medicines and try to avoid any treatments until after the third month of pregnancy. X-rays are also best avoided and you should do your best to give up smoking and drugs (legal or otherwise). Tell your doctor and dentist you are pregnant.
- **Food and drink**: Cut down on alcohol and caffeine (the latter has been linked in some studies to miscarriages) and avoid soft cheeses, pâté, soft-boiled eggs and cold prepared meats which carry a risk of listeria which can cause birth defects. Give up liver and vitamin A tablets.
- **Folic acid**: Take supplements, which can reduce the risk of spina bifida, as soon as you want to conceive and for the first twelve weeks of pregnancy.
- **Cats**: Ask someone else to change the cat litter, and wear gloves when gardening as there is a risk of toxoplasmosis carried in cat faeces which can harm a developing baby.

PART THREE
THE CAST

9

Bride and Bridegroom: Coping with Stress

Psychologists believe that getting married is one of the most stressful times in our lives – only divorce and death of a close family member lead to greater anxiety. Weddings have a habit of spawning other stressful situations, too – leaving home or at least moving house, money worries and the emergence of old family sores. The most effective way of dealing with stress is to recognize you're suffering from it and determine who and what you can turn to for help.

Brides in particular may feel under great stress: they're the centre of attention and a great deal of the organizing will often fall to them. Probably more than men, they may want to try new ways of relaxing.

WAYS OF COPING: THE ART OF DELEGATION

People love being involved, and even complete strangers are flattered to be asked for help. Mention a wedding and you're more likely to get the hotel room you want, the shop assistant will miraculously be able to find an extra reel of the ribbon you're looking for, and the engineer may even turn up on time to fix your boiler.

Look at your friends' talents: someone who likes sewing might be prepared to make waistcoats, a friend who's keen on computers might design the invitations, someone else could decorate the church. Once you've delegated, let people get on with their tasks and don't interfere – unless they ask your opinion. If you're not prepared to trust them, it's pointless asking for their help in the first place.

MONEY

When you start to budget for your wedding, decide which aspects you don't want to scrimp over and which you are happy to pare back to the minimum. Then look carefully at how this compares with your parents' expectations.

It is still customary for parents (usually the bride's) to foot a large chunk of the bill (see page 139, 'Who pays for what'). But many parents will be shocked at how much everything costs, simply because things were probably much simpler when they got married.

One compromise is for the couple to offer to pay for the areas of expenditure which parents deem extravagant – perhaps the dress, the honeymoon or the attendants' outfits. On the other hand, you might want to meet the entire cost of the day yourself, either because you have the resources or simply because you don't see why your parents should pay. But bear in mind that your parents might feel excluded or insulted – they will probably be asking many of their friends and to some extent acting as hosts, and they may also have been saving for years for your wedding. You might like to ask them to pay for a specific item – the marquee, the drinks, the flowers or the invitations – so that they don't feel left out.

CASE STUDIES

Weddings have a tendency to remove a sense of proportion. A bridegroom was jailed for five years for robbing two petrol stations so that he could pay for his wedding and honeymoon. The 47-year-old was arrested at a register office in South London as he waited for the ceremony to begin.

A NO-FRILLS WEDDING

Charles, a 26-year-old builder, and Mandy, a 25-year-old teacher, didn't want a big wedding. He wore his best suit and she bought a white bridesmaid's dress. Their guests – parents, one best friend each and a sister – were invited by word of mouth to the register office in Colchester and to a restaurant afterwards. Their honeymoon was a day trip to Brighton.

A LAVISH AFFAIR

A dozen committees were set up to organize the triple wedding of three brothers from one of Britain's richest Asian families, the Hindujas. When Dheeraji, 23, Ajay, 27, and Ramkrishan, 24, married in Bombay, 10,000 guests from over fifty countries attended. They were showered with twenty baskets of rose petals at the Royal Western Turf Club, and 1,200 staff prepared the wedding banquet. The entrance to the club was transformed into a grotto representing the Himalayan home of the gods, complete with dry ice for waterfalls. Foreign guests, who were given silk Indian costumes to wear during the three-day celebrations, were transported by elephants and white horses and watched the ceremony on giant video screens.

HOW TO MEET THE BILL

- **Savings**: Look out for accounts with high interest rates but leave yourself plenty of time to take the cash out – some accounts penalize you if you give insufficient notice, while others only allow one withdrawal in a set time.
- **Borrowing**: A wedding is seen by most banks and building societies as a legitimate reason to lend money, but shop around for the best rates and compare APRs (annual percentage rate – the true measure of the interest you are paying on a loan). Credit cards are generally an expensive way of raising finance.
- **Friends and family**: Borrowing from someone you know can put a strain on a relationship – especially if the lender doesn't agree with the way you spend the money. Make sure you know exactly the terms under which the money is being lent: for example, when you will pay it back.

WORK

Try to arrange your wedding so that it doesn't clash with any big projects or busy periods. Ideally, take at least a week off beforehand so that you can unwind, enjoy the run-up to the day and spend time with guests who arrive early.

Don't bombard colleagues with every detail of the wedding – especially if they're not invited – and limit the amount of work time you spend making wedding arrangements. If you need to phone the florist or caterers, make the phone calls in one go so that you're not too distracted, and try to do it in a lunchbreak.

INSOMNIA

HOW MUCH SLEEP DO YOU NEED?

Insomnia is a vicious circle – the more you worry about lack of sleep the harder it becomes to doze off. But once you acknowledge that the body can adapt to less sleep than it's used to, you're on the road to a good night's rest.

Remember how little sleep you got by on when you were first in love, or the times you've been forced to work late to meet a deadline. In both cases the adrenalin kept you going. Getting married is exactly the same: if you feel in a state of perpetual excitement you may not actually need as much sleep.

Even if you don't manage a good night before your wedding, the thrill of the event will be enough to carry you through the day. Think about it . . . how often have you heard a bride and bridegroom described as 'glowing' or 'radiant' and how rarely have they looked 'tired' or 'drawn'?

ADOPTING A SLEEP ROUTINE

Take a good hard look at where you sleep. Is it too hot, too cold, too noisy? How comfortable is your bed, and how often do you turn your mattress?

Use the few hours before you go to bed to prepare for sleep – listen to music or read a magazine or book (but avoid something like a thriller that might keep you awake). Don't take work to bed with you, or make phone calls that are likely to make you anxious, and only go to bed when you feel sleepy. Exercise can help, but don't do it too late in the day otherwise it might wake up your whole system.

Cut down on alcohol, tea, caffeine (not just coffee, but cola drinks) and smoking. Don't eat too late in the evening, or go to bed hungry.

FIGHTING INSOMNIA

- **Timing**: Some people find it helps to get up at the same time every day and avoid the temptation to snooze during the day. Others prefer a ten- to twenty-minute power nap after lunch.
- **Frustration**: If you can't sleep, get up and go to another room. Read a book or magazine, or write a letter (but don't do anything connected with an issue that's bothering you – this is not the time to attempt the seating plan for your wedding reception). Only go back to bed when you feel sleepy.
- **Medicines**: Doctors are reluctant to recommend sleeping pills as they can be addictive and may lead to side-effects such as – ironically – insomnia. There is a plethora of over-the-counter sedatives to choose from in your local pharmacist's. Many, though, are based on antihistamines which can cause drowsiness during the day and should not be seen as a long-term solution.
- **Alternatives**: Other remedies mix herbs traditionally used to treat insomnia such as hops, valerian, lemon verbena or camomile (which can also be taken as teas).
- **Relaxation**: Try yoga or meditation. Acupuncture also helps some people.

Tip Put a few drops of lavender oil in your fabric conditioner when you wash your sheets, or keep some lavender in your linen drawer.

ANXIETY

THINGS TO DO WHEN IT BECOMES TOO MUCH

- **With your wedding party**: Watch some live comedy; play hide-and-seek, rounders or Frisbee; go to the seaside and ride the dodgems.
- **Just the two of you**: Book a weekend away together a few weeks before the wedding (this may seem hard to stick to as the day approaches but will pay dividends); ban any talk of the wedding for twenty-four hours; go to the sea or for a walk in the woods.
- **By yourself**: Allow time to relax; soak in an aromatherapy bath (see Further Reading, page 271) surrounded by brochures of where you'll go for your honeymoon; swim regularly.

A HELPING HAND

- **Worries**: Guatemalans line up seven dolls and tell each of them one of their worries before they go to sleep. Since there are only seven dolls you are only allowed seven worries.
- **Massage**: This can be emotionally and physically purging. Aromatherapy uses essential oils, while Shiatsu works on the pressure points of the body to redirect energy in the body. Reflexology concentrates on the feet.

VIDEOS TO EXORCIZE THOSE DEMONS

A few weeks before the wedding you may feel you're in danger of losing your sense of humour.

Four Weddings and a Funeral
Guaranteed to make you thankful Rowan Atkinson isn't conducting the ceremony, and to remind you that a bridesmaid's dress tucked into her knickers certainly diverts attention from the bride.

Father of the Bride (original Spencer Tracy or Steve Martin version)
If your father's tempted to buy a fake designer jacket or your mother wants a wedding organizer who insists on ice sculptures in your garden, this is the film for you.

The Philadelphia Story
Marriage second-time around will seem a doddle compared with this screwball comedy starring Katharine Hepburn, Cary Grant and James Stewart.

Plaza Suite
Should you feel like locking yourself in the hotel bathroom before your wedding, Walter Matthau's frenzied portrayal of the father of the bride will be enough to make you see sense.

Muriel's Wedding
One bride's battle to prove that a nightmare family needn't stop you fulfilling your wedding dreams.

ON THE DAY

No matter how nervous you feel, you will be surprised at the speed with which the day passes. If you feel yourself becoming anxious, take deep breaths and try to concentrate on your honeymoon.

- **Breakfast**: Yoghurt, together with cereal such as Jordan's Oat Crunchy, fresh fruit and a piece of toast (if you're not prone to bloating) will provide a nutritious start to the day. Herbal tea will calm your nerves, whereas coffee may set your heart racing. If you really can't face food, try a fruit milk shake. As one nutritionist said, you wouldn't expect the bride's car to arrive with an empty petrol tank, so don't start your own day without some sort of fuel.
- **Alcohol**: Just because it's your wedding day doesn't mean you can't have a drink – especially if you know it will calm your nerves. Plan to incorporate it into the celebrations: a quiet drink in a relaxing hotel bar around the corner from the register office, or a glass of champagne at home with your chief bridesmaid, rather than a desperate dash to the pub opposite the church.
- **Snacking**: Nuts such as almonds or dried apricots, or a snack bar like Jordan's Fruesli will give you a quick boost.

HOW THE ROYALS COPE

Royal weddings are usually portrayed as the epitome of poise, when everything goes like clockwork. But Royal Households are similar to any other on a wedding morning.

- On the Queen's wedding day on 20 November 1947 the bride's orchids went missing and were eventually found in the fridge (put there by a footman). The Queen Mother's tiara needed last-minute repairs and the Queen's pearls were left behind at St James's and had to be fetched. Prince Philip, convinced he had overslept, grabbed a piece of toast and coffee and leaped into a car – only to be reassured by a policeman and sent back for a calming gin and tonic.

- When Edward, Prince of Wales, married Princess Alexandra of Denmark in 1863 at St George's Chapel, Windsor, the travel arrangements for guests proved less than adequate. The 'special' train was so over-crowded that Lord Palmerston, the Prime Minister, had to travel third class and Benjamin Disraeli was forced to sit on his wife's lap.

10

The Minders: Best Man or Woman; Ushers, Bridesmaids and Pageboys

THE ROLE OF THE BEST MAN OR WOMAN

The ideal best man or woman should be at the hub of the wedding without stealing the limelight; he or she must be a good organizer and trouble-shooter without appearing bossy; should be able to calm the couple's nerves without revealing his or her own, and should treat everyone, from a guest who complains of the cold in the church to another who doesn't like where he or she is sitting at the reception, with equal charm.

If all that sounds like a tall order, remember that as best man or woman you are only being asked to fill the role for one day (which is bound to pass very quickly) and, since everyone knows how demanding the job can be, the guests will all be on your side. Afterwards, too, you will be able to bask in the reflected glory of a happy wedding.

Exactly how involved you become in the preparations depends on the couple. If one, or both, of them enjoys making arrangements, your duties may be confined to the wedding day itself. But it is still a good idea to offer to help – even if it's just arranging the stag or hen night.

You might find, too, that while the couple insist they want a low-key wedding, their parents will only be happy if everything is done 'properly'. It is best to make this discovery before the wedding rather than on the day.

A good best man or woman will also spot the first signs of wedding tension, discuss what is bothering the bride or groom, and see if there is anything he or she can do. You might take them out for a special evening, or pamper the bride with a treat such as a manicure or massage, and the groom with something like a night in with the boys (see page 117, 'Anxiety').

If you manage to escape with a fairly light load in the run-up to the wedding, the day itself will be a different matter. Even the most organized bride and bridegroom will not be able to cope with every unexpected development – nor should they since their job is to be the centre of attention. Make sure they are aware of this and stress that, for one day in their lives, you are their slave.

THE BEST WOMAN AND CHIEF BRIDESMAID

The idea of the best woman, either fulfilling the traditional role of the best man alone or side by side with their male counterpart, is becoming more and more popular. Chief bridesmaids, too, are often asked to do more than simply look after the other bridesmaids and pageboys and may end up acting, at least in part, as an unofficial best woman (sometimes even making a speech).

The biggest obstacle you face as best woman is making your position of authority clear to everyone at the wedding. A best man is easily identified by his 'livery' – the suit that shows he is part of the same team as the bridegroom, ushers and father of the bride. Although best women have been known to wear a morning suit, this might be a bit too radical for some weddings. Many best women find the answer is to wear something that makes them stand out from the other guests: a distinctive hat, or one with a very large brim, or a dress or suit in a vivid colour.

It also helps if the key members of the wedding party such as parents and minister are told that there will be a best woman and asked to refer to, and introduce her, as such, rather than as a bridesmaid. The person who speaks before the best woman at the reception should make a point of introducing her so that the guests realize she has a legitimate reason for being there.

If the best woman is sharing the role with a best man, the two should discuss how to divide their responsibilities. The most natural division is that the best man looks after the bridegroom, and the best woman the bride.

THE HEN AND THE STAG PARTY

One theory about hen and stag parties is that, like many wedding customs, they developed as a way of warding off ill luck. If evil spirits could be tricked into doing their worst *before* the wedding, the couple would have an auspicious start to their married life. It is up to the best man or woman to make sure evil spirits aren't given *too* much scope for fun.

Hen and stag parties are now rarely held the night before the wedding but, as on the wedding day, the best man or woman must be sober enough to make sure nothing disastrous happens. It may seem a good idea to strip the bridegroom, wrap him in brown paper and put him on a train to Manchester with a Red Star label stuck to his forehead, or to dye his hair a shade of pink which takes weeks finally to disappear, but the joke will usually have worn thin by the next day.

If the best man or woman has agreed to arrange the stag or hen night he or she should ask the bridegroom or bride what sort of celebration they want (even if the details are kept from them). The bride, for example, may want a mellow day culminating in a picnic and out-door concert, whereas the best woman may be planning a night out clubbing.

The bride and bridegroom should also be consulted about who is coming to the party. Usually it is their closest friends, but they might want to use the event as a way of introducing a partner of a friend to other wedding guests. The bride or bridegroom might also want their parents to come, depending on their relationship.

One way of making the hen or stag day memorable is to tailor it to the bride or bridegroom's interests. Richard, who was best man for his brother Graeme, started the day with a trip to watch Leyton Orient, a football team their grandfather had once played for. Linda held a hen party for her friend Rosemary at her own home which she decked out with sunflowers – Rosemary's favourite.

KEEPING THE MOMENTUM GOING

The secret of a good hen or stag party is that guests pace themselves. One way is to ensure that you manage to have some food before you become too drunk, but choose a restaurant to suit everyone's budget. If you decide to go on a pub crawl, ring up one of the stopping points in advance and arrange for some sandwiches to be laid on for when you arrive.

Ask guests to arrive at different stages, or arrange to travel to a place where the bride or bridegroom lived or worked in the past and still has friends. Many stag and hen nights meet up at the end of the evening, which has the added advantage of making it easier for people to find lifts home and also gives a focus to the day.

If either the bride or bridegroom is particularly outgoing he or she will enjoy letting everyone know he or she is on their hen or stag night. One group of women in York made a hen outfit for the bride-to-be: a long paper cape with feathers painted on it and a pink washing-up glove on top for the hen's crown. You could ask each guest to wear a wig (you can buy them at charity shops) or to come dressed in the same (bright) colour.

THINGS TO DO

- Take to the road: tank-driving; go-carting; off-road vehicles.
- Outdoor options: llama trekking; paintballing (where teams 'shoot' each other with paint); open-air concerts; bungee jumping.
- Make a weekend of it: visit Amsterdam, Hamburg or Dublin for the night life (and stock up on duty free – see page 156, 'Drink'); take a trip to Disneyland Paris or go on a Murder Mystery Weekend.
- Live entertainment: stand-up comedy; a drag act; a night at the dogs.
- Something more sedate: a tea dance; health farm (or beauty treatments at a hotel); an unusual museum (like Cadbury World in Birmingham); or a distillery (such as Bushmills in Northern Ireland); ten-pin bowling; Turkish baths.

Your local tourist information centre will tell you what's available in your area (see also Stockists, page 287).

The best man or woman should make sure plenty of photos are taken during the course of the day (you could even hire or borrow a video camera) and that he or she knows of a late-night café or bar where the guests can finish the evening if it goes on beyond normal closing hours.

STRESSBUSTER

Give everyone the telephone number of someone (perhaps a parent) who has promised to stay in on the stag or hen night. If anyone gets lost they can call the number and leave a message to say where they are.

IF TEMPERS FLARE

Too much drink can sometimes lead to angry words, or you may come across someone who doesn't see the funny side of a stag party. If one or more of your charges is squaring up for a fight:

- Move them away from their audience and disco strobe lights (which can sometimes inflame tempers further), but without touching them. Try: 'I'm sorry I can't hear you, can we move to a quiet corner?'
- Listen carefully to what they're both saying – sometimes people just want a chance to sound off.
- Reassure in a quiet voice – don't shout.
- A joke aimed at yourself or another member of the party can often defuse the situation.

COUNTDOWN FOR THE BEST MAN OR WOMAN

DUTIES IN THE RUN-UP TO THE WEDDING

(TH = thoughtful, not essential)

- Ask if there is anything in particular you can take responsibility for. Meet both set of parents, if you don't already know them, and the ushers and other attendants.
- Check the date of the wedding with the local police to see if it clashes with any major events such as a gala procession or RAF training exercise.
- The best woman may be asked to come along to any dress fittings, or to help the bride shop for an outfit. (TH)

TWO MONTHS BEFORE

- Make arrangements for your outfit, whether it is hired or bought (see page 87, 'Finding the right fit, and hiring suits').
- Ensure bridegroom and ushers have made similar arrangements for their clothes. The best woman or chief bridesmaid should also help make arrangements for the other attendants.
- Run through the guest list so that you are aware of any potential trouble-spots, for example: someone coming from a long way who may be late; any ill-feeling between particular guests; anyone with

particular needs, such as a mother with a young child or a disabled guest. Make sure, too, you know the names of close family and if there is a doctor or nurse among the guests.

- Arrange stag or hen night. (TH)
- Visit the place where the wedding will be held and meet the person who will be taking the service. Check out: parking; rules on confetti; where photos are usually taken (and options if it rains).
- Take the couple along to the reception venue and meet the person who will be in charge. Check out: parking; a room for the couple to change in; the seating arrangements; a table for gifts and whether a microphone will be available; where the seating plan will be displayed.
- Liaise with the best man or woman and other adult attendants. Divide tasks and arrange to meet again before the wedding.

ONE MONTH TO GO

- Time the length of journey from where the bride and bridegroom will be staying to the wedding venue and then on to the reception at the same time of day that the wedding will take place.
- Start work on your speech.
- Brief ushers on any difficult guests (see previous page), and make sure they know who the key players are. If you think parking will be a problem, enlist their help.
- Arrange transport to church for yourself and the bridegroom. Make sure you have means of getting to the reception and home afterwards. If the bridegroom's car is being used on the day, make sure it has been serviced.
- Buy ribbons to decorate the car (check with the couple over the colour) and arrange for posies or white heather for the interior. Collect old cans for the going-away car and buy string and balloons (twice as many as you think you'll need – you're bound to burst several).
- Have hair cut when necessary.
- Make sure the right number of buttonholes have been ordered.
- Buy a small present for the day. If you are the best woman, or chief bridesmaid, ask the bride if you may buy her garter. (TH)
- Check on the format for the reception: will there be a receiving line; what sort of entertainment is planned; when will drinks be served? Help draw up the seating plan so that you have an idea who most people are (see page 230, 'Seating').

TWO WEEKS BEFORE

- Finish writing speech, time and practise it. Liaise with the other speakers to make sure it doesn't overlap.
- Check that ring(s) have been bought.
- Compile a list of local taxi firms and find out how long it would take them to arrive in an emergency.
- Ask if there are any family celebrations you can help with. (TH)
- Best woman should check on bridesmaids' and attendants' outfits. Help deliver and store bride's dress and accessories if necessary. (TH)
- Draw up a list of photos to be taken and who will be in them. (TH)

ONE WEEK TO GO

- Attend rehearsal.
- Make sure the licence/banns certificate has been collected.
- Check that the couple have all the documents for the honeymoon, and photocopy their itinerary in case you need to reach them.
- Confirm arrangements with car hire firm or taxi.
- Arrange for friends to decorate and clean the car on the day (if not hired).
- Decide when to collect any hired clothes for groom and best man.

THE DAY BEFORE

- Collect order of service sheets and pass on to ushers.
- Make sure the couple's luggage and going-away outfits are ready for the honeymoon and will be taken to the reception venue. Arrange for presents for the couple's mothers to be taken to the reception.
- Check all cars being used have sufficient petrol, oil and water.
- Ensure the car the couple are using after the reception is in the right place and filled with petrol.
- Pack emergency kit for the day and decorations for going-away car.
- Arrange for alarm call.
- Make sure the bride's family knows where you will be next morning.
- If the best woman or chief bridesmaid will be taking care of the bride's make-up, make sure everything you need is laid out on a tray and that you have found a well-lit area in which to apply it.

KEEPING THE BRIDE AND GROOM CALM

The best man or woman often spends the night before the wedding with their charge. Although there may still be tasks to do, they should make sure the bride or groom gets to bed at a reasonable hour (but not artificially early) and that they avoid caffeine.

If the house is crammed full of people, you could play charades or old family games like Sorry!, Pictionary or Animal Twister, or watch a video or cine-film of the bride and bridegroom as a small child. The bedroom should be made as relaxing as possible: fresh flowers, a few drops of aromatherapy oils on the pillow, soothing music and good ventilation all help.

On the day, make sure the bride or groom is given priority in the bathroom and try to persuade them to have breakfast. Some people, especially men, feel a full cooked breakfast sets them up for the day, even if they feel nervous. Others will hardly be able to touch a thing (see page 119, 'On the day').

The bride will need most of the morning to get ready, whereas the bridegroom may find himself at a loose end. Best men have taken their charges fishing and golfing on their wedding day, or for a brisk walk. Others have treated them to a breakfast at a nearby hotel in their full wedding gear (to get them into the spirit of things), or to a quick drink (see page 119, 'On the day'). Whatever you decide, make sure you leave enough time and weigh up the chances that something might go wrong (this could be the one time in your life a golf ball hits you in the eye).

Remember to keep telling the bride and bridegroom they look great, and make sure they are not late (guaranteed to increase tensions). Traditionally, the best man is meant to ask the bridegroom whether he still wants to go through with the wedding. This is probably best avoided – it may either cause offence or provoke a panic reaction.

STRESSBUSTER

Avoid hanging the wedding dress or suit so that it is the first thing the bride or groom sees if they wake up in the middle of the night.

Five videos to relax the bride the night before

Bringing up Baby
Strictly Ballroom
Some Like It Hot
Gregory's Girl
Thelma and Louise

Five videos for the bridegroom

101 Great Goals (BBC Videos)
The Odd Couple
Withnail and I
Airplane!
The Blues Brothers

ON THE DAY

- Make sure the groom gets up in time and has: certificate of banns or marriage licence; passport; tickets; ring(s); car keys; luggage in right place.
- Give the bridegroom the once-over: check his collar isn't sticking up; his buttonhole is secure; he's wearing matching socks; the sleeves of his jacket aren't showing too much shirt and his tie is straight.
- The best woman or chief bridesmaid should help the bride dress. This includes (throughout the day) looking out for details like smudged make-up or a visible bra strap.
- Ring the ushers and make sure they remember the order of service.
- Collect buttonholes (usually at the bride's house) and distribute. Collect any telegrams from the bride's house and see if there is anything you can help with.
- Put ring(s) and documentation in a safe place.
- The best man should arrive at the church about twenty minutes before the service.
- If there is a best man and a best woman, the best woman will usually travel with the bridesmaids and the bride's mother.

AT CHURCH

(See Chapter 16, 'The Ceremony')

- Make sure the ushers are doing their job.
- Hand over the banns certificate.
- If the best woman does not arrive with the bridegroom but will be handing over a ring, she should sit in one of the front pews with the bride's family.
- On the bride's arrival the best man should stand a little behind the bridegroom and to the right.
- Church fees may have to be paid.
- Help the photographer to organize the photos by assembling the appropriate people. Check again that everyone, especially the bride and groom, look their best. Make sure the photographer does not take too long (see page 184, 'Avoiding waiting at the church').
- Escort the bride and bridegroom to their car.
- Leave for the reception (usually with the bridesmaids).

STRESSBUSTER

Some people prefer to keep the ring in its box until they're inside the building where the service will take place. They then transfer it to a clean handkerchief. Don't fiddle with the ring and don't stand near a grid on the floor in case the ring is dropped.

REGISTER OFFICE

The main duties at a civil wedding are to get the couple there on time (they may arrive together or separately) and to remember the rings. Since many of the new venues have reception facilities nearby, the task of transporting the wedding party to the celebrations is much easier (see Chapter 16, 'The ceremony').

AT THE RECEPTION

(See Chapter 18)

- The best man or woman, or chief bridesmaid, may be asked to join the end of the receiving line. They may even be required to announce guests as they arrive.

- Make sure there is a table for wedding gifts.
- Mingle with guests and make sure everyone has a drink. Check that the bridal couple aren't cornered by anyone.
- Guide guests to the seating plan, and help anyone who looks lost.
- Decide when the cake should be cut.
- Dance with your opposite number once the bride and bridegroom are on the dance-floor, and dance with as many people as possible – especially parents.
- Make sure the going-away car is packed and decorated, and announce that the couple are leaving. Check the couple have everything for their honeymoon, and leave them a surprise such as flowers, chocolates, Polaroids of the day. (TH)
- Check that nothing is left at the reception and gather up the couple's formal clothes, if they have been left.
- Collect a few mementos of the day to give to the couple: label from champagne bottle, menu, seating plan, balloons.

AFTERWARDS

Make sure all the gifts are safe and that any hired suits are returned on time (remind ushers). Ring up both sets of parents, who may be feeling a little flat after the wedding. Tell them how wonderfully the day went and ask if there is anything more you can do.

Keep an eye on the couple's home while they are away and make sure there is something waiting for them on their return: flowers, some pictures of the day, or the keepsakes you collected at the reception.

EMERGENCY KIT FOR BEST MAN OR WOMAN

This might include: whistle (to help round up guests for photos); headache remedy; handkerchief; comb; plenty of change; cheque-book; phone-card; mobile phone (switched off during ceremony); golf umbrella; make-up bag (see page 105, 'Your kit for coping') or grooming bag.

Telephone numbers of: person taking ceremony; transport firm; spare taxis; photographer; florist's; person in charge at reception; entertainment; hotel where the couple will spend the first night of their honeymoon; main members of wedding party; nearest casualty unit and doctor.

THE SPEECH

(See also page 235, 'Speeches')

The speech is the part of being a best man or woman that people dread most. It needn't be. The audience appreciates that it's not an easy task, they've had a good meal and a drink and they're ready to enjoy themselves. Savour the chance to hold sway over a whole room, and don't be afraid to sound enthusiastic.

Content

If you can't think of what to say, collect a few anecdotes from the couple's friends, or ask what they like most about them. Is there anything unusual about the way they met? If you mention any of the guests in your speech, acknowledge them (unless they are painfully shy) as this will help to draw in your listeners.

You're allowed to poke gentle fun at the bride or bridegroom, but only do so in an affectionate way. Anecdotes are much better than jokes because they're more personal and less nerve-racking as you're not conscious of the punchline looming ahead for you to trip over.

Traditionally, the best man is supposed to say how beautiful the bride looks, but only do this if you can use words that come naturally to you. Find out in advance if there is anyone in particular the couple would like you to thank.

After the toast the telegrams are read. If there are too many, choose ones that come from close family or friends, or ones from abroad (have a quick word with parents beforehand). Telegrams with cryptic messages should be jettisoned first if you're running out of time – you can always pin them up afterwards for people to read.

To be avoided

- Too many references to your own wedding.
- Jokes in dubious taste. (You would have to be pretty sure of yourself to attempt, 'What's the difference between a bride with PMT and a fanatical terrorist? – You can reason with a fanatical terrorist.')
- 'In' jokes. Remember that you are speaking to an audience of different ages and tastes, and that some people may not even know the bride or bridegroom very well.

- Money.
- Ex-lovers.
- Past arguments.

Hits

The most effective speeches are the ones when the best man or woman are themselves. You're not auditioning for *Saturday Night at the London Palladium* and the occasional corny joke will be taken in good spirit.

- **Advice from old-fashioned books on marriage**: You can usually find this sort of book in car boot sales, or even tucked away on a bookshelf at your granny's house. Reading out extracts should have your audience in fits of laughter – partly because of the old-fashioned tone of the writer and coy way of alluding to sex, but also because of the image of the man as the hunter/gatherer and the woman as the little housewife whose greatest ambition in life is to make sure her husband's slippers are properly warmed.
- **Mock telegrams**: If the bridegroom is a football, classical music or comedy fan, for example, invent a message from their heroes (especially good if you can do impersonations), for example, 'Just my sort of bash – plenty of tears and free beer' (Gazza); 'Married at 27 – no more nights out with the lads . . . do I not like that' (Graham Taylor).
- **References to any (minor) hiccup in the wedding arrangements**: One best man alluded to the fact that the church was 60 miles away from the reception venue and that several of the guests had lost their way. 'Jayne has asked me to say that she's enjoyed organizing today so much that she's available for weddings, funerals and bar mitzvahs – but only if the service is 60 miles away from the reception. And for those of you who got lost and are watching this via a satellite link from Barnsley . . . welcome.'
- 'There's an old Chinese proverb that says the best way to start a best man's speech is with an old Chinese proverb . . .'
- 'Last night my brother took me to one side and said I could tell any stories about him I liked but there was one thing I mustn't, under any circumstances, reveal. (Pause, to look at bridegroom.) So we'll come back to that later.'

Misses

- Mentioning the bride's previous marriage – a piece of information that was new to most guests.
- The speech that centred around the share price of the two families' companies.
- A reference to an argument that the bride and bridegroom had only recently patched up (the bride ran out of the marquee in tears).

Preparation

Most people think that if they forget about the speech it will go away. It won't, so don't leave preparation to the last minute. You'll feel more confident if you're sure of what you're going to say.

Visit the room where you will be making the speech and test its acoustics. Imagine the room full of people and try speaking from the exact spot where you will be on the day. Find out whether you will be competing with any other noises like air-conditioning.

If you decide to type out your speech in full, don't use only capital letters which are difficult to read, but underline words you want to emphasize. Use line-spacing of one and a half or two, and turn pages at the end of an anecdote or a natural pause (even if this means having only a few lines on one page). Alternatively, if you feel more confident, write down the key points on prompt cards and tie them together (in case you drop them). Keep a spare copy of the speech in your pocket or with a friend.

Either way, try to memorize the opening and closing lines of the speech and practise saying the whole thing out loud several times. Run it past a friend who knows the couple and tape-record it so you can play it back to yourself.

Delivery

Avoid alcohol and caffeine beforehand as these will make you jumpy. Chocolate and biscuits can also clog up your throat.

Before you stand up, take three deep breaths. When you rise to speak, take a good look round the room and pause until the hubbub dies down. If there's a sudden disruption, acknowledge it, rather than trying to compete for attention. If the marquee is suddenly buffeted by a storm, point out that rain on a wedding day is lucky.

Stand with your feet slightly apart and in a relaxed position. Remember to breathe through your mouth – it's more energy-efficient and will keep your throat open. Aim to speak for no longer than five to seven minutes – unless you are an accomplished public speaker – and make regular eye-contact with your audience. One way of combating nerves is to imagine you are speaking to a room full of aliens with two heads and blue antennae.

THE ROLE OF THE USHERS

The ushers are the best man or woman's troops on the ground. There is normally about one usher to every fifty guests, although this is a very broad rule of thumb. Having the same number of ushers as bridesmaids means each usher can escort a bridesmaid, but this is not strictly necessary.

Nowadays more women are being chosen as ushers, but like the best woman, they must overcome the problem of identifying themselves to the guests. However, a prominent buttonhole, a pile of orders of service and an air of authority should give most guests the right idea.

It helps if the usher has a car available for any last-minute errands, and carries a large umbrella.

COUNTDOWN FOR THE USHERS

THREE MONTHS TO GO

- Meet the best man or woman to establish how they can help.
- Meet the family and the person taking the service. Find out about problem guests from the best man or woman.

ON THE DAY

- Collect the order of service from the bride or best man or woman.
- Pick up buttonholes for guests not staying with the bride or bridegroom.
- Arrive one hour before the service.
- One usher is given the task of dealing with car parking.

AT THE CHURCH

- Take order of service sheets to the church or make sure they will be there on the day.
- Greet guests at the door with order of service, hymn book and prayer book (if needed). Advise guests on whether or not photos are allowed.
- Gather guests together for photographs.
- Ask people not to throw confetti if this is against the church's rules.
- Make sure everyone has transport to the reception and that nothing is left in the church.
- Collect order of service sheets.

Seating

Traditionally the bride's friends and family sit on the left (facing the altar) and the groom's on the right, but it is up to the ushers to make sure the guests are fairly equally distributed. Any latecomers should be discreetly given a seat, and people with children should be positioned so that they can make a quick escape if necessary.

The first one or two front pews are reserved for close family. The groom's family sits in the second pew from the front and the bride's mother, who is the last to arrive, is escorted by the chief usher or a male member of the family to the front pew on the left where her husband will join her, if he is giving away the bride.

If either of the couple's parents are divorced, but not remarried, they usually sit together. Etiquette suggests that if either mother is remarried she will sit with her new husband in the front pew and a remarried father will sit in the second pew with his new wife. The most sensible option, though, is to discuss seating beforehand to avoid any unseemly scrums at the front of the church.

THE ROLE OF THE BRIDESMAIDS AND PAGEBOYS

Originally, bridesmaids were intended to act as decoys for evil spirits planning mischief aimed at the bride. For this reason they wore dresses similar to that of the bride. An adult bridesmaid, whether a matron of honour – a married bridesmaid – or not, may be asked to sign the register. She should also hold the bride's bouquet in church and look after it at the reception.

Chief bridesmaids are in charge of the other bridesmaids and pageboys and will help the bride choose their outfits. If the attendants don't know one another, try to arrange for them to meet before the day. Having lunch or breakfast together and changing in the same room can be a bonding experience.

The chief bridesmaid will also help the bride get ready, arrange her dress and veil before she enters the church, and help her change into her going-away outfit (see Chapter 16, 'The ceremony').

HOW PARENTS CAN HELP

Like any other member of the wedding party, bridesmaids and pageboys need to be well briefed. If they know that they must be quiet in church and stand still for the photos but can run wild at the reception, they are more likely to behave for the important bits. Books such as *My Day as a Bridesmaid* and the short story 'Alfie and Annie Rose' will help prepare young children (see Further Reading, page 271).

Either the bride's parents or the bride herself usually pay for the bridesmaids' and pageboys' outfits. But before parents offer they should establish the cost, or set a limit as it may come as a bit of a shock. If the outfit is being made, children should try on the whole ensemble, including footwear, at least two weeks in advance so that there is plenty of time for the inevitable alterations to be made.

Young children like being in the midst of the excitement, so there's no reason why they shouldn't be sent on errands in the bride's home on the day of the wedding – even if it's simply distributing cups of tea. On the other hand, you might think it wise to take them out for a walk if tensions are mounting.

Temper tantrums are normally triggered by hunger or cold, so keep a snack on hand to stave off those pangs before the reception. Bridesmaids' dresses can also be cold and impractical, so take a cardigan for when the photos are over.

If you can afford to, buy any siblings a special outfit so they don't feel left out, and make sure you treat the whole day as a party everyone can enjoy.

(See page 26, 'Choosing attendants' for suggestions for bridesmaids' and pageboys' presents and how to avoid offending people not chosen.)

11

Parents, Friends and Family

PARENTS

The wedding of a child can be a difficult time for parents. Whether they are paying for all or part of the day or not, the bride's parents may feel responsible for everyone having a good time. The bridegroom's parents may also feel anxious to help without appearing to interfere.

For some parents, seeing their child's name on a wedding invitation can spark off a whole series of feelings, from reflections about whether they sent them to the right school, to an analysis of their own marriage, to intimations of mortality. On top of these mixed emotions they are being asked to share the intimate experience with another family they may not know very well.

SMOOTHING THE WAY: HOW BRIDE AND BRIDEGROOM CAN HELP

The two sets of parents should try to meet as soon as possible. If you can engineer it, a low-key meeting before you even announce you're getting married can be a painless way of making introductions. Neutral ground such as a restaurant or the bride's or groom's home is often better than leaving the catering up to one set of parents.

Keep conflict to a minimum by drawing up a list of decisions to be taken – before you discuss them with parents. Sort the items into two columns: things you feel strongly about and things that you are prepared to compromise over.

So, for example, you might have a hankering for an elegant cake decorated with sunflowers. Your parents think this is laughable and will settle at nothing short of a full-blown, three-tiered traditional wedding cake. Since the cake is not integral to your view of the wedding you concede, which makes it easier to stand your ground over the choice of dress for the ushers.

STRESSBUSTER

If someone is dominating the conversation, focus on an object such as an ashtray as a way of allowing everyone to have their say: whoever has the ashtray 'has the floor' and no one else can speak until the ashtray has been passed on.

Parents should resist the temptation to turn their home into a hotel. Pay for someone to come in and tidy up while you're at the wedding so you don't return to a bedraggled home full of dirty washing-up and bitter-sweet memories.

MEETING THE COST

(See also Chapter 3, 'Gifts')

It is no longer automatically assumed that the bride's family will pay for the bulk of the wedding. The groom's parents might want to contribute (it is more tactful to offer to pay for a specific item or items such as the wine rather than simply to write out a cheque), or the couple might prefer to pay for the whole thing. If the latter is the case the couple should normally accept any token contributions such as an offer to pay for the flowers graciously – especially as this may help parents to feel more involved.

WHO PAYS FOR WHAT (TRADITIONALLY)

(* = room for flexibility)

Bride's family	Budgeted cost	Actual cost
Bride's clothes		
Outfits for bridesmaids, pageboys (and ushers*)		
Flowers for ceremony and reception		
Hire of venue or marquee (including decorations, lighting and equipment such as tables and chairs)		
Catering and wine		
Decorations, e.g. balloons, candles		
Cars (to the wedding) for the bride and father, bridesmaids and bride's mother		

	Budgeted cost	Actual cost
Music and entertainment		
Photographs and video		
Invitations and other stationery		
Wedding cake		
Gifts for bridesmaids		
Press announcements*		
Groom's family		
Groom's outfit		
Best man's outfit*		
Ceremony (e.g. minister, verger, bellringer, choir, marriage licence, reading banns, register office paperwork)		
Rings (engagement and wedding)		
Bouquets, corsages, buttonholes, bridesmaids' flowers and headdresses		
Gift for best man		
Car to church for groom and best man		
Car to reception for bride and groom		
Honeymoon*		
Going-away transport		

CASE STUDY

Retired bus driver Lorenzo, from Swindon, estimates the weddings of his eleven daughters cost him £50,000, but he and his wife Sylvia say they had always planned to spend their savings on huge, Italian-style celebrations and don't regret a minute of it.

DIVORCED OR SEPARATED PARENTS, AND STEP-PARENTS

No matter how acrimonious the separation may have been, most couples will find it possible to keep their feelings in check for one day. This will be easier if potential flash points are discussed beforehand: who will sit where (at the service and the reception), who will stand next to whom in the photos (see page 184, 'Who goes where'), who will pay for what, who will give the bride away and who will make speeches.

REMEMBERING FAMILY MEMBERS WHO HAVE DIED

A wedding can lead to mixed feelings if a parent or other close family member has died, but don't worry that a few tears will spoil the day – they're entirely natural at such an emotional time.

Some people find it helps to make a special visit to the grave, whilst others prefer to remember the person in the service by choosing their favourite hymn or reading. A more public acknowledgement is to ask the minister to say something like, 'We remember . . . in our prayers', or 'We rejoice in the memory of . . .' Another option is to ask the minister to mention them in the introduction to the service or in the sermon.

If the person has died fairly recently it might seem artificial not to make some allusion to them, but there is a thin line between remembrance and commemoration. The minister may not think it is appropriate to dwell too long on this in case the service becomes in danger of sounding too much like a funeral.

You might prefer to mention the deceased in the speeches. Bernard, for example, said one of the reasons he regretted that his father had not lived to meet his bride, Ruth, was that they both shared the same sense of humour (he then went on to tell a funny and affectionate story about his father).

THE FATHER OF THE BRIDE

(See also 'Bridegroom and male guests', page 85; Chapter 16, 'The Ceremony'; page 132, 'The Speech' and page 235, 'Speeches'

STRESSBUSTER

If the prospect of making a speech is likely to ruin the entire day for you, you might consider asking someone else (a godfather, friend of the family, uncle or the groom's father) to do the honours.

Giving the bride away

The notion of giving the bride away is an old-fashioned one and, taken at face value, could be seen as offensive. But, as with most traditions, what counts is what the custom means to you. For many brides, even those who view themselves as staunch feminists, walking down the aisle on their father's arm represents a passage from life as a single person to a life shared with someone else. Other brides see the tradition as a way of acknowledging their parents' love and support for them as a child.

One bride decided to ask her father to accompany her up the aisle for this very reason. It was also important on another level because her father had suffered brain damage in a car accident a few years before and she wanted to stress to him that she still saw him as someone more than capable of fulfilling the traditional role of a father.

Other brides have walked down the aisle alone, but taken time to explain to their fathers beforehand that they wanted to do this because they disagreed with the notion of being treated like a chattel rather than because they felt they had had bad fathers. One bride asked both her parents to walk behind her up the aisle because she didn't like the idea of being given away but still wanted to say a public thank-you to both her parents.

The bride's father is also the only person to spend any time alone with the bride immediately before the service. You may want to say something special to your daughter, but remember that she is probably already walking an emotional tightrope.

MOTHERS

The mothers of the bride and groom are, after the bride, the most important female members of the wedding. Because of the mother of the bride's special role, the groom's mother may feel a bit left out. The bride's mother should be aware of this and encourage the groom's mother to become involved in the arrangements – if she senses she would like to be. The bride could, for example, arrange a shopping trip or day at a health spa for herself, her mother and future mother-in-law.

STRESSBUSTER

Parents should try not to deluge the bride and bridegroom with countless queries but instead do their best to find the answers elsewhere. One mother of the bride, for example, was concerned that her rather extravagant hat would be too wide for the door of the wedding room at Brighton Pavilion. Rather than pester her daughter she phoned the wedding organizer who, after taking measurements, was able to reassure her.

What to wear?

- Consult with your opposite number to avoid the same colour, one that clashes, or identical outfits.
- Remember the wedding's colour scheme and, if possible, take a swatch of the dress material from the bridesmaids' outfits when choosing what you'll wear.
- Don't 'dress your age' – if you do, you'll look ten years older.
- Black is no longer the colour of mourning and can make an elegant choice.
- Navy blue is popular among guests.
- Be very careful with bold printed patterns – especially if you are on the large side. They can make you look like a settee.

Hats

Mothers are no longer expected to wear hats and it doesn't matter if one of you decides to wear something on your head and the other doesn't. But ask – if your counterpart has chosen an extravagant creation, it may give you the confidence to alter your original plans, or make you realize you don't want to be outdone.

Unless you fall in love with some wonderful piece of millinery, it is sensible to leave buying a hat until after you've chosen the rest of your outfit.

Planning your strategy

Choosing your outfit should be fun – a reward for arranging the wedding or simply bringing a child to adulthood. (If you're a step-mother this is your chance to show how happy you are to be part of the family.)

Leave yourself plenty of time to find the perfect outfit and remember that next season's styles start appearing in the middle of the previous one. Incorporate a shopping trip into a weekend away, or build the day around lunch in a chic department store coffee shop, or end the day with a sauna.

Where to go for inspiration

If you want help in choosing your outfit you might consider 'personal shopping' (a service which is normally free). Many large department stores (such as Dickins and Jones, Harvey Nichols, Harrods and Selfridges) offer the service, whereby customers can relax in a special suite and discuss their clothing needs with assistants trained to spot what will suit them. The assistant will then go round the shop gathering clothes while you sit back and relax.

You will be able to try on an entire outfit, from shoes, tights and underwear to gloves, jewellery and hat. The advantages are that you will feel pampered and the assistant will probably suggest something which you might never have tried on but which looks fabulous.

CASE STUDY

Jo, a 57-year-old primary teacher from Stroud in Gloucestershire, didn't have a clue what to wear for her daughter's wedding. She had spent a life-time in simple, practical clothes.

When she visited Dickins and Jones in London's Regent Street the assistants recognized that because she was tall and had striking blonde hair she would look stunning in a black outfit.

After trying on a wide range of outfits she chose a black Max Mara suit with three-quarter-length sleeves and a fitted, knee-length brocade skirt. She wore black, patent-leather high-heeled shoes, large pearl earrings and a matching necklace, ivory gloves and sheer tights in a natural colour. The whole ensemble was topped with a large black hat which had a transparent rim and large bow to ensure the black did not become too overpowering.

MONEYSAVER

If you can't afford a new outfit, splash out on a scarf to pep up an old dress or suit.

AN OUTFIT FOR THE WHOLE DAY

- **Feet and legs**: You will spend a lot of time on your feet: posing for photographs or dancing. Make sure your shoes are comfortable and try to wear them in beforehand. Consider support tights, but don't feel you have to stick to black or other dark colours which can have the effect of 'dragging down' an upbeat outfit.

- **Evening**: If you choose a suit, wear a top under your jacket which will give you another look for the reception.
- **Underwear**: Foundation garments are no longer the instruments of torture they used to be.

(For make-up, see page 101, 'Beauty')

SIBLINGS

As brother or sister you may be heavily involved in the wedding – as best man, bridesmaid or usher. If your role is less prominent, there is still much you can do behind the scenes (see 'Friends' below). You may also be in a position to smooth things over with parents if any misunderstandings arise.

FRIENDS

A wedding can be as much a rite of passage for friends as for the couple themselves. They may feel anxious that being married will endanger the friendship, or they may even feel a little jealous.

Weddings can also bring friendships into sharp focus. You may finally realize that in fact you've been growing apart for several years. Or you might feel disappointed and hurt that a friend doesn't become more involved in your wedding preparations. But for every friend who doesn't quite live up to your expectations there will be someone who proves to be unexpectedly thoughtful.

HOW FRIENDS CAN HELP

- The bride and bridegroom may be wary of asking you to do too much. Acknowledge this by saying that they should feel free to ask three favours of you.
- Plan treats, either at home or away – a facial, a massage, or a night in watching videos.
- Don't wait to be asked – if you can see anything you can help with, suggest you do it.

- If you're married yourself, tell your friend that the hardest thing about being a bride is believing the wonderful things people say about you – but that she must promise to accept all the compliments as genuine.

PART FOUR

MAKING YOUR MARK

12

Planning the Reception

A wedding celebration is different from most big parties because of the spread of ages and the range of intimacy among the guests. Deciding what sort of refreshment to offer and where will depend on three main factors: your resources (budget and quality of catering available); the needs of your guests (their age, expectations and how far they have travelled); and your own vision of the day (which doesn't have to be sacrificed to the first two).

THE VENUE

QUESTIONS TO ASK

1. Who will be in charge on the day – and do you feel comfortable with them?
2. Will there be any other functions on that day – if so at what time and in what part of the hotel?
3. How much parking is available and will anyone help direct drivers?
4. Where will the bride and groom change before going away? Does the hotel offer a special rate for guests staying there or for the couple?
5. How much is corkage and water – does it have to be bottled, how many people will be serving?

CHECKLIST FOR A RECEPTION AT HOME

Several taxi numbers
Wine bins
Ashtrays
Corkscrews
Glass-holders to clip on to plates (if food is to be eaten standing up)
Flowers to decorate toilets
Several dustbin liners
First-aid box

CALCULATING SPACE

- Allow 1.10 square metres/12 square feet per head for a sit-down meal and 0.56 square metres/6 square feet per guest for standing (take into account doors, columns). Each guest should have 45–60 cm/1½–2 feet of table space.
- Round tables: a 90-cm/3-ft table will hold six people; a 105-cm/3½-ft table seven people; and a 120-cm/4-ft table eight people.
- Leave about 45 cm/18 in of space around each table for chairs, and 30 cm/12 in for the waitress to get past.

Tip Keep a list of the crockery you hire and what you need it for so that you don't serve up twenty pâtés on a plate originally earmarked for dessert.

ENLISTING HELP

- **Wedding organizers**: If you're too busy to organize your wedding yourself, or if you want to have a slightly different celebration, or simply need reassurance, professionals can help. They should be able to secure you discounts on some wedding services.
- **Before the reception**: Ask someone to be at the venue to take deliveries. They should have some extra cash (in case they need to tip someone to do some extra lifting), a clipboard with letters confirming different deliveries, and if possible, a mobile telephone.
- **Waitresses**: Contact your local pub, restaurant, club or catering firm (see Stockists, page 285) to hire extra help. Remember to serve food from the left and clear and serve wine from the right. Keep your waitresses happy and you'll keep your guests smiling – make sure they have plenty to eat and drink, somewhere to put their valuables, and safe transport home at the end of the day.
- **Numbers**: If guests are served at table you will need one server for every six guests.

  A buffet will need one server for every twenty-five guests (or fifteen if the server is inexperienced).

  Canapés will require one server per thirty-five people.

  Don't forget someone to tend the bar.

- **Afterwards**: Pay for someone to help you clear up and, if the reception was held in a hired hall, make sure you know where to put the rubbish.

MARQUEES AND TENTS

If you need some extra space but don't have room for a marquee, consider a framed tent. The sides won't billow in the same way as a marquee but it should be able to fit into most spaces because you won't need the extra 3 m/10 ft around the perimeter for guy-ropes.

As a rough rule of thumb, you will need the following space for a reception of about 150 people at which your guests will have enough room for a sit-down meal and dance:

- Framed tent: 24 × 12 m/80 × 40 ft.
- Marquee: 30 × 18 m/100 × 60 ft.

If you want a dance-floor you will need an area of about 37 square metres/400 square feet – depending on the liveliness of your guests.

Check that the marquee is covered for insurance purposes, or take out your own, and make sure the marquee or tent is made of fire-retardant material.

CHECKLIST

(* = Optional extras)
Lining*
Lighting
Flooring – wooden boards with matting and/or carpeting with underlay*, and dance-floor*
Heating* (this can be ordered at the last minute, depending on availability)
Tables and chairs
Public address system*

DECORATIONS

Your marquee could be as utilitarian as an agricultural tent, or so sophisticated that air-conditioning or thermostatically-controlled heating and dimming switches will make guests forget they are outdoors.

PUTTING ON THE STYLE

Coloured linings can be designed to fit in with your overall scheme, or you can choose a marquee company that specializes in themed events to provide you with painted backdrops and props. One couple wanted a rustic look and commissioned a background of blue skies and swallows and asked the hire company to install a rusty country gate. Another wanted a Venetian look with archways, gondoliers and fountains.

STRESSBUSTER

When choosing a marquee company, check that they have someone available (preferably round-the-clock) to help if something goes wrong.

FOOD

CATERERS

Look at sample menus within different price ranges and ask if you can taste some of the dishes. If you're given the chance, bring along your parents or whoever's paying, so they have a say in planning the menu. Oriental canapés dressed with seaweed may sound the height of sophistication to you, but will come as a shock to parents expecting meat and two veg. Set yourself a budget and ask for written confirmation of everything. Remember that travel will push up the cost.

THE MAIN FOOD CHOICES

- **Canapés and finger buffet** (usually passed round or put on table): *Pros*: bite-sized food easy to eat and sophisticated to look at; guests have chance to mingle; often suitable for small, low-key weddings or to keep guests going before a more substantial meal. *Cons*: some people may feel cheated and hungry (although a finger buffet is more filling); also fiddly and time-consuming to make; little can be prepared in advance; standing up is tiring.

- **Buffet**: *Pros*: more substantial; need for fewer servers; opportunity to make the table a focal point by decorating it with flowers and with butter, vegetable and ice carvings; food can be prepared in advance. *Cons*: queuing; table can look dishevelled for later guests; if eaten standing up can lead to spillages (elderly will need seats).
- **Sit-down**: *Pros*: guests feel they've had a proper meal; relaxing; more time for dancing which is good for breaking the ice. *Cons*: expensive; experienced waitresses needed; tables take up room.

MONEYSAVER

There will be times – after the service, or the middle of the evening – when all your guests really want is a cup of tea (you might supply sausage rolls, sandwiches, or cakes if you wish too). Quenching guests' thirst will also keep the wine bill down.

CASE STUDIES

- *Sue, 26, who works in a large department store, and Tim, 30, who works for a car manufacturer, decided to give their reception an oriental theme as Tim's father is from China. They decorated the garden of their home in Surrey with Chinese lanterns and ordered a special celebration from their local Chinese restaurant.*
- *Phil, 28, and Greta, 29, who both work in public relations, wanted to build their wedding round the county of Sussex because they had spent their happiest times together there. They chose a Jacobean manor on the county border for the ceremony and reception. The menu was Sussex smoked salmon and trout, locally reared lamb, and Sussex Pond Pudding.*
- *Former sailor and keen surfer, Barry, 37, and his bride, June, 38, held their reception in Harry Ramsden's fish and chip restaurant in Cardiff.*

DOING IT YOURSELF, OR ASKING A FRIEND TO HELP

Taking on the task of preparing the wedding food is a big responsibility which includes making sure there is enough to go around, that it looks and tastes wonderful, and that no one goes down with salmonella (a common risk at summer weddings). Before you agree to help, ask yourself the following questions:

1. Will it ruin my own enjoyment of the day?
2. Do I have the experience (especially in planning menus)?
3. Do I have the time? (Much of the food should be prepared in advance.)
4. Do I have the resources? (Extra equipment can be hired or borrowed, but is your oven big enough, for example, to cook a very large turkey?)
5. Where can I go for help – can I persuade friends to lend a hand, where can I find other helpers?

DECIDING ON A MENU

Remember that you are probably catering for a wide range of people who may have very different tastes.

- **Special diets**: How many vegetarian guests are there, and how many eat fish? Will there be any Jewish, Hindu or Muslim guests and how closely do they stick to religious practice (see overleaf)? Are any of your guests diabetics, recovering from an operation or following a gluten-free diet? If you're planning a buffet, try to keep food for guests with special dietary requirements to one side or make sure there are greater quantities of it. No one should feel singled out because of their diet – if it's a sit-down meal put a discreet sticker on the back of a guest's chair to denote special requirements and try to ensure their food arrives at the same time as everyone else's.
- **Variety**: Will your food have a mixture of texture and colour, or will it appear predominantly yellow and slop-like? Make sure you vary the main ingredients – a creamy soup, chicken with a rich sauce and a Pavlova for dessert will be too heavy for most people. Likewise, vary canapés so that they are not all pastry- or bread-based. Include at least one hot dish if the weather is likely to be chilly.
- **Cost**: The greater the choice, the bigger the bill. Intersperse a few expensive ingredients such as smoked salmon with a staple food like rice (see overleaf for canapé ideas).
- **Suitability**: Avoid anything too temperamental – a dessert that is prone to collapse, or a delicate soufflé. Choose food that can be wholly, or partly, prepared in advance.
- **Timing**: If the wedding is immediately after lunch your guests won't expect a huge meal at the reception, but if the ceremony is in the late

afternoon they will probably want more than a caviar egg balanced on a sliver of salmon.

PUTTING ON THE STYLE/ MONEYSAVER

Canapés are an elegant way of feeding guests and a wide range will give an impression of generosity. Try mixing cheap and simple morsels with more expensive and elaborate fare. Recipes for the following can be found in *Leith's Cookery Bible* (see Further Reading, page 275):

- **Simple**: Stuffed dates; cocktail sausages with mustard; cheese straws; cherry tomatoes, avocado and mozzarella kebabs.
- **Lavish**: Drop scones with caviar; tartlets with quail's eggs and smoked salmon; smoked oyster tartlets; Peking duck coronets.

RELIGIOUS DIETARY REQUIREMENTS

- **Hindu guests**: Most are vegetarian and some do not eat eggs. Cheeses should be avoided as they are usually made with animal rennet (the Cornish cheese Yarg is an example of a vegetarian alternative). Hindus are not permitted to eat dripping or lard.
- **Jewish guests**: Strict Orthodox Jews will only eat in a restaurant that has been authorized by a rabbi. Shellfish (including squid and octopus), pork and rabbit are forbidden, but beef, lamb, goat, turkey, chicken, duck, goose, pheasant and partridge are permitted, so long as they are kosher, that is, killed by Jewish methods. Animal and dairy products cannot be combined or served together and dairy foods can only be served after meat if there is a certain gap between the two.
- **Muslim guests**: Pork and the meat of other carnivorous animals are not allowed. Meat should be slaughtered in accordance with Muslim law and come from a halal butcher. Strict Muslims will avoid cakes, biscuits and many desserts if they contain fat or lard from animals not slaughtered in this way. Alcohol is not allowed, so avoid tipsy trifles.

Tip If you are including an RSVP card with your invitation you could add a line saying something like 'Please let us know if you have any special dietary requirements', or 'The main course will be . . . but please tell us if this is unsuitable for your dietary requirements'.

CASE STUDY

Sophie, a 35-year-old cook, and Stephen, a 36-year-old biologist, married in a small church in Monmouth late in the afternoon. Invitations told guests to come 'dressed for dancing'. Tea, scones and sandwiches were served in a barn and followed by wine and speeches. Once the dancing had started, Sophie's friends prepared a barbecue on two large oil-drums borrowed from a local school. As well as traditional barbecue food they also prepared grilled Mediterranean vegetables and spicy sauces. The wedding cake was a carrot cake.

DRINK

WHERE TO BUY IT

Expect to be fêted by the large off-licences. Most will offer sale or return on part, if not all, of your purchase, and several (for example Victoria Wine, which has over 1,500 outlets) will offer a discount on bulk orders. A chain will also give you the chance to order from a shop near you for delivery in another part of the country (Victoria Wine has a special telephone order line – 0800 526 464). You should also be able to hire glasses for a small, refundable deposit and several shops offer a free delivery service within a certain radius.

Some shops, such as Majestic Wine Warehouses, pride themselves on their staff's knowledge of wines and will be happy to help you pick suitable wines. Majestic will often open bottles for you to taste (even of sparkling wines), although they will need to be convinced that you aren't simply looking for a free drink (they will be more willing to do this on a Friday since they stand more chance of using it up over the weekend).

A trip to France (perhaps as part of the stag and hen celebrations) can also save you money. Each person is allowed 90 litres (80 bottles) of table wine (60 of which can be sparkling), 10 litres of spirits, 20 litres of fortified wine and 110 litres of beer without questions being asked. But make sure you do your sums first to see whether you really are saving money.

- **Cost of transport**: Will you need to hire a minibus? Look out for special ferry offers.
- **Exchange rate**: When deciding on where you will buy the wines, check the exchange rate being quoted. How does it compare with the cost of your francs?
- **Corkage**: Most hotels and catering companies charge per bottle, which can wipe out any savings from the trip abroad.

Customs officials may challenge you and even impound the alcohol if you have more than your allowance and they believe that you intend to sell it on. A wedding invitation is not sufficient proof of your good intentions, but an invoice from a reception venue and the minister's phone number should help.

WHEN TO SERVE

- **The welcome**: A good dry champagne is best appreciated on its own, but you might want to offer cocktails as an alternative (see below).
- **The food**: Your choice of wine will, to some extent, depend on the food. Don't try to be too ambitious. Consider matching red and white duos from Australia or California.
- **The toast**: This is the time to crack open the champagne – although you can easily get away with a good sparkling wine, indeed some people prefer it. In some cases you will get more for your money by buying a good sparkling wine rather than a cheaper champagne. Try Freixenet Cordon Negro Brut or Yalumba Angas brut or rosé.
- **Afterwards**: At Greek and Jewish weddings it's common practice for the bar to be free. In other communities it is perfectly acceptable for the guests to buy their own drinks. Alternatively, as a compromise, the host can put a certain amount behind the bar or foot the bill for the first hour or so.

PUTTING ON THE STYLE

Cocktails, Pimms or a fruit punch make an elegant alternative to wine and you can concoct non-alcoholic versions of the punch and cocktails. Remember, however, that cocktails can be lethal – especially if it's a hot day and people don't realize exactly what they're drinking. Mulled wine, sherry or a hot punch will warm up guests in the winter and you might offer them a mince pie if it's near Christmas. **Cocktail suggestions**: Buck's Fizz (champagne or sparkling

wine and orange juice); Kir (crème de cassis and sparkling wine); Kir Royale (cassis and champagne); Between the Sheets (equal measures of rum, Cointreau and brandy and a splash of lemon); a Manhattan (one measure whisky, half-measure vermouth, a few shakes of Angostura bitters and a green olive); elderflower cordial and sparkling wine.
Non-alcoholic drinks: Shirley Temple (ginger ale, grenadine and maraschino cherries); real lemonade (juice of a large lemon, two level tablespoons sugar, water and lemon peel to decorate); Cranberry Refresher (unsweetened cranberry juice and tonic or sparkling water); elderflower cordial and sparkling water.

STRESSBUSTER

Give the cocktails or punch a trial run with your close family and friends beforehand.

QUANTITIES

- **Wine**: Generally, people drink more white wine than red (for every ten bottles drunk roughly six will be white) and the average guest will consume about half a bottle during the wedding breakfast. But if you know most of your friends are heavy drinkers and prefer red wine to white, or that your relatives only drink whisky, or a large number of people will be driving, factor this knowledge into your calculations.

  Expect to get six glasses from a 75-cl bottle of wine and twenty-four measures from a 70-cl bottle of Pimms. Each guest should have one glass of champagne or sparkling wine for the toast.
- **The bar**: Quantities for a bar will depend on how much your guests have drunk so far, and whether you have invited a second tranche to the evening celebration.

Suggested line-up for a bar serving 100 people

Spirits: two bottles each of four or five different spirits.
Fortified wine: one or two bottles of sherry.
Beer/lager: 100 large cans (including low-alcohol, depending on the number of drivers).

Soft drinks: at least 10 litres (of which four should be cola) – more if there are several children.
Mixers: tonic water, orange juice, lemonade. (Allow 2 litres for each 70-cl bottle of spirits.)
Wine: four red and six white.
Non-alcoholic drinks: People are currently drinking much less alcohol than they used to, so make sure there is plenty of fruit juice and mineral water. This should also discourage people from drinking alcohol when what they really want is something to quench their thirst.

KEEPING YOUR COOL

Use the bath to chill bottles and fill lined dustbins with ice and water (most off-licences sell ice and some like Majestic Wine Warehouses hire out dustbins). Red wine should be opened and allowed to breathe an hour or so before serving. Create your own clear ice-cubes by using cooled, boiled water. You can also include a rose petal or sprig of borage or mint before freezing.

MONEYSAVER

Don't chill too much wine in advance as bottles left in ice for a long time will lose their labels, making it difficult to return them if they are unopened.

THE CAKE

You may view the cake as no more than a useful photo-opportunity at the end of the wedding breakfast, but in fact the bride cake, as it was known until Victorian times, was loaded with heavy symbolism long before it became loaded with royal icing.

The original cake was round, flat and spicy and was thought to bear mystical properties. Its ingredients were carefully chosen – nuts were seen as a potent symbol of fertility and still survive in the modern wedding cake through the almond paste (marzipan) and sugared almond bonbonnière. The cake was crumbled over the bride to promote fertility and girls passed bits through the wedding ring and then put the cake under their pillow for three nights running to dream of their future husband. Cutting the cake has been seen as symbolic of the bride's forthcoming loss of virginity.

CHOOSING A CAKE AND CAKEMAKER

Cakemakers will show you examples of their work and even offer samples to taste. Place your order at least four months before the wedding, or if you know a cakemaker is in demand, make a provisional booking as far as a year in advance.

The number of tiers can range from one to about five, and they can sit directly on top of one another or be supported by square or round columns. Cakes come in a wide range of shapes, the most common being square, round and heart-shaped, but more unusual-shaped tins can be hired. Square cakes are easier to cut and more economical.

Most wedding cakes are made of the traditional rich fruit cake, although sponge is also common. Chocolate makes an interesting alternative but can be unpredictable in warm weather.

PUTTING ON THE STYLE

The French wedding cake, or croquembouche, is also becoming popular. This dramatic pyramid of choux buns filled with crème pâtissière is probably beyond the reach of most amateur cooks but can be ordered from pâtisseries.

QUANTITIES

Approximate number of servings for a fruit cake. (The same sizes of sponge cake will serve about half the number.)

Size	Square	Round
13 cm/5 inches	15	14
15 cm/6 inches	30	20
18 cm/7 inches	40	30
20 cm/8 inches	50	40
22 cm/9 inches	60–80	50–60
25 cm/10 inches	90–100	70–80
30 cm/12 inches	100–130	80–90
40cm/15 inches	150–200	120–160

Remember that you may want to send cake to people who couldn't come to the wedding (most stationers, such as W. H. Smith's, sell boxes for this purpose); to take some in to work; or reserve a whole tier for a future christening, house-warming or special birthday.

For a very big wedding a simpler version of the wedding cake can be ready-cut in the kitchen, rather than trying to dismantle a multi-tiered structure in a short time.

MONEYSAVER

If you don't want to pay for a towering cake you'll never eat you can follow the American practice and make a few faux layers out of cardboard.

CAKE-BAKING COUNTDOWN

(This has been adapted from *Leith's Book of Cakes*)

1. Bake the cake(s) at least three months before the wedding. Wrap in greaseproof paper and kitchen foil and store in a cool, dry, place.
2. A month before the wedding, cover with marzipan and leave to dry, uncovered, in a cool, dry place for one week.
3. Base-ice the cake three weeks before the wedding.
4. Decorate one week before and cover the cake with soft tissue to prevent dust from collecting.

EQUIPMENT CHECKLIST

Cake tins (never use a new tin)
Greaseproof paper
Tissue paper
Icing nozzles
Foil
Icing scraper or comb
Icing ruler or comb
Serrated knife
Cake boards*
Icing turntable
Decoration for top of cake (e.g. small vase)
*For each tier: one thin board of the exact size and one larger than the tier and strong enough to take its weight.

Square cake sizes		15 cm/ 6 in	18 cm/ 7 in	20 cm/ 8 in	22 cm/ 9 in	25 cm/ 10 in	28 cm/ 11 in	30 cm/ 12 in
Round cake sizes	15 cm/ 6 in	18 cm/ 7 in	20 cm/ 8 in	22 cm/ 9 in	25 cm/ 10 in	28 cm/ 11 in	30 cm/ 12 in	
glacé cherries	45 g/1½ oz	70 g/2½ oz	85 g/3 oz	110 g/4 oz	140 g/5 oz	225 g/8 oz	285 g/10 oz	340 g/12 oz
chopped mixed peel	30 g/1 oz	55 g/2 oz	55 g/2 oz	85 g/3 oz	110 g/4 oz	140 g/5 oz	200 g/7 oz	250 g/9 oz
rais ins	140 g/5 oz	225 g/8 oz	340 g/12 oz	450 g/1lb	620 g/1lb 6 oz	790 g/1lb 12 oz	1.12k g/2lb 8 oz	1.35k g/3lb
sultanas	55 g/2 oz	85 g/3 oz	110 g/4 oz	200 g/7 oz	225 g/8 oz	370 g/13 oz	425 g/15 oz	500 g/1lb 2 oz
currants	55 g/2 oz	85 g/3 oz	110 g/4 oz	200 g/7 oz	225 g/8 oz	370 g/13 oz	425 g/15 oz	500 g/1lb 2 oz
grated lemon zest	¼ lemon	½ lemon	1 lemon	1 lemon	1 lemon	1½ lemons	1½ lemons	2 lemons
blanched almonds – chopped	30 g/1 oz	55 g/2 oz	55 g/2 oz	85 g/3 oz	110 g/4 oz	140 g/5 oz	200 g/7 oz	250 g/9 oz
butter	85 g/3 oz	140 g/5 oz	170 g/6 oz	285 g/10 oz	340 g/12 oz	500 g/1lb 2 oz	590 g/1lb 5 oz	790 g/1lb 12 oz
soft brown su gar	85 g/3 oz	140 g/5 oz	170 g/6 oz	285 g/10 oz	340 g/12 oz	500 g/1lb 2 oz	590 g/1lb 5 oz	790 g/1lb 12 oz
e g gs	2	2½	3	5	6	9	11	14
pla in flour	10 g/4 oz	170 g/6 oz	225 g/8 oz	340 g/12 oz	450 g/1lb	560 g/1¼ lb	675 g/1½ lb	790 g/1lb 12 oz
ground mixed spice	¼ teasp	½ teasp	¾ teasp	1 teasp	1½ teasp	2 teasp	2½ teasp	2¾ teasp
black treacle	½ tblsp	½ tblsp	1 tblsp	1½ tblsp	2 tblsp	2½ tblsp	3 tblsp	3½ tblsp
brandy (can be added after cook in g)	2 tblsp	3 tblsp	4 tblsp	4½ tblsp	5 tblsp	5½ tblsp	6 tblsp	6½ tblsp
cook in g time	2 hours	2½ hours	2¾ hours	3¼ hours	3½–4 hours	4–4½ hours	5–5½ hours	6–6½ hours

METHOD

The table will give you the ingredient quantities for different-sized cakes.

1. Preheat the oven to 150°C/300°F/gas mark 2. Grease and line the base and sides of the cake tin with a double layer of greaseproof paper and protect the sides by tying a couple of layers of newspaper around the outside of the tin.
2. Cut the cherries in half and mix with the mixed peel, raisins, sultanas, currants, grated lemon zest and blanched chopped almonds.
3. Cream the butter until soft, add the sugar and beat well until light and fluffy. Beat the eggs and add gradually, beating well between each addition. If the mixture looks as if it might curdle, add a spoonful of flour.
4. Sift together the flour and mixed spice and fold into the mixture with the treacle.
5. Fold in the fruit and nut mixture. The brandy can be added now or it can be poured over the cake once it is baked.
6. Put the mixture into the prepared tin and place in the centre of the oven. Bake for the required time (see table). If it is a large cake (i.e. larger than 25 cm/10 in square or 28 cm/11 in round) you should turn the oven temperature down to 140°C/275°F/gas mark 1 after three-quarters of the baking time. If the top is getting too dark, cover with a piece of damp greaseproof paper. Test by inserting a sharp knife or skewer into the centre. If it comes out clean, the cake is ready.
7. Remove from the oven and allow to cool completely in the tin. When the cake is cold, remove from the tin but keep it in its greaseproof paper. Make a few holes in the top of the cake and pour over the brandy, if using or not already added. Wrap the cake well in the kitchen foil and store in a cool, dry place.

WACKY WEDDINGS

- A scientist who was a keen palaeontologist chose a fruit cake in the shape of a dinosaur.
- Cakemaker Kate Poulter of Pat-A-Cake was asked to make a wedding cake which had two tiny snails on it because the bridegroom's first present to his girlfriend had been a brass snail.
- Rachel Mount, who specializes in novelty cakes, made a three-tier cake for a couple who had conducted their courtship across the Atlantic. One tier showed his home in Birmingham,

another her base in Los Angeles, and the third depicted telephone lines across the Atlantic.

- One couple chose a cake in the shape of the Eiffel Tower because it was the scene of his proposal. Another bride and groom chose a gondolier-shaped cake to remind them of his proposal in Venice.
- One bridegroom insisted that a tier of the cake should be a pork pie as this was his favourite food.

CAKES THAT TRAVEL

Holiday companies normally include the cake in the package deal, but they can be of poor quality, and many resorts wheel out the same battered and chipped bride and bridegroom for the top of the cake.

Flyaway cakes by Pat-A-Cake are specially designed and packaged to be carried as hand luggage. Their most popular designs are: a two-tiered blue iced cake littered with shells and starfish (ideal for a beach celebration); two suitcases with gold handles one on top of the other, and lucky horseshoes and a piece of veil on the top (the cake can be personalized with 'Mr and Mrs—' on the luggage label and your honeymoon destination); and the bride and bridegroom riding an elephant for African weddings. (See Stockists, page 280.)

Remember to check with the airline that it's happy for you to transport your cake as hand luggage (often the cake will have a better seat than you if there is one free) and when you arrive at your hotel keep it out of direct sunlight. Some couples reserve the cake for a second celebration at home.

Tip Companies who specialize in moving fine art and antiques will often guarantee the safe delivery of your cake within this country – but at a cost.

STORING THE CAKE AFTERWARDS

If you want to save a tier for a christening or other big occasion wrap it in greaseproof paper and foil and store in a tin or freezer. The smallest tier might seem like the most obvious choice but can look rather miserly at a big celebration.

Don't be put off if the icing turns yellow – this is simply the oil from the marzipan seeping through, and if you're worried about how it looks you can have it re-iced.

PLANNING FOR THE WORST

WEATHER

Several services offer a short-range forecast for your region which will give you the choice of adapting your plans accordingly – the marquee company might be able to let you have a few heaters if the weather looks like turning arctic, or you might want to swap your open-top car.

The Met Office provides a telephone information service that will predict four or so days in advance what the weather will be like. Ceefax and Teletext also offer regional breakdowns of weather forecasts for the next few days.

Another way of taking the sting out of a bout of bad weather is to place a bet on it. William Hill says the vicar's word is usually taken as sufficient proof. The odds given depend on how close the wedding day is.

INSURANCE

Do you have a nagging doubt that the hotel could go bust the day before your wedding, that your little brother might turn your ivory dress into a tie-dye creation while you're not looking, or that you might lose your job? If you do, you could benefit from wedding insurance.

Read the small print closely: some companies cover the cost of any supplier going bust; others limit insurance to the venue only; some will pay for photos to be taken again but not for a video to be reshot. Most insurance companies don't include change of heart – or 'disinclination to marry' as they prefer to call it.

13
Flowers

Flowers don't need to be expensive, and often one grand gesture – a sheaf of arum lilies or a top table draped with garlands of blossom – can be as effective as a series of painstakingly constructed decorations. Whatever you choose, the florist's arrival with your bouquet and a tray of buttonholes may be the first time the fact that you're getting married really sinks in.

THE FLORIST

When choosing a florist bear the following in mind:

- Look for the logo of the Society of Floristry (the Society will also provide details of your nearest qualified florist: see also Stockists, page 284); see Useful Addresses, page 273.
- Consider personal recommendations.
- Most florists will have an album of photos showing their work. You could also ask to visit the shop early on the day of another wedding to look at the bouquet.

Show the florist fabric from your dress and the attendants' outfits, and if possible a drawing or picture of what you'll be wearing. Describe how your hair will look on the day, and if you'll have a veil, how long it will be.

Order the flowers at least two months in advance and confirm the arrangements a week before. The florist may also need a contact name and telephone number for the wedding and reception venues if they will also be making arrangements for these parts of the day.

MONEYSAVER

If you're on a tight budget ask if the florist offers any special bridal packages for a set price. This will usually provide the basics but you may be restricted to certain colours, flowers that are in season, less complicated designs and a small number of buttonholes.

SUPERSTITIONS

You may think you're holding a bouquet of beautifully coordinated colours, but to your ancestors you are clutching a bundle of carefully coded messages. Even in the language of flowers there are different dialects – some flowers carry several (sometimes conflicting) meanings, whilst others have no hidden message at all (perhaps because the flowers have only become popular recently).

Peonies, for example, denote shame, while azaleas represent temperance. Lilies mean majesty, but some people view them as unlucky because of their association with funerals. A red rose and white snowdrop separately mean love and hope – but for the superstitious red and white flowers together represent blood and bandages and are to be avoided at all costs.

FLOWERS IN SEASON

Advances in horticulture mean that most flowers can be grown in this country, or flown in from abroad – both of course at a price. New variations on old favourites are being developed all the time, too. The cerise and white 'Zebra' rose is about as far removed from the traditional English rose as you can imagine and the sunflower has come in from the cold after a virtually pollen-free breed was developed.

Spring

Amaryllis
Anemone
Azalea
Bluebell
Broom
Camellia
Clematis
Crocus
Daffodil
Forsythia
Freesia
Fruit blossom: apple, cherry
Heather
Lilac
Mimosa

Muscari
Narcissus
Polyanthus
Primrose
Ranunculus
Tulips: variegated, red, yellow

Late spring

Delphinium
Heather
Jasmine
Lily of the valley
Queen Anne's lace
Rhododendron
Stocks
Sweet pea
Waxflower

Summer

Aster
Blue freesia
Cornflower
Delphinium
Echinops (Globe thistles)
Fuchsia
Gardenia
Gerbera
Gladiolus
Heather
Hollyhock
Honeysuckle
Jasmine
Larkspur
Lilac
Lily
Lily of the valley
Lupin
Marigold
Magnolia

Peony
Rhododendron
Rose
Scabious
Stock
Sweet pea
Sweet William
Tiger lily

Autumn

Copper beech leaves
Dahlia
Feverfew
Heather
Hydrangea
Love lies bleeding
Michaelmas daisy
Morning glory

Winter

Christmas rose
Freesia
Gentian
Holly berries
Poinsettia
Red carnation
Snowdrop
Trailing ivy
Winter jasmine

CHOOSING YOUR FLOWERS AND OTHER MATERIALS

- **Exotic**: Amaryllis, anthurium, calla lily, celosia, Columbian rose, heliconia, orchid, palm leaf, safari sunset, stargazer, waxflower.
- **Fragrant**: Freesia, honeysuckle, jasmine, lavender, lilac, mimosa, sage.
- **Fruit and vegetables**: Aubergine, ornamental cabbage, chilli pepper, cranberry, currant, fig, grape, miniature leek, radish, squash, baby turnip.

- **Rustic**: Aster, broom, catkin, clematis, cornflower, daffodil, gerbera, honeysuckle, larkspur, lavender, lilac, phlox, poppy, primrose, scabious, sweet pea, tulip.
- **Sophisticated**: Lenten rose, orchid, peony, Peruvian lily (or other varieties), ranunculus, sunflower.
- **Traditional**: Anemone, carnation, freesia, gypsophila, lily of the valley, rose.

WACKY WEDDINGS

Don't be afraid to ask the person who arranges the flowers in the church to do something slightly different – most churches incorporate fruits and vegetables into their displays at harvest time. Red and yellow peppers crammed into a glass vase, for example, provide a colourful way of hiding long stalks.

BOUQUET – SHAPE AND SIZE

Bear in mind your skin tone, hair colour, build, and the style of your dress. The Society of Floristry recommends that a bouquet should represent about a third of your height.

Since a long, trailing shower or waterfall bouquet draws the eye from top to bottom it can have a slimming effect, but if you're short it may appear overwhelming. By contrast, a posy-style bouquet draws the eye from left to right and will accentuate your hips and middle. This sort of bouquet can also look out of proportion on a very tall bride. A shower bouquet can seem unbalanced with a mini or knee-length dress.

Hold the bouquet at waist level or below. If the front of your dress is very ornate and you are anxious not to hide it, ask the florist to construct a bouquet that lies across your arm.

POLLEN STAINS AND HAYFEVER

A good florist should deal with troublesome stamens beforehand, but if you're unlucky, avoid wetting the pollen, instead flick or lightly brush it away.

Hayfever sufferers will know which plants affect them most. You might even consider dried or silk flowers if you want to avoid a running nose on the day. Try to plan the wedding when pollen will be less troublesome (see page 14, 'Timing').

BUTTONHOLES

An extra hole for a flower started to appear in the top left lapel of men's suits from the 1840s.

- **Who wears one**?: The groom, best man, ushers, and fathers of the bride and groom usually have buttonholes in their left lapel. Other guests such as uncles, grandparents and close friends (of both sexes) are sometimes also honoured.
- **Flowers**: The most common choice is a carnation or rose, but the bridegroom may want to wear something different (perhaps picking out a flower from the bride's bouquet).
- **Securing the buttonhole**: The stem is fitted through the buttonhole on the lapel and fixed with a pin behind (if you want to avoid any sign of the pin simply thread the pin through one thickness only of the lapel material).
- **Corsages**: These are usually bigger than buttonholes and are worn by the mothers of the bride and bridegroom. They are chosen to match their outfits.

PUTTING ON THE STYLE

The buttonhole can blend in with the theme of the wedding – for example sweet peas and cow parsley if you're looking for a rustic look, or heather and thistle if you're getting married in Scotland.

MAKING YOUR OWN BUTTONHOLES

This can be a therapeutic way of spending the early hours of your wedding day. One bride sat down with a friend, her mother and grandmother to help her.

1. Cut the flower to leave a stem of about 5 cm/2 in.
2. Thread thick florist's wire through the base of the flower/top of the stem.
3. Push the flower about two-thirds of the way along the wire.
4. Bend the wire so that both ends are parallel with the stem of the flower.
5. Wind the longer end of wire around both the stem and the shorter strand of wire.

6. Wrap green gutta tape (available from florists and garden centres) around the stem and wiring.

Foliage or other flowers can be added after preparing them in a similar way and the arrangement taped together with more gutta tape. Leaves can be supported by using wire to make a small, horizontal stitch in the central vein at the back. Draw both ends of the wire down into a hairpin shape, parallel to the stem, and twist one wire round the other end of the stem. Cover with gutta.

CARE AND FIRST AID FOR FLOWERS

All the flowers to be worn or carried should arrive on the morning of the wedding boxed, well sprayed and covered with Cellophane to protect them. Whoever delivers them should give you instructions on how to unpack them and, if treated kindly, the flowers should not droop during the next few hours. If they do, call the florist immediately or spray and water them.

Resist the temptation to keep touching the flowers and put them somewhere safe that's cool, and away from direct sunlight, children and animals. Putting them in the fridge is a bit risky as it may be too hot or too cold. A garage is usually suitable.

FLOWER ARRANGEMENTS

If you have a friend or member of the family who is a flower enthusiast you will save a lot of money, and know that you have a personal service by handing all or part of the job over to them. You still need to plan the flowers closely – you might, for example, decide to buy a few exotic but key flowers and gather the rest from the countryside or your garden.

WHAT YOU'LL NEED

- **Flowers**: Buy from florists; flower stalls or markets; wholesale markets or flower specialists. Look for supplies in your garden or friends', keep an eye out for inspiration in the countryside (fruit blossom can be spectacular and abundant), respecting the country code by taking care not to overpick, cause any damage or, most importantly, take rare plants.

- **Equipment**: Chicken wire; florists' foam; sharp scissors; spray; gutta tape; twine; ribbon; knife; secateurs; various-sized wires; bucket and watering can.

PREPARATION

Give your flowers a good dose of flower food before the wedding and remove damaged and unwanted leaves.

- **Woody stems** (e.g. lilac, rhododendron): Hammer the bottom 2.5 cm/1 in of each stem, scrape off the same amount of bark. Place in boiling water for about half a minute and move to cool water.
- **Milky stems** (e.g. poppy, euphorbia): Cut stems, dip in tepid water for half a minute to seal, or singe ends with a match or candle.
- **Hollow stems** (e.g. delphinium, lupin, amaryllis): Fill stems with water and plug with cottonwool.
- **Roses**: Remove thorns. Split ends and plunge bottom 5 cm/2 in in boiling water for two minutes, then put up to their necks in cold water. (This method also revives wilting roses.)
- **Foliage**: Hammer ends and soak in water for several hours.

QUANTITIES

Break down individual arrangements into: the focal flowers (the key flowers to which the eye is drawn); the transitional flowers (the 'in-fill' flowers); and the foliage. Multiply each group by the number of arrangements you plan (for example six table decorations or three pew ends).

THE CHURCH

Churches are ideal for floral decorations because they usually contain architectural features such as columns and wide window-ledges that are perfect to build arrangements around. They are also already geared up for flowers: many have special equipment available and, more importantly, skilled arrangers who are keen to make their church look attractive (especially if they are given a slightly bigger budget than normal).

Ask the minister where you can put arrangements. Most churches will be grateful for the free flowers but others don't like arrangements on the altar or during Lent or Advent. If someone from the church is helping, remember to give them a thank-you present.

A friend or family member who has agreed to arrange the flowers will need to know:

- Who keeps the key to the church.
- Equipment the church has – pedestals or other containers, for example.
- Where the water source is.
- Where the rubbish is put and where vacuum-cleaners and dustpan and brushes are kept.

Making the most of the church

When deciding on colours, think about the backcloth: are there any stained-glass windows or a brightly patterned carpet, stonework or wooden choir stalls?

It is usually better to concentrate on a few large arrangements. Since your audience will be standing up, sitting down and kneeling, try to put arrangements at eye-level for maximum visibility. But don't waste flowers if an arrangement won't be seen from all sides.

- **Lychgate**: Hanging arrangements such as flower balls or baskets, garlands and swags of blossom look spectacular.
- **Entrance**: As lychgate, but consider also making arches (the church may have the necessary trelliswork). An arch entirely of foliage can look stunning. Topiary trees draped with ribbons may be placed either side of the entrance (some flower clubs will sell or hire out the containers). You can also decorate the windows or a bench or use a pedestal – but make sure there's enough room for the guests to pass.
- **Pew ends**: Either tie swags to the ends or make special wooden and foam holders (also available from florists). Attach to alternate pews, or every third pew if the aisle is long.
- **Window ledges**: Allow to drape over the edge. You may want to miss out stained-glass windows or to pick out one colour.
- **Columns**: Hang garlands or swags vertically.
- **Altar and chancel**: Consider the steps leading to the altar. A pedestal could be put either side of the altar, or garlands draped on the choir stalls.

OTHER PLACES FOR FLOWERS

- **Jewish wedding**; You may want to decorate the chuppah (see page 214, 'Jewish weddings').
- **Register office**: Most wedding rooms have their own decorations, but some will allow you to use your own. Try to make them easily portable.
- **Tables**: Swags can be draped over the back of chairs. Small topiary trees or decorations based around candles also make a change.
- **Marquees**: Small topiary trees can lead the way to the reception. The poles can also be decorated or decorations hung from ropes. Bear in mind where eye-level will be most of the time.
- **Home/new wedding venues**: Hang swags from doors, drape garlands round mantelpieces, suspend flowers in stairwell or fix decorations to bannisters.

FLORAL MEMORIES

- **Bouquet**: There are several ways of preserving your bouquet – either in one piece or as a mounted decoration (See Stockists, page 284). One way of doing it yourself is by air-drying the flowers: simply hang the bouquet upside-down in a warm room out of direct sunlight for about two to three weeks.
- **Cuttings**: Princess Anne's flowers contained a sprig of myrtle from Queen Victoria's bouquet. To take a cutting from a stem, make the cut immediately below a node or joint and plant in compost. You might also want to use a root-promoting hormone. When roots begin to form, put in new pots. Gradually move the plant into cooler temperatures before putting it in the garden. Tell your florist of your plans in advance as some flowers are treated in a way that makes them unsuitable to take cuttings from.

MONEYSAVER

Dried petals make a cheap and environmentally friendly confetti.

FLOWERS CHECKLIST

Type	Number	Budget	Price
Bridal bouquet			
Headdresses			
Buttonholes			
Corsages			
Other flowers for attendants			
Church or other venue for wedding ceremony			
Reception			
Bouquets/plants for mothers			

14

TRANSPORT

How you arrive at your wedding will depend on the distance you have to travel, your budget, and whether you want to travel in style or just arrive quietly with minimum fuss. You could argue that, since most of your guests won't actually see you arrive, an extravagant gesture would be wasted. On the other hand this could be a chance to fulfil your wildest dreams – to arrive in Chitty Chitty Bang Bang or a horse-drawn carriage, and to savour the experience of stopping Saturday shoppers in their tracks and holding up the traffic.

If your priority is to arrive safely and on time, your best bet is to choose a local taxi firm or to ask a friend with a reliable car to pick you up. But if calling a cab seems too dull you could always hire a white version or a New York-style yellow taxi.

Asking a close friend to drive you to your wedding can be reassuring, especially if they have a calming aura and won't expect you to make small talk. Check they've had their car recently serviced and it has a tank full of petrol. Ask them to drive at a sedate pace and make sure they know the area reasonably well. If you arrive too quickly it's helpful to have a loop of road in mind to give your guests a chance to overtake you.

GETTING THE MOST FROM YOUR MOTOR

Start looking for your wedding car about eight months before the day and expect to put down a deposit of about a quarter of the price. Whether you want a sedate Rolls or a racy Aston Martin, or fancy jumping into the Batmobile or Roy Orbison's white Cadillac convertible, bear the following in mind (see also attendants' duties in Chapter 10 and Stockists, page 289):

- Make sure you know what the cost involves. Ask about VAT, mileage, decorations. Although some hire agencies are based in the South-East of England, many offer a nationwide service.
- Older vehicles tend to be more expensive, partly because they're usually gas guzzlers but also because the cost of upkeep is high.

- If you are based near the venue you may need only one car to do several journeys, but make sure the firm knows about this. Don't be tempted to save money at the cost of extra anxiety over whether everyone will arrive on time.
- Check that the car is big enough for both you, your dress and your hairstyle. You will almost certainly need a four-door model.
- Find out if an open-top car has a pull-up roof in case it rains. Also, remember that open-top cars will have to drive slower to preserve your hairstyle.
- Consider the colour of the vehicle and how it will look as a backdrop for your dress. A white car could, for example, drain the colour from your dress in photos.
- Ask what sort of back-up the firm has if your car breaks down (not such a remote possibility if it's a vintage car – see below).
- Find out if the car will be used for any other weddings that day and when they will be held.

CASE STUDY

Anne and David, both 34, were left stranded outside Bristol City football ground just as fans were arriving for a derby match with Swindon Town. The couple's vintage Rolls-Royce had broken down between the church and reception and eventually a police van took them with lights flashing and sirens screaming to their reception in a community hall. They were twenty minutes late.

Tip If you discover the ride to the service leaves you dishevelled and uncomfortable, ask the driver if it's possible to swap cars for the trip to the reception. On a quiet day hire firms often have cars sitting empty.

OTHER FORMS OF TRANSPORT

- **Horse and carriage**: Find out what the driver will be wearing and what sort of protection is offered against the weather. Check that the roads are suitable – you don't want the horse to collapse halfway up a 'one-in-two' hill, or find your route blocked by a motorway. Travelling along fume-filled roads may also make you feel a bit queasy and destroy that just-washed feeling.
- **Hot-air balloons**: One of the most romantic, but least reliable forms of transport. You've probably got a fifty/fifty chance that weather conditions will be suitable depending on where you are (bear in

mind it's generally wetter in Ireland and the west of Britain). The best time to fly is first thing in the morning or early evening because winds are more predictable, but there's no guarantee where you'll touch down and how long it will take to get there (someone will have to follow you by road). Your pilot should have a licence from the Civil Aviation Authority and be fully insured. They will also be able to tell you whether your proposed flightpath steers clear of restricted air space – for example, if you're near a stud farm where horses might be frightened by the balloons, or near an airport or city.

- **Helicopters**: A convenient, if expensive, way of getting from the church to the reception or to the airport to start your honeymoon. Many hotels have enough room for a helicopter to land, but remember that you're paying for the helicopter to come from its base to pick you up. Your luxury transport may also be hit by poor weather.
- **Walking**: A relaxing way to start the day or to mark a change of tempo after a church wedding, but make sure your clothes are suitable and you have a fall-back plan if the weather turns nasty. Not suitable if you have to negotiate muddy paths. Equally exhilarating for town and country.

PUTTING ON THE STYLE

Robert, 46, a journalist, and Katherine, 43, who works in PR, decided to walk from the church where they had their blessing (Katherine had been married before) to their reception a few miles away across the busy streets of West London. As Robert is Scottish they hired a piper to lead the way playing 'Marie's Wedding'. All their guests, except an elderly aunt, walked with them. Traffic stopped to let the procession cross the roads, cars honked their horns, passers-by cheered and a man on a balcony accompanied them on his tin whistle.

DOING YOUR OWN THING/MONEYSAVER

Most people know someone who has a sports or classic car they will be proud to drive for the day (you could inquire at car enthusiast clubs) – but check it over beforehand for oily patches or sharp edges which could damage your clothes. Smaller cars are more suitable for going away as you're both likely to be wearing slightly more practical clothes, but make sure there's enough room for your luggage. If you want to drive a borrowed car, insurance can usually be arranged for the day.

Decorate the car with ribbons outside and flowers on the inside backshelf, but make sure it stays clear of lipstick and shaving foam. You could also ask the driver to dress up in clothes to suit the car: Teddy boy outfit for a Cadillac convertible, as James Bond for a 1960s Aston Martin, or a simple peaked chauffeur's cap for any shiny, upmarket car.

WACKY WEDDINGS

Some couples have gone even further when personalizing their mode of transport. Beatles fans Tim, 38, and Jean, 37, asked a carpenter friend to make a 3-m/10-ft wooden yellow submarine with holes in the bottom so that they could walk along wearing it to the register office in Bishop Auckland, Durham.

Another couple, who married in Glamis Castle in Scotland, left for their honeymoon on a steam-roller. Mick and Jane, both truck-drivers from Southampton, decorated their trucks and drove them to the register office.

Jerry, a 34-year-old former Royal Marine, was shocked when his best man transported him to the church in Weston-super-Mare in an 11-tonne armoured personnel carrier which had been painted pink for the occasion.

WHO TRAVELS WITH WHOM

Traditionally, the bride's mother travels with the bridesmaids and pageboys in the first car. The bride and her father follow in the second car (or one car can make several trips).

If one of the bridegroom's parents is alone, make sure they have someone to travel with – another family member, for example.

After the service, the bride and bridegroom take the first car to the reception followed by the bride's parents and attendants. The best man or woman should make sure that every other guest has transport and then try to reach the reception as soon as possible.

If the reception is a long way away, or you want to encourage guests to relax and not worry about staying sober, you could hire transport for them – a double-decker bus, minibus, coach or old-fashioned omnibus. You might even be in a position to transport people by boat or barge. Whichever form you decide on, talk to the driver about the best return route so that they can drop off as many guests as possible at their homes, hotels or B&Bs.

WHAT TO AVOID ON THE WAY TO THE WEDDING

According to superstition, the following are bad omens:

- A monk or nun (because of their association with chastity and poverty)
- An open grave or funeral
- A pig, hare or lizard

If you're unfortunate enough to catch sight of any of these, a chimney sweep (who carries strong associations with hearth and home), or a black cat, will go a long way to cancelling out the effect.

15
MEMORIES: PHOTOGRAPHS, VIDEOS AND OTHER MEMENTOS

PHOTOGRAPHS

Why do you need wedding photographs – to please your parents, to send to someone abroad who couldn't come to the wedding, to provide an instant family heirloom, or as proof of how wonderful you and your dress looked on the day? The answer will, to some extent, dictate the style and number of photographs you choose.

Often the most memorable wedding photographs are those which are neither posed nor taken by professionals. But relying on amateur snaps takes courage. One compromise is to employ a professional photographer, but to encourage keen amateurs among your guests to make free with their cameras.

CHOOSING YOUR PROFESSIONAL PHOTOGRAPHER

Make sure you feel at ease with them and that their work is in sympathy with the sort of vision you have of your wedding. Bossy or aggressive photographers who work to their own agenda can spoil the day.

Personal recommendations work well if they come from someone who has similar tastes, and professional bodies will recommend photographers in your area and indicate any specialist skills such as hand-tinting (see Useful Addresses, page 274).

Visit the photographer in their studio and have a good look at their portfolio. Make sure the photos cover different weddings and that one of them was recent.

- Is there a good mix, or are they very similar?
- Do they convey the spirit of the occasion, or are they stiff and bland?
- Does everyone look happy, and are they all looking at the camera?
- Is everyone neat and tidy, or is a collar sticking up or a bridesmaid standing at an odd angle?

Ask if the person you see for your initial consultation will be there on the day and if they are a member of a professional association. Find out what type of qualifications they have and which area of photography they cover. Discuss where the photos will be taken if it rains and make sure they have professional indemnity insurance to cover the cost of retaking the whole lot if disaster strikes.

MONEYSAVER

Most photographers are open to negotiation, so don't be afraid to make suggestions that fall outside the standard package. Photographers usually feel they have to present their work in lavish albums which can cost hundreds of pounds (and which they won't make much money from). If you have no desire for a padded white album with your initials embossed in gold, negotiate a price that covers just the photos.

Likewise, photographers normally charge a lot more for travelling long distances, but if you get married on a Friday in November rather than a Bank Holiday weekend in August, they might be prepared to lower their prices in what is traditionally a quiet period for them.

Reprints can cost more than the original photos, so it pays to take time calculating in advance how many copies you will need. Photographers own the copyright to the photos but must ask your permission to reproduce any shots of your wedding. They usually like to hold on to the negatives (partly to retain some control over the quality of reprints) but will sell them if you have a convincing argument such as you are going to live abroad.

AVOIDING WAITING AT THE CHURCH (OR OTHER WEDDING VENUE)

Good wedding photography is one-third talent and two-thirds crowd control.

- **Limit numbers**: If you want group shots of everyone from your Sixth Form metalwork class to your local pub quiz team, you run the risk of turning your guests into a horde of cold, hungry and disgruntled onlookers.
- **Planning**: Draw up a list of shots and a schedule.
- **Early shots**: Start taking photos while the guests are spilling out of the building. In some weddings such as a Jewish service or a register office affair it may be possible to take some shots of the couple beforehand. It can be reassuring to have photos taken before the service when you know you look your best.
- **Single-mindedness**: Avoid chatting to guests until after the photos are taken. Take shots in a systematic way – a photo of the bride, bridegroom, ushers, best man and bridesmaids, followed by the two sets of family with the bridesmaids and best man (rather than calling the bridesmaids back when you get round to the family shots).
- **Discipline**: Brief two friends (one for each family), or ushers (if the best man or woman is in several shots), to round people up.

WHO GOES WHERE

If either of your parents is divorced or separated, discuss with them how they want the photos to be arranged and brief the photographer. Often couples who have split up are happy to appear together. In some cases it eases tensions to mix up a couple's parents so that separated parents don't have to stand next to one another.

- **Core list of shots**: Bridegroom (alone); bridesmaids; bride and her father; signing the register; bride and bridegroom (full-length); bride and bridegroom (head-and-shoulders); bride, bridegroom, best man and bridesmaids; bride (full-length); bride and best man; bride, bridegroom and both parents; bride and bridegroom leaving in or standing by their car; the couple cutting the cake.
- **Other suggestions**: Male attendants; the first dance; school friends; work colleagues; groups of relatives (for example uncles, aunts or

cousins); different generations (for example mother, daughter and grandmother); the oldest and youngest guest (if for example your guests include a very new baby and someone who is proud of their longevity); a group shot of everyone.

Tip Usually formal photographs are taken at the church and less formal ones at the reception, but if you are getting married in one of the new venues or a rather bleak register office you might prefer to have all the photos taken at the reception. Guests can have a drink or retreat to a warm room, and children can let off steam.

PUTTING ON THE STYLE

Reportage-style photography tells the story of the wedding through a series of relaxed and largely unposed photos. At its best it has the advantage of combining the fly-on-the-wall intimacy of photographs taken by friends with the technical expertise of a professional.

Pictures taken in this style might, for example, include: the bride at home wrapped in a towel waiting for her nail varnish to dry; an adult bridesmaid in an unguarded moment puffing on a cigarette behind a tree; a flower girl and pageboy locked in earnest conversation under a table at the reception; two guests with their heads thrown back in abandonment at a good joke; your wedding shoes wrapped in tissue still in their box.

Since the photographer will be with you in your most intimate moments – probably from the time the hairdresser arrives – it is even more important to make sure you feel comfortable with and trust them. Make sure, too, that they include some more formal shots, to please relatives and provide a contrast. (See Stockists, page 287.)

BLACK AND WHITE, OR COLOUR?

Ironically, couples who have grown up in a world of high-quality coloured photographs increasingly want their wedding depicted in monochrome, while their parents, who often had no choice when they got married, will only be satisfied with colour. One compromise is to use a colour film but to have a set of photographs developed in black and white.

If you've spent hours coordinating the colours for your wedding, or you want to remember the exact hues in your bouquet or the lime-green trouser-suit your best friend wore, then you will need colour prints. Black and white serves a different purpose. It can look wildly romantic and timeless, and you may feel that, without the distraction of colour, the expressions on people's faces are more clearly defined. Black and white can also be more flattering, hiding blemishes and uneven tones.

Hand-coloured prints are usually more expensive because the technique is so time-intensive, but adding colour to details of a favourite black and white photo (the confetti, flowers in a bouquet or a buttonhole) can give a photo a dream-like quality.

TIPS FOR THE AMATEUR PHOTOGRAPHER

Someone who is well known to the guests will have the advantage of putting them at their ease. Before you ask a friend to take your photographs, think hard about whether the responsibility will ruin the day for them, and how you (and your parents) will feel if the film doesn't come out.

- **Setting**: Look for anything that will make an interesting backdrop – a bright red church door, an unusual arch, a stone wall, a hedge, a ruin or a lake. Think about where you would take the photos if it rained. Ask before taking photos inside.
- **Film**: Invest in a good-quality film and make sure it isn't past its sell-by date. 400 ASA is suitable for most conditions, 100 ASA is better for group photos taken with a more sophisticated camera as enlargements will be superior.
- **Equipment**: Take a spare camera, batteries and film and make sure you have read through the instructions and are familiar with the equipment. Use a tripod to steady yourself or rest the camera on a car or wall, or lean against a tree.
- **Composition**: Make sure your subjects fill the frame and look out for any unsightly additions – telegraph poles growing out of heads, rubbish bins, a mirror that will reveal the person taking the photo, exit signs or fire extinguishers. Check that people aren't looking straight into the sun and squinting. A fully shaded area should reduce distracting shadows, but take a light-meter reading of their faces if possible.

INVOLVING GUESTS

Photographs taken by guests will give you a novel view of your wedding, either because they are taken from a different angle or because they show parts of the day (for example chatting outside the church before the ceremony starts or the dying moments of the reception) from which you, as bride and bridegroom, are excluded.

Often, though, guests take a handful of snaps and then wait until their summer holidays to have the film developed, by which time they assume you won't be interested in seeing the wedding photographs.

- Ask guests to send you either two of their favourite photographs of the day or, if you know they are good photographers, a complete set.
- Leave disposable cameras on tables at the reception.
- Make a large wooden or cardboard frame and encourage guests to pose in it.

SALVAGE WORK

Modern technology means that even if you rip up a photo in a fit of pique the chances are it can be salvaged. The vampire look can be expunged with a retouching pen available from most specialist photographic shops. To avoid red eyes in the first place look into a bright light just before the photo is taken or fix on the photographer's forehead so that the flash doesn't bounce into the eye.

Aunt Rachel didn't make it from Rwanda, or your best friend's boyfriend who subsequently ran off with her mother appears in every shot? New technology means that absent guests can be included in wedding photos (or unwanted people removed). Computer magic means a bride's eyes can be opened and a lightning rod removed from the groom's head. (See Stockists, page 287.)

VIDEOS

Deciding whether or not to have a video of your wedding and which parts should be included is an even bigger decision than choosing the style of photographs. Do you really want to see every second of your wedding through someone else's eyes or would you prefer to rely solely on your own memories? You may remember your father's speech as faultless – will a video remind you that he stumbled over his words? Will it become an important document for your children – a rare example of your whole family together?

Advice for finding a good photographer applies to choosing a video-maker. They should also have a licence to cover copyright of music and readings, and professional indemnity insurance. The Association of Professional Videomakers will recommend someone in your area and in some cases can help you find someone suitable abroad (see Useful Addresses, page 274).

If you decide to ask a friend to video the wedding, make sure you're not putting too heavy a burden on their shoulders (both literally and metaphorically). You may, however, reap greater pleasure from a less polished reminder of your day: your father trying discreetly to slip payment into the piper's sporran without disrupting his playing; the bridegroom winking at the camera; or the person making the recording confusing the names of guests.

TIPS FOR THE AMATEUR

You can hire a video camera from most branches of Radio Rentals, or from several other shops found in your local telephone directory. Remember to book well in advance, especially if the wedding is in the summer.

- **Practice**: Make sure you feel comfortable with the camera and take it to the rehearsal.
- **Top positions**: Near the church door so that you can film guests as they arrive; close to the altar; in a balcony or organ loft. (Always ask permission first.) Use the time devoted to the official photographer to capture guests standing around and the main members of the wedding lining up. You might also consider interviewing guests.
- **Timing**: Individual shots should be between seven and ten seconds – longer if you're filming words (such as the name of the church or the register). Read anything you're filming to yourself silently as a guide.
- **Composition**: Leave room between people's heads and the frame. See also page 186, 'Tips for the Amateur Photographer'.
- **Posture**: Stand with your feet apart and your weight evenly distributed, or kneel on one leg with your arm propped on the raised knee. Sit astride a chair and rest your arms on its back – good for filming children or people sitting down (for example at the reception).
- **Panning**: Rehearse a vertical or horizontal pan before shooting and

hold the first and final images for about three seconds. Move the camera slowly and at a steady speed. Use the technique sparingly (it's most effective to show the relationship between things or people, such as a child staring in amazement at a bride). Pan *with* any action – not against it – for example the bridal car arriving at the church.

MEMENTOS

Other ways of remembering the day:

- A cassette recording of the service.
- Passing round a book at the reception and asking everyone to add their messages.
- A montage of mementos from the day: a champagne label, place setting, confetti, order of service, scrap of material from your dress. Helen Atkinson will mount them in a special frame that can even have fragments of the speeches woven into it (see Stockists, page 286).

You can arrange the above yourself or ask a professional to design something especially for you – for example a book covered in the same material as your dress whose pages can be detached and put on each table for everyone to sign.

WACKY WEDDINGS

Forever Yours harnesses multi-media technology to allow you to choose a series of memorabilia – from your wedding video to invitations and photos – and combine them with music, backgrounds and titles. The result is converted to a CD-ROM disc (you click on a pair of cherubs to move backwards and forwards) and more conventional video. If you feel like it, you can add to the disc and build up a complete story of your life: from your first child to your golden wedding. (See Stockists, page 286.)

PART FIVE

THE DAY

16

THE CEREMONY

See also Chapter 4 'Choosing the Ceremony and Making Preliminary Preparations'

THE CHURCH OF ENGLAND WEDDING CEREMONY

THE ARRIVAL OF GUESTS

One hour before:
Ushers (see page 135, 'Countdown for the Ushers') arrive carrying the service sheets. They hand these out to guests and guide people to their seats – bride's family and friends on the left-hand side (facing the altar) and groom's on the right. Close family are seated nearest the front. A space should be left for the bride's parents and for the best man (who sits in the front right-hand pew).

Thirty minutes before:
Church bells ring out and organist plays introductory music.

Twenty minutes before:
Best man and bridegroom arrive and may chat briefly to guests. Photos are sometimes taken and the best man discreetly pays the minister (this may also be done afterwards). The best man and bridegroom take their place in the front pew on the right – the best man to the right of his charge. They may sit or stand depending on which feels more comfortable.

Ten minutes before:
Attendants and bride's mother arrive and wait in the church porch for the bride and the person giving her away to arrive.

Five minutes before:
The bride and her giver-away arrive. A few photos may be taken. The bride's mother or the chief bridesmaid adjusts the bride's veil (if worn) and gown and makes sure that her engagement ring has been transferred to her right hand.

Just before the service starts:
The bride's mother is escorted to her seat (the front row on the left) by the chief usher or a male member of the family. Her arrival is a signal that the service is about to begin.

STRESSBUSTER

Waiting for the bride can be a nerve-racking time for the bridegroom – especially if she is late. Don't feel you have to take your seat as soon as you arrive if you would rather walk around. You could wait in the vestry, although being amongst your guests may help to relax you. Some churches (especially Scottish ones) have rooms in the tower where you can wait until you spot the bridal car in the distance.

THE SERVICE BEGINS

The organist starts to play the processional music, or a hymn may be sung. Ushers take their seats and the best man and bridegroom rise and stand at the top of the aisle – the best man on the bridegroom's right and a step behind him. The congregation stands up.

Bridesmaids and pageboys either form two lines at the main door through which the bride and giver-away pass, or they line up behind her. If the choir and minister are to form part of the procession, they gather at the church entrance. Otherwise the minister may appear briefly to greet the bride.

Giver-away and bride walk slowly down the aisle, the bride on the giver-away's right arm. If there is a flower-girl she will walk in front scattering petals or confetti (if allowed). Other attendants follow the bride in pairs – usually the youngest first.

Bridegroom and best man may turn to greet the bride, or wait until she arrives at the steps of the chancel (the part of the church where the altar or communion table is situated).

AT THE ALTAR

The giver-away leads the bride to the left of the groom and then takes a pace backwards. Other attendants remain in their processional formation. The bride's train is lowered.

If there is a chief bridesmaid or best woman (in addition to the best man), she lifts the bride's veil and takes the bouquet and any gloves until the register is signed. Otherwise the bride will lift the veil herself and the giver-away will pass the flowers and any gloves to the bride's mother or someone similar, or put them on the front pew. Whoever receives the bouquet returns it to the bride after the register has been signed.

Altar

Minister

Bride   Bridegroom

Giver-away/bride's father   Best man

Chief bridesmaid

Attendants

Bride's family   Bridegroom's family

Tip Traditionally, the bride walks down the aisle with her veil lowered – but this is up to you. Usually the veil is lifted when you arrive at the altar but you may prefer to do this during the ceremony (after you are pronounced man and wife can be a dramatic moment) or in the vestry when you are signing the register.

THE SERVICE

The minister normally starts with a few words of welcome. The service takes about thirty minutes, depending on whether Communion is celebrated, how many readings, psalms, prayers and hymns there are, and the length of the minister's address (which may take place at the beginning of the service or after the vows).

The order of service will vary slightly from church to church and depending on which form you choose. Some ministers like to complete the wedding ceremony before any hymns are sung, although you may have one after the processional.

THE VOWS

First, the minister will explain the basis of Christian marriage and will then ask if anyone knows of a reason why you cannot marry. After pausing just long enough for a frisson of expectation to circulate round the church the minister will then ask the bridegroom if he takes the bride to be his wife, to which he replies 'I will'. The bride is asked the equivalent.

The minister either asks who gives away the bride, or the giver-away simply steps forward, depending on the form of service. The giver-away takes the bride's right hand and gives it palm-down to the minister who places it in the right hand of the bridegroom. The father, or other giver-away, then takes his place in the front pew (or he may wait until after the exchange of rings).

The couple face one another. The minister says the vows slowly, phrase by phrase, for the bridegroom to repeat. They loose hands and the bride takes the bridegroom's. The bride then repeats her vows in the same fashion.

They loose hands and the best man puts the ring(s) on the minister's open prayerbook. The best man may return to his seat at this point or remain standing. The minister blesses the ring and gives it to the bridegroom who places it on the fourth finger of the bride's left hand. While holding the ring, he repeats words said by the minister. If the couple exchange rings the bride repeats this part of the service. If not, the bride acknowledges the symbolism of the ring.

The minister pronounces the couple man and wife and they may kiss. The best man takes a pace backwards and to the right. The couple kneel for a blessing.

STRESSBUSTER

If you find your mouth becomes dry just before the vows try, very gently, biting the tip of your tongue. This will moisten your mouth.

CASE STUDY

Stella and Richard learnt their vows off by heart and simply turned to each other and said them without the help of the vicar. They decided to do this so that it would make them think hard about what they were saying and so that they would be able to repeat them to one another in the future. You may find this too nerve-racking, but remember the minister is there to help you out if you lose your place. If you're superstitious, avoid practising the vows beforehand.

SIGNING THE REGISTER

The bride takes her husband's left arm and attendants take up her train. The minister leads them to the vestry or side table where the register is signed. The best man gathers up his and the groom's hats and gloves.

The most usual form of procession is as follows, but there is room for flexibility if you have an odd number of people or parents who have split up. Strictly speaking, the bride and bridegroom are the only couple who link arms. Any other witnesses should also be part of the procession and attendants may also join in.

Procession:	Minister
	Bride and bridegroom
	Chief bridesmaid and best man
	Bride's mother and bridegroom's father
	Bride's father and bridegroom's mother
Signing the register:	Minister
	Bride (using her maiden name)
	Bridegroom
	Two adult witnesses

The witnesses are usually the best man or woman, chief bridesmaid, one or more parent or close friend. A few photos are usually taken. The congregation is often entertained by a singer, solo instrumental piece or organ music.

LEAVING THE CHURCH

The bride picks up her bouquet and takes the bridegroom's left arm. Attendants hold the bride's train and proceed down the aisle – usually to jubilant music. They can nod at friends but should not pause for a chat.

The chief bridesmaid and best man follow behind the bridesmaids and pageboys. Parents of the couple come next in the same order as in the procession to sign the register. Guests join them, those in the pews at the front leaving first.

An archway is sometimes formed for the couple to walk through outside the church: soldiers holding up swords; schoolchildren if one of you is a teacher; or a team associated with a sport or hobby.

OTHER TRADITIONS

In parts of Italy rice is used to trace a heart on the ground outside the church for the couple to stand in and pose for photographs.

WACKY WEDDINGS

Jason and Eve, from Birmingham, arranged for a vicar to conduct a blessing in the skies over Gloucestershire. All three dressed up in their wedding clothes and were strapped, standing up, to two biplanes.

THE CATHOLIC WEDDING CEREMONY

The service is similar in content to the Anglican ceremony. It begins with a welcome and the congregation is invited to make the sign of the cross. Prayers and Bible readings follow and the minister talks about the ideals of marriage.

Everyone stands and the minister addresses the couple. He asks them three questions: 'Have you come here freely and without reservation to give yourself to each other in marriage?', 'Will you love and honour each other as man and wife for the rest of your lives?' and 'Will you accept children lovingly from God and bring them up according to the law of Christ and his Church?' (The final question may be omitted if inappropriate.) The couple answer in unison: 'We have/We will/We are.'

They then take one another's right hand and say the marriage vows – the bridegroom first. The wedding rings are blessed and exchanged.

During the Prayer for the Faithful the congregation prays for the couple's future happiness, their family, all married people and the world at large.

If Mass is to be celebrated it will take place now (see page 53, 'Roman Catholic weddings'). If not, there is a nuptial blessing – a prayer for the couple's happiness. The Lord's Prayer and a blessing for everyone who has witnessed the wedding follows. The register is signed.

THE WEDDING CEREMONY IN SCOTLAND

(See Chapter 4)

CASE STUDY: A SCOTTISH BEACH WEDDING

The idea of getting married in a field near the sea had started off as a joke but eventually seemed like the best solution for Jean and Ewan who live in a small village in south Scotland. They had wanted a religious wedding but thought a church service would have been hypocritical as they rarely went to church.

They chose a field with a big oak tree which would protect at least the bride and bridegroom during the ceremony. About fifty guests came and the women were warned not to wear high-heeled shoes which would have sunk into the earth. Ewan cut the grass in the field and bought tubs of flowers to decorate it.

Jean wore a traditional, long white wedding dress and Ewan his kilt. The local minister, who had married Jean's parents, came out of retirement to take the service and they played music by Eric Clapton and Bryan Adams on a tape-recorder. Photos were taken on the beach. Their only regret was that they didn't buy any midge repellent.

THE SCRAMBLE

In Scotland it is still traditional for the bridegroom and best man to empty their pockets of small change in the street at the church or outside their homes, for children to scramble after.

QUAKER WEDDING CEREMONY (RELIGIOUS SOCIETY OF FRIENDS)

Quaker weddings can take place at any time and at any venue, but the ceremony is usually held at one of the Society of Friends' regular meetings and is very simple. Attendants are not necessary and the bride does not usually wear a special dress. There are no hymns.

The couple stand up and make a simple vow. The wedding certificate is signed by the bride and bridegroom and two witnesses and read aloud.

CIVIL WEDDING CEREMONY

REGISTER OFFICE

Although the register office wedding is only about twenty minutes long, most registrars try to make the ceremony as personal as possible. Many produce brochures to explain the structure of the ceremony and other facilities available at the register office: where you can take photographs; any taped music you can borrow; or if silk flower arrangements are used to decorate rooms. At Haringey in North London, for example, the marriage ceremony is available in over forty different languages (although the legally binding words must be in English or Welsh) and couples can choose from a wide range of taped music.

Wedding rooms also vary in the number of people they can hold. Haringey has room for fifty guests seated and the same number standing, but many register offices have much smaller rooms or rooms that range in size.

There is no reason why you can't have bridesmaids and pageboys, and someone to give the bride away if you wish. But if you're planning anything too outlandish check with the registrar beforehand to avoid potential problems on the day.

Since the wedding ceremony is brief and register offices are often fully booked, it is important not to be late – aim to arrive at least ten minutes before your ceremony is due to start. Detailed descriptions about where to park and where guests should wait are usually included in information supplied by the register office. You can arrive together or separately, but the registrar will normally want to see you alone to check that the details to be entered in the register are correct, and to collect fees.

Certain parts of the ceremony must, by law, be followed, but beyond that the registrar is allowed considerable freedom in adapting the words. Following an Act of Parliament due to be introduced in April 1997, you can also now choose a more modern and simpler version of the words that you must, by law, say as part of the ceremony. The main difference is that instead of saying: 'I do solemnly declare that I know not of any lawful impediment . . .' you simply say: 'I declare that I know of no legal reason . . .'

Some registrars will also allow you to add your own words (but remember to check this with them beforehand and make sure there is no religious content). If English isn't your first language you may repeat the vows in your native tongue.

The registrar normally begins by welcoming you and your guests and by stressing the importance of the vows you are about to take. The couple stands and the bridegroom is asked to confirm his name. The same question is asked of the bride.

The bridegroom, repeating words said by the registrar, then declares that he knows no reason why he cannot marry. The bride makes the same declaration. The couple are usually allowed to include their own, extra words at this point if they wish.

Guests stand and the bridegroom takes his bride by the hand (or puts a ring on her finger) and says: 'I call upon these persons here present to witness that I, — — do take thee, — — to be my lawful wedded wife.' The bride makes a similar statement.

The registrar stresses the solemnity of the vows just taken and declares the couple man and wife. Guests may congratulate the couple and then return to their seats while the register is signed.

APPROVED BUILDING

A ceremony in a licensed venue follows the same format as the register office wedding, except that there is greater scope to make it more personal. There will be time for readings and music and more room for guests to sit comfortably. Normally, seats are arranged to form an aisle in the traditional American style of weddings seen in films.

MUSIC

Many couples choose music for their wedding because it has a special significance for them, or simply because it's their favourite piece. The Music Publishers' Association (see Useful Addresses, page 274) will help you track down most sheet music, but if it doesn't appear on their database they should be able to suggest archives where you might find it, tell you who owns the copyright, or at least recommend where you will find a sound recording of it.

CHURCH WEDDING

Arrival of the bride: suggestions

Arrival of the Queen of Sheba (Handel)
March (from *Scipio*) (Handel)
Trumpet Tune (Purcell)
Bridal March from *Lohengrin* (Wagner)

Entrance/processional: suggestions

Water Music (Handel)
Sonata Number Three (first movement) (Mendelssohn)
Wedding March from *The Marriage of Figaro* (Mozart)
Fanfare (Purcell)
Grand March from *Aida* (Verdi)

CASE STUDY

Catriona, 35, was so worried that she would rush down the aisle rather than walk at a sedate pace that she chose a piece of plainsong for the processional in the hope that it would slow her down.

Signing of the register: suggestions

Ave Maria (Bach/Schubert)
Air from *Water Music* (Handel)
Romanze from *Eine Kleine Nachtmusik* (Mozart)
Traumerei (Schumann)
Chorale Prelude on Rhosymedre (Vaughan-Williams)

CASE STUDY

Andrew, 31, and Stella, 33, both journalists, married in a Catholic church in Harrogate. During the signing of the register the organist played the theme to Casablanca *(the first film they saw together) and* Three Coins in a Fountain *(he proposed to her at the Trevi Fountain, Rome).*

Exit/recessional: suggestions

Pomp and Circumstance March Number Four (Elgar)
Music for the Royal Fireworks (Handel)
Wedding March from *Midsummer's Night Dream* (Mendelssohn)
Toccata (Widor)
Toccata in C (Pachelbel)

CASE STUDY

John, 34, and Dinah, 31, asked the organist to play 'Bring me Sunshine' – the theme from the Morecambe and Wise show – as they walked down the aisle because they thought it was a happy, optimistic piece to end with.

FAVOURITE HYMNS

Bear in mind the talents of your congregation, the choir and the organist. If these are limited it is best to avoid high notes and unfamiliar hymns.

'Lead Us, Heavenly Father, Lead Us'
'Father, Hear the Prayer We Offer'
'Love Divine, All Loves Excelling'
'Praise, My Soul, the King of Heaven'
'Now Thank We All Our God'
'The Lord's My Shepherd'
'O Jesus I Have Promised'
'The Day Thou Givest, Lord, is Over'
'O Lord and Father of Mankind'
'Come Down, O Love Divine'
'Morning is Broken'

Ministers can be surprisingly broad-minded about non-religious music, but always check with them beforehand. One couple were relieved when their vicar allowed them the romantic theme to the film *Robin Hood, Prince of Thieves* (Bryan Adams's 'Everything I Do, I Do it For You'), but horrified when the organist struck up the rollicking tune 'Robin Hood, Robin Hood Riding Through the Glen . . .' from the television series.

CASE STUDY

Steve, 23, a zoologist, and Louise, 24, a teacher, who married in a small Anglican church in Warwickshire, asked if they could leave the church to 'Heard It on the Grapevine' and sign the register to 'Green Tomatoes'. The vicar was more than happy to allow both their choices but drew the line at 'Jerusalem' because he said it pretended to be a hymn but was in fact unreligious in its content.

CIVIL WEDDINGS

The only caveat here is that you mustn't choose anything with religious connotations – even if the words aren't sung. For this reason, a registrar in Norfolk refused to allow a couple who married in a school to have 'Amazing Grace' in the ceremony (they chose The Carpenters' 'I'm on Top of the World' instead).

Other people, though, have had string quartets, a rap singer, a harpist or a recording of classical music, and many register offices have tapes for you to chose from (although you unlikely to be offered anything too unusual – Vivaldi's *Four Seasons*, for example, is popular). One couple who married in Brighton Pavilion arrived to the music from the Guinness advertisement in which a man dances round a giant pint glass.

If you're getting married in one of the new venues you will probably have slightly more time to incorporate music into the service. Favourite songs have included Cole Porter melodies, and 'True Love' from *High Society*. Finding non-religious songs for group singing is difficult and you might prefer to ask a friend to sing a solo or to hire a professional. One couple, for example, asked a professional opera singer to perform for them.

SUGGESTIONS

'That Old Devil Called Love'
'Can't Help Loving that Man'
'When I'm Sixty-four'
Balcony and marriage scenes from *West Side Story*
Ode to Joy (from the finale of Beethoven's Ninth Symphony)
'You'll Never Walk Alone'
'Keep Right On to the End of the Road'

MUSIC AND THE LAW

The law regarding copyright and weddings is hazy, but strictly speaking you may be infringing a composer's rights if you reproduce their music (for example on a service sheet) without their permission. The Music Publishers' Association and, in the case of video recordings, the Mechanical Copyright Protection Society (see Useful Addresses, page 274) will advise you of where you stand.

The other area of potential difficulty is in musical arrangements. If the organist plays 'The Teddy Bears' Picnic' from sheet music (he or she may even improvise slightly) there is generally no problem. But if you produce a special arrangement, say for a string quintet, you might upset the composer (if he or she ever found out). Generally, all you need to do is to seek permission to use the music, which is rarely refused.

READINGS

FROM THE BIBLE

New Testament

Ephesians 3:14–end
A prayer that we should know the love of God.

Ephesians 5:21–end
A description of the different ways husband and wife should love one another. Includes advice that wives should submit to their husbands.

1 Corinthians 13
Paul describes the qualities of Christian love.

1 John 4:7–12
A description of the nature of Christian love and how you can only know God through loving someone.

John 2:1–11
The miracle of water turned to wine at the wedding in Cana.

John 15:9–12
Includes the Commandment that we should love one another as God loves us.

Mark 10:6–9
Jesus explains how man and woman become one.

Matthew 7:21, 24–7
Jesus compares the person who heeds God's words to someone who builds a house on firm foundations.

Romans 12:1, 2, 9–13
A description of the Christian way of life.

Colossians 3:12–17
A plea for couples to love one another as Christ loves and to be quick to forgive one another after a quarrel.

Old Testament

Genesis 1:26–8, 31
A description of how man was made in God's image to become master of the earth and to go forth and multiply.

Psalm 84:1–7
Verses in praise of God's House.

Psalm 121
A reminder that God is there to protect his people.

Song of Songs (Song of Solomon) 2:8–10, 14, 16; 8:6–7
Beautiful piece describing 'my Beloved'.

NON-RELIGIOUS POEMS AND READINGS

So long as there is at least one biblical reading, many ministers will allow an extract from a book or a poem. Some couples choose something for its sentiments, or because it has a special meaning for them, or simply because they enjoy it as a piece of writing. Anthologies of love poetry are useful places to look for inspiration.

One couple wanted a poem about a rose garden because it described the setting for their Humanist wedding ceremony. Another couple, who met in a pub where she was a barmaid and he was a customer, chose 'A Drinking Song' by W. B. Yeats:

> Wine comes in at the mouth
> And love comes in at the eye;
> That's all we know for truth
> Before we grow old and die.
> I lift the glass to my mouth,
> I look at you, and I sigh.

Other suggestions:

- Thoughts on marriage by the Lebanese poet Kahil Gibran found in *The Prophet*.
- W. H. Auden's 'Oh, tell me the truth about love'.
- Edwin Morgan's sexually charged poem, 'Strawberries'.
- Shakespeare's sonnet CXVI, which featured in the film of *Sense and Sensibility*:

> Let me not to the marriage of true minds
> Admit impediments. Love is not love
> Which alters when it alterations finds;
> Or bends with the remover to remove . . .

- Robert Frost's 'The Road Not Taken'
- Bertrand Russell's views on marriage.
- Philip Larkin's 'An Arundel Tomb'.
- John Donne's 'The Anniversary'.

CASE STUDY

Vicky, a 33-year-old painter, and Stewart, a 34-year-old musician, chose an extract from Brian Keenan's book, An Evil Cradling, *as one of the readings at their church wedding. The piece described the moment when the hostage is brought oranges as a surprise supplement to his bland and meagre diet. Instead of gobbling them down, he lingers lovingly over their colour, smell and texture. As well as admiring the piece of writing in itself, both Vicky and Stewart felt the sentiment of savouring the present carried an important message for their relationship – particularly as they were both self-employed and had a tendency to worry about the future.*

GETTING MARRIED ABROAD

A good tour operator will make you feel as if you have your own personal wedding organizer: someone to turn to if something goes wrong and to tell you exactly what to do on the wedding day.

CASE STUDY: WHEN THINGS GO WELL

Gemma, who works in a building society, and Paul, who sells office furniture, decided to get married abroad because they couldn't agree on the guest list and they were nervous about saying their vows in a packed church.

The couple, who are both 23, chose a package deal with Thomsons to the Dominican Republic. Flowers, photographs, champagne (other than the one complimentary bottle) and hairdressers all cost extra but were much cheaper than at home.

Twelve of their closest friends and family flew out to the August wedding. The size of the group meant that they secured a hefty discount and that there was a party atmosphere on the plane.

The wedding took place halfway through their three-week stay and Gemma was quite brown. She kept make-up to a minimum (eye shadow, lipstick and no foundation) and wore a three-quarter-length cream chiffon dress, headdress, silk shoes and bare legs. Paul wore a white grand-dad shirt and beige linen suit. Guests dressed quite informally (except for the parents).

The ceremony was conducted in a secluded part of the hotel garden and was over in a few minutes. Gemma liked the fact that she could walk to it from her hotel room, that she only had to say 'I do' and that their parents were mentioned by name.

Their wedding cake, which was meringue, melted in the heat, but Gemma and Paul kept cool in a horse and carriage which took them down to the beach for their official photographs. They celebrated in a local Italian restaurant.

The day after they arrived home they threw a party for 200 people in a marquee in Gemma's parents' back garden. Paul and Gemma wore the clothes they had got married in, and their best man and Gemma's father made speeches.

Paul and Gemma celebrated their first anniversary in Portugal and the same twelve wedding guests joined them for a holiday.

CASE STUDY: WHEN THINGS GO BADLY

Barnie and Tessa from Newcastle arranged their own wedding in Grand Cayman. But when they arrived they had to pay extra for the chapel, beach and view they thought they'd already booked. The witness did not arrive and a passer-by had to be asked to step in. During the service a young boy with an airbed walked through the middle of the proceedings and the champagne was sent to the wrong hotel.

HUMANIST WEDDINGS

CASE STUDY

Alison, a 29-year-old researcher for the BBC, 'gave up religion at the age of seven' and thought that the decision had meant she had also forfeited the chance of a white wedding. But both she and her boyfriend of ten years, Peter, a 30-year-old computer support engineer, weren't keen on the idea of a register office wedding because of the restriction on numbers and because it seemed impersonal.

The British Humanist Association put them in touch with a celebrant, Sue, and they met two months before the wedding. Sue discussed with them issues such as whether they wanted children, their family backgrounds, and their expectations of marriage. She sent them a draft of the ceremony and they adapted it so that it expressed their feelings exactly, and was 'slightly less hippy'.

On the wedding day they tied up the legal formalities in a register office in London wearing jeans and T-shirts and accompanied only by Alison's sister and the best man.

At the Humanist ceremony that afternoon Alison wore a full-length white dress and tiara, and was accompanied by five bridesmaids and a pageboy. She arrived with her father in a coach and horses at Lauderdale House in Waterlow Park, Highgate, North London. They walked down the aisle in a timbered room with a long gallery illuminated by autumnal sunlight and decorated with ivy gathered by friends.

Sue welcomed guests and explained briefly what Humanism was and how Alison and Peter viewed their commitment. She then asked Peter if he would take Alison to be his wife: 'Will you love her, comfort her, honour and protect her, and forsaking all others, be faithful to her as long as you both shall live?' The same vow was put to Alison.

Peter then placed a ring on Alison's finger and said:

'I give my love to you, and will be open to your love in return.
I would like to share in your dreams and for you to share in mine;
To give help when you need it and to ask for help when in need;
To support you in all your endeavours;
To share in your joys and sorrows.
In the presence of our family and friends, I ask you, Alison,
To be a friend, companion and lover throughout my life.'

Alison repeated the vow to Peter.

As Alison and Peter were keen not to offend anyone they asked Sue to include moments of silence in the ceremony when she would make it clear that anyone who wanted to pray could. Everyone sang 'Jerusalem' and 'Drink to Me Only with Thine Eyes'. A friend also sang 'That Old Devil Called Love'. Other friends read a piece from The Prophet, *an extract from a wedding ceremony by American Indians, and a Celtic benediction.*

Both their parents enjoyed the ceremony and Alison's mother in particular was pleased that her daughter's wedding had been more meaningful than her own rather bleak register office affair. Some members of her father's family who were Irish Catholics were dubious beforehand, although most were won over by the ceremony. One distant aunt, though, couldn't resist making the sign of the cross over them with handfuls of confetti.

SINGLE-SEX WEDDINGS

CASE STUDY: A LESBIAN CEREMONY

The idea of a life commitment ceremony to celebrate their relationship evolved for Frances, a 31-year-old nurse and acupuncturist, and Alison, a 33-year-old clinical psychologist, six months after they had met.

They chose Hove Town Hall in Sussex because they wanted somewhere people would take seriously (register office weddings are held there). About 110 friends and family came to the ceremony. They were careful only to invite guests who they knew would genuinely want to celebrate their commitment, rather than anyone who was attending through curiosity or a sense of duty.

Both sets of parents were initially wary of such a high-profile event, but were eventually won over (arranging for both families to meet helped) and contributed to the cost of the day. One of Frances's sisters acted as celebrant and her brother-in-law drove them to the Town Hall in his sports car. As they were on a tight budget they wore their favourite suits – which happened to be green – and jazzed them up with a new waistcoat, scarf and designer shirt.

Chairs were arranged to form an aisle for the ceremony, which took place at 6 p.m., and each guest was given a candle and a yellow or red carnation by the four ushers. The couple arrived together with their best women and walked down the aisle. During the ceremony a local female group performed 'And I Love Her', and 'Nobody I know could love you more than me', and another song, 'Walking forward'. Frances's sister, Sonia, read from The Prophet *and a friend read poems and extracts on love and commitment which she had chosen herself. The third friend read a piece she found in the* Essential Guide to Lesbian and Gay Weddings *(HarperCollins).*

The lights were dimmed and the ushers lit the candles given to each guest. Frances said the first line of the vows and Alison repeated each line:

'Alison, I promise you today in front of your family, my family and all our friends that I will love and care for you all my days. I will strive to always respect and value your thoughts and feelings; and do all that I

can to help you realize your goals and dreams. I will be your faithful lover and endeavour to be open and honest with you always. I undertake to work through conflicts and problems and do all that I can to resolve them. I promise to love and to cherish you, to stand by you in joy and in sorrow, in good times and in bad, and to be there for you always.'

As they exchanged rings they said: 'This ring is my symbol of commitment to you. As I place this ring on your finger I pledge my faithful love to you for ever.'

The guests gave one another flowers and then pinned them to their lapels.

Another 90 people were invited to a buffet in the Town Hall during which there were speeches by Alison and family members. Celebrations included a cake in the shape of the scientific symbol for women, and a disco.

17
WEDDING CEREMONIES IN OTHER FAITHS

Church weddings can seem almost drab compared with the ritual and intricate customs involved in the marriage ceremonies of the world's other main religions. The increase in mixed-faith marriages has also added another layer of colour to ceremonies already rich in traditions.

GREEK ORTHODOX WEDDINGS

Celebrations vary from family to family, but usually close friends and relatives visit the bride and bridegroom separately on the morning of the wedding. Traditional songs are sung, often accompanied by a fiddler or clarinet player.

The bridegroom may also be ritually shaved using a brush and razor from an old wooden box which he will leave open for coins to be thrown into as payment for the barber. At the end of the performance paper money is stuck to the by now moist foreheads of the musicians. A dish of incense may be passed three times round the bride and bridegroom's heads.

In Greece the bridegroom will pick the bride up from her home, but in this country it is more usual for the couple to meet outside the church where the bridegroom will present the bride with her bouquet. The priest welcomes them and asks if they are marrying of their free will. Then, singing a hymn, the priest will bring the couple into the centre of the church. Bridesmaids may wait inside the church holding candles. The guests move closer to create an intimate circle around the couple.

The service is divided into two parts: the blessing of the rings and the crowning of the couple. The priest blesses the rings by placing each to the forehead of the couple three times. The sponsor, who may be male or female and fulfils the role of best man (there are sometimes more than one), puts each ring on the bride and bridegroom's finger three times in turn. A psalm is sung and prayers may follow before the priest places two garlands or crowns on the couple's heads. The sponsor(s) then put(s) each of the crowns or garlands on the couple's heads three times and later sign(s) the white ribbon hanging from the garlands as a memento of their role in the day.

Readings from the Gospels and the Lord's Prayer follow and then the bride and bridegroom drink from a common cup to symbolize their commitment to share the bitter and the sweet in life. The priest leads the couple, their sponsor(s) and any bridesmaids and pageboys in a procession, the Dance of Isaiah, three times round the table from which the service has been conducted. Guests sometimes shower them with rice, flowers, coins or sugared almonds. The final blessing follows and the priest congratulates the couple. The register is signed and the couple leave.

JEWISH WEDDINGS

Before the eleventh century the Jewish wedding took the form of two distinct ceremonies: betrothal (erusin or kiddushin), which established a legal bond between man and wife, and the marriage itself (nissu'in). The two ceremonies might be separated by as much as a year, during which time the woman lived with her parents. The couple were considered married after the first ceremony, although the wedding was only consummated after the second.

Under Jewish teaching marriage is seen as the ideal human state, although there is no specific Hebrew word for marriage. The bride and groom are treated like royalty during the wedding ceremony, and in some communities for a whole year afterwards.

WHERE TO MARRY

Jewish people have for a long time had the freedom to marry where they wish in Britain, including gardens and other open-air venues. The marriage takes place under the chuppah, a lavish canopy supported by four poles which has been described as symbolizing the nomadic history of the Jewish people, the couple's wedding chamber, and the home they will build together.

Many couples marry in hotels, while others feel this setting doesn't convey the right atmosphere. In some communities it is customary to erect the chuppah outside to represent the hope that the couple's descendants may be as numerous as the stars in the sky.

WHEN TO MARRY

Weddings are not held on the Sabbath (from sunset on Friday till sunset on Saturday), nor on various special days such as festivals or days of public mourning like Tishah Be'Av or Yom Hashoah (Holocaust Memorial Day). Check with your synagogue to see whether the day you had in mind falls on a significant date that is best avoided as it may cause offence to guests.

Tuesday is a popular choice because it was on the third day of Creation that God twice said: 'It is good.'

WHO CAN MARRY

A Jewish wedding can only take place between two Jewish people. Converting to Judaism is a lengthy process and instruction normally takes between eighteen months and two years, but can take as long as five years.

Rabbis are usually reluctant to offer a blessing at a marriage ceremony in which one person is not Jewish, although mixed-faith couples who devise their own ceremony often incorporate Jewish readings.

If you are both Jewish, but one of you has been divorced, the rabbi will want to see proof of your get (the Jewish divorce document).

WHO CAN OFFICIATE

Weddings in synagogues are recognized as civil marriages so long as the legal formalities are completed on the day. You will still have to contact the register office where you live beforehand (see page 44, 'Civil weddings').

The wedding is normally taken by the synagogue's rabbi but they often allow another rabbi to officiate – perhaps someone who conducted your barmitzvah or similar important ceremony.

GUESTS

Anyone attending the wedding should cover their heads – either with a hat or a scarf. In some synagogues it is traditional for men to wear bowler hats. In an Orthodox service men and women sit on opposite sides of the synagogue.

Witnesses to the ketubah, or marriage contract (see below), must be Jewish, but other attendants and witnesses to the civil certificate need not be.

THE RUN-UP TO THE WEDDING

The bride and bridegroom normally don't see one another for at least a day (but sometimes as long as a week) before the wedding. On the Sabbath before the wedding the bridegroom (and bride in Reform Synagogues) says the blessings over the Torah and the rabbi says a special blessing over the couple. Sometimes this is held in the parents' synagogue if this is different from the place chosen for the wedding.

OTHER CUSTOMS

- **Ritual immersion**: The mikveh (ritual bath) has been practised by Jewish brides for centuries as a way of preparing for a period of transition and moving to a higher state of holiness. Some bridegrooms also now go through immersion (see Useful Addresses, page 276).
- **Fasting**: Some couples abstain from food on the day.
- **Bedeken** (putting on the bride's veil) – see page 77, 'The Jewish tradition of bedeken'.
- **Yichud**: The couple spend about twenty minutes alone together after the ceremony in a special room. Originally this was when the marriage was consummated but now it provides a time when you can reflect on the vows you have just taken, catch your breath before the festivities begin, and break your fast together.

THE MARRIAGE CONTRACT (KETUBAH)

The ketubah was originally a contract signed by two witnesses which outlined the husband's duties towards his wife and fixed a price to be paid to the woman if the marriage ended in divorce.

Although the document was not viewed as an equal contract between man and wife, it gave the woman considerable rights at a time when her position in society was far from equal. Rabbis believed, for example, that in fixing the divorce price at the very beginning of the marriage when relationships between the couple were sweetest, they would secure the greatest financial security for her if things turned sour.

In Reform Synagogues the ketubah is a joint statement of the couple's mutual love and their hope to support one another and build a Jewish home together. Many modern ketubot are beautiful documents written in calligraphy and decorated with lavish illustrations of Jewish symbols or themes of special significance to the couple and their families.

The Reform Synagogues of Great Britain sell silk screen and hand-printed ketubot, and many Jewish craftsmen and women also design documents which can be displayed at home after the wedding (see Useful Addresses, page 276). It is important to check the details of the wording with your rabbi in advance.

THE SERVICE

The bridegroom arrives first and may be escorted by his father, best man, both fathers or his parents. The bride may be escorted by both her parents, the two mothers or simply her father.

It is deemed a great honour to escort the couple to the chuppah – an act which God first performed when he brought Eve to Adam. Although the unterfuhrers are normally parents, you may choose a close friend or another member of your family.

The bride stands to the right of the groom under the chuppah and in some communities circles her future husband three or seven times.

The ceremony begins with two psalms and a welcome, prayers and wedding address. The couple then drink from the same cup to symbolize that from now they will share their lives (at this point the veil is lifted). Some people choose kiddush (wine) cups that have been part of a family's observance for generations.

The groom places the ring on the index finger of the bride's right hand and makes a declaration to which the bride does not, in traditional synagogues, reply. (She can then transfer the ring to her left hand.) The ketubah is read aloud and the rabbi says the Seven Benedictions (or they are sung), after which the couple sip wine from the same glass. The groom then crushes it underfoot and everyone shouts *mazel tov!* (good luck).

The couple sign a covenant, there is then a blessing and a psalm of praise. If there was no register wedding the civil register is signed, as well as the synagogue's register.

WEDDING CLOTHES

Most brides wear a white or ivory wedding dress and veil similar to those worn at a church wedding, but should not wear any jewellery (not even an engagement ring), to show that under the chuppah riches count for nothing. Generally, too, dresses are more modest at Jewish ceremonies and it is best to avoid anything that is low-cut or off-the-shoulder.

The groom may wear a morning suit, dinner jacket or a lounge suit. He may also wear his tallit (prayer shawl) or kittel (the white robe worn at significant times such as Yom Kippur, Passover, and finally as a shroud). Some couples wrap themselves in a large prayer shawl, creating a chuppah within a chuppah, and some brides choose to wear a kittel.

RINGS

(See also Chapter 7, 'Rings')

The ring must belong to the bridegroom and should not include any precious stones or be pierced as either might distort its value. It is usually gold, although it can be made of any material so long as it is worth more than a perutah (the smallest denomination of currency in Talmudic times).

Popular engravings include: 'Dodi Li V' Ani Lo' ('I am my Beloved's and my Beloved is mine') from the Song of Songs in the Bible.

See also Chapter 18 'Keeping guests happy at the reception'.

ASIAN WEDDINGS

Wedding ceremonies can vary enormously within the main Asian religions, not simply due to the different sects within one faith but also because of the cultural differences which exist in such a vast geographical area. This means that an Asian wedding in, say, Bradford, can be different from a wedding in London – not just because one is Shi-ite and the other Sunni, but also because one family might have originally come from Pakistan and the other from Saudi Arabia.

Several customs, such as the Mehndi or henna party (see page 219, 'The Mehndi party') and the tradition that the bride should wear bright colours, are common to different faiths. Many brides make special shopping trips to India and Pakistan for the wedding, while others use the services of UK-based wedding suppliers, many of whom advertise in the Asian bridal magazine, *Wedding Affair*.

Arranged marriages remain common, but more families are accepting that their children may not want this and may marry someone from a different faith – or with no faith at all.

An increasing number of temples and mosques have the authority to register a wedding, but the norm is still that a couple will have to attend a register office before their religious wedding.

THE MEHNDI PARTY

The tradition of using henna to trace intricate patterns on the hands and feet started several thousand years ago. In hot countries the henna has a cooling effect and is used for many religious festivals.

Anointing the bride, and any other guests who want to take part, has grown into a fine art, and the patterns have become more and more intricate. Indian henna work is usually dark brown and concentrates on tiny flowers, peacocks, mangoes and other traditional symbols. In North Africa designs are more geometric, whilst Arabic artists prefer floral designs. Some contemporary artists have adapted Celtic and oriental motifs, and even cartoons. The artist will often bring a big book of designs with her for you to choose from.

The Mehndi (sometimes spelt Mendhi) party usually takes place the night before the wedding and is held at the home of the bride. Normally it is a time exclusively for the bride's family, but sometimes the bridegroom can't bear to be left out and turns up uninvited. Since the bride has to sit still while the henna is applied it can be a very relaxing experience, and since the patterns take weeks to fade you will instantly be identified as a newly-wed long after the wedding.

ARRIVAL

At Indian weddings the bridegroom often arrives on a white horse (ghori), which is itself draped in brightly coloured hangings – often gold and red. The bridegroom normally wears a long white coat called an achkan and white leggings called chooridar. He sometimes also has a veil of flowers, called a sahra, which his sisters put on him as a sign of his new responsibility.

HINDU WEDDINGS

Choosing an auspicious time for the wedding is important and some families consult an astrologer. If the wedding is an arranged one, the couple's horoscope will also be studied to make sure they are a suitable match.

THE BANGLE OR CHURA CEREMONY

This usually takes place before the Mhendi and is organized by the bride's mother's brother (mama), or a similarly close friend or relation. A priest leads prayers and blesses the bangles which, in the Hindu religion, carry a significance similar to a wedding ring. Traditionally the bangles are not removed for forty days and even after this period it is seen as unlucky to leave home without your bangles. If a woman is widowed, she usually breaks her bangles.

THE WEDDING CEREMONY

The religious ceremony takes place under a mandap, which can be a plain canopy decorated with flowers or a fabulous structure draped with bright-coloured materials and a backdrop depicting Hindu gods. The service is solemnized in accordance with the Vedas (ancient Hindu holy books) and performed in the Sanskrit language.

The order of service is usually something like:

1. The bride greets the groom by placing a garland round his neck.
2. The sacred fire is lit and the couple and parents undergo purification rites.
3. The parents of the bride declare that they, under their own free will and in accordance with the wishes of the bride, give the hand of their daughter to the groom.
4. The bride and the bridegroom are joined by the tying of the sacred cloth.
5. Parikrama – the couple walk round the sacred fire seven times.
6. Saptapadi – they take seven symbolic steps for sustenance, physical well-being, prosperity, knowledge, to be blessed with children, for integrity and for fidelity.
7. The groom puts vermilion in the bride's hair – the mark of a married woman.
8. Prayers for peace.

WACKY WEDDINGS

Poppy, 24, and Gez, 26, from Leicester followed their register office wedding a few months later with a Hindu ceremony in a private jet 2,000 feet above St Paul's Cathedral. Guests met in an

Indian restaurant in their home town for the first part of the service before the bride left in a chauffeur-driven Rolls-Royce for Coventry airport and Gez took a helicopter.

A second part of the service was performed at the airport, leaving the vows to be said on the plane with thirty of the couple's closest friends and family. They had to obtain special permission to circle above the cathedral, which they chose because they felt it was a most romantic setting.

Tip Florists are usually able to create Asian-style garlands and other decorations if you show them photos of what you want.

SIKH WEDDINGS

THE SERVICE

Prayers are said at the bridegroom's family home before his guests set off in a procession or barat. They are either entertained at the bride's home (if practical), where they will spend the night before an early-morning ceremony the next day, or go straight to where the marriage is to be held.

The wedding can take place in a Gurdwara (Sikh temple), at the bride's home, or somewhere else where the Guru Granth Sahib (the Sikh holy book) has been properly installed. Any Sikh man or woman can officiate at the ceremony – and usually a respected and learned person is chosen.

Hymns are normally sung and then the bride takes her seat on the bridegroom's left. The couple and their parents stand to show their consent to the marriage, while the congregation remains seated. A blessing is said and a hymn follows.

The person who officiates gives a talk about marriage and then the marriage hymns or lavan are sung. The couple bow before the Guru Granth Sahib to show that they accept their marital duties. The bride's father places a garland on the holy book and on bride and bridegroom. He also puts one end of a garment known as a patka in the groom's hand, passes it over his shoulder and puts the other end in the bride's hand.

A short hymn follows and a piece is read from the Guru Granth Sahib. The same verse is then sung by musicians while the couple walk slowly round the Guru Granth Sahib, the groom leading in a clockwise direction with the book on this right. The bride, holding the patka, follows, doing her best to keep in step with the bridegroom. When they reach the front of the book, they both bow and take their seats. The whole process is repeated for each verse of the lavan.

The ceremony ends with more singing and a prayer in which the whole congregation joins. Another extract from the Guru Granth Sahib is read and the congregation is served with the sacred food.

CASE STUDY

Tarun, a 27-year-old lawyer and Sikh, and Ritu, 28, who is also a lawyer and a Hindu, had three wedding ceremonies, each hosted by Ritu's family. The first was in February at a register office in London and was purely practical – the lease on Ritu's flat was running out and she wanted to move in with Tarun but didn't want to live with him outside marriage. Seventy people attended the service.

Six hundred people attended the Sikh wedding in August at a Gurdwara (temple) in Leicester followed by a traditional meal on langar (sheets spread on the temple floor).

The Hindu wedding took place a week later at Ripley Castle in Yorkshire. A drummer led Tarun and a procession (barat) of about seventy of his family, extended family and friends to the castle. Tarun, wearing a white shot-silk tunic and trousers, sahra (veil of flowers) from a florist's in Leicester, sword and red sash, rode a white horse hired from the local stables and bedecked with scarlet and gold trappings specially made from photos of Indian weddings. Several villagers also followed the barat as far as the castle gates.

Ritu's parents welcomed the barat at about 4.30 p.m. and the ushers (who were dressed similarly to Tarun but with red turbans) escorted guests to their seats, giving each a scroll which explained the form the service would take and its significance. Ritu had five attendants who, as a concession to the European idea of a bridesmaid, were all dressed in the same colour pink silk lehenga (dress).

A champagne reception followed the ceremony during which a pianist entertained the 250 guests who wore either dinner jackets or national dress. There was a sit-down meal of Indian food, and speeches by the groom, best man (a college friend who wore a dinner jacket) and Ritu's father.

ISLAMIC WEDDINGS

The basis of the Muslim marriage contract ceremony, or Nikah, is very simple, although the celebrations afterwards can be ornate and usually take in the traditions of different Muslim communities.

An increasing number of mosques are permitted to carry out the civil side of the wedding, but if yours doesn't, you will also have to arrange for a register office ceremony before or after the religious event. Many mosques prefer you to complete the civil side of the wedding first.

The imam (Muslim priest) usually officiates but a friend of the bride or bridegroom or another well-respected Muslim might fulfil the role. Arranged marriages remain common in this country, although more Muslims are turning their backs on the tradition. A Muslim woman may only marry another Muslim, although a Muslim man can marry a Jewish or Christian woman.

Before the ceremony begins the imam must ask the couple if they are marrying of their own free will. The bridegroom must also give the bride a gift which is hers and hers alone. The choice of gift should not cause hardship to the bridegroom, and can range from the materialistic – money or a television and video recorder – to something more ethereal such as a promise to make her a garden or to teach her to read the Koran.

The bride and bridegroom sit in front of their friends and family and two Muslim witnesses in two separate rooms (as male and female are usually separate in a mosque). The imam carries out the ceremony twice in front of each group. A sermon in Arabic is usually followed by a reading from the Koran and sayings of the Prophet. A second sermon may follow and then final prayers. Sometimes there are two celebrations after the religious ceremony held on different days: one hosted by the bride's family and one by the bridegroom's. This tradition dates back to the times when families lived a long away apart and travel was difficult. The room where the celebration takes place is normally richly decorated and the bride and bridegroom often sit like king and queen on a raised dais.

GUESTS

It is traditional for guests to remove their shoes when entering a mosque, but this is more for practical than religious reasons, as a lot of time is spent sitting on the floor. In some mosques visitors are only required to remove their shoes when entering the carpeted prayer area. If in doubt, it is best to watch what everyone else is doing.

CASE STUDY

Ali converted to Islam when he was 18 and ten years later felt ready to marry. He asked friends to arrange a marriage for him with a Muslim woman. Sangeeta, 24, had also decided she wanted an arranged marriage but that she didn't want a husband from her parents' original home in Bangladesh who probably wouldn't speak English.

Sangeeta and Ali found out about each other by asking questions of their mutual friends until they felt ready to meet. Sangeeta's brother arranged the first meeting because her father was not happy about the idea.

They decided to marry after about five months but it took another five months to win round Sangeeta's father. Ali's mother was also concerned about the marriage because she felt arranged marriages were unromantic. She grew used to the idea, though, as she saw how happy Sangeeta and Ali were.

The wedding was held in an East London mosque and the imam made a special effort to explain to the older members of the mosque that, although Ali was a convert and did not come from their place of birth, his faith was what mattered.

Ali's gift to his wife was the promise to take them both to Mecca – a commitment he has not yet been able to fulfil since children arrived early in their marriage and he is still saving.

Ali wore a long, Arab-style shirt and jacket and Sangeeta was eventually persuaded to wear a traditional, colourful sari and green wedding scarf with gold and silver tinsel. As Sangeeta is very religious she had at first been reluctant to wear anything so ostentatious but the imam persuaded her that it would be an important gesture of compromise to the community.

They also agreed to a celebration afterwards but tried to keep it as low-key as possible, although the room was decorated and traditional sweets served.

BUDDHIST WEDDINGS

While the Buddha recognized that marriage should be a partnership of two equals he did not prescribe either monogamy or polygamy. There is no specific marriage ritual laid down in Buddhist teaching, but services have developed throughout the world for Buddhists who feel the need for a ceremony.

The wedding emerged out of the practice of asking monks to chant sutras after the civil or home ceremony. In 1924 the International Buddhist Institute of Hawaii published a marriage service which has been used by different sects throughout the world. The ceremony, which includes the exchange of vows and leaves scope for the giving of rings, often takes place during a normal Buddhist meeting, and the Buddhist Handbook includes a shortened version of the ceremony.

Another version of the Buddhist marriage blessings ceremony consists of:

1. An offering of flowers.
2. Recital of the Homage to the Buddha.
3. Recital of The Three Refuges.
4. Recital of The Five Precepts.
5. Offering of lights.
6. Sermon by priest and description of the duties of husband and wife.
7. Chanting by monks.
8. Meditation.

Aspects of the Thai wedding ceremony have also been used by European Buddhists. This sometimes includes wrapping a large ball of cord three times in a counter-clockwise direction round the base of the Buddha's image. One end is threaded through a window and round the building, eventually to return to the Buddha. The other end is wound thrice round the presiding monks who hold the thread while reciting the sacred text. The thread is seen as a sort of mystical telegraph wire carrying the sacred words chanted by the monks to everyone present.

CASE STUDY

Graphic designer Sandy, 46, married Sue, 32, an occupational therapist, in a colourful ceremony at the ornate temple at the

Samye-Ling Tibetan Centre, near Eskdalemuir in Scotland. They decided to marry there as Sandy had worked at the centre for seventeen years and helped to decorate the ceiling of the temple. Sue had also spent several years looking after cattle in the grounds.

A hundred guests attended the ceremony at which the Tibetan Buddhist monk and abbot of the centre, Dr Akong Tulku Rinpoche, acted as registrar – he is one of two Buddhists licensed to perform weddings in Scotland. The couple sat cross-legged in front of him during the ceremony while cymbals tinkled in the background and prayer-wheels spun.

WACKY WEDDINGS

Actress Gillian Anderson (Special Agent Dana Scully in the television series about the paranormal, *The X Files*) married Clyde Klotz (assistant director of *The X Files* on the seventeenth hole of a Hawaiian golf course. The ceremony was conducted by a Buddhist priest.

18

KEEPING GUESTS HAPPY AT THE RECEPTION

Your guests' first impressions of the reception will help set the tone for the rest of the day, so take care not to send them the wrong, or conflicting, signals. If they are handed a glass of champagne and their arrival is announced by a toastmaster in red tails, they will naturally assume they are attending a formal occasion and will behave accordingly. A bouncy castle and a cup of tea will tempt them to loosen their ties and remove their jackets and hats.

THE RECEIVING LINE

As hosts, the bride's parents traditionally stand at the beginning of the receiving line. Attendants may or may not be included. The usual order is:

Mother of the bride, father of the bride, mother of the groom, father of the groom, the bride and groom, chief bridesmaids, other attendants and best man or woman.

Tips for the perfect line-up:

- Whittle down the bridal party if you're worried about how long it will take. A minimalist line-up will include the couple and their parents, or even simply the bride and bridegroom. (The best man or woman can help make sure there are no stragglers and that guests know where to go after the line-up.)
- Enlist a few close friends to start the process and encourage other guests to follow suit.
- Don't be tempted to spend too long talking to one person.
- Keep an eye on the person next to you and rescue them if the guest seems reluctant to move on.
- Be ready to jump in with an introduction if you can see another member of the line-up is struggling to place a guest.

- Make sure guests have a drink while they wait to be greeted or for the line-up to finish.

A JEWISH GREETING

Guests wait in the dining area for the bride and bridegroom who are announced and then clapped in. The traditional hora dancing usually starts immediately. Female guests may link arms in a circle and the male guests form a circle either around the women or next to them. Alternatively, men and women can mix in together, or groups such as the ushers and best man might link up. After ten or fifteen minutes' dancing everyone is much more relaxed.

TOASTMASTERS

The best toastmasters should blend into the background and help guests to relax by keeping them informed of what is happening where. Their main tasks include: announcing the guests; bringing the bride and bridegroom through; announcing or saying grace; making the loyal toast; announcing the cutting of the cake and introducing each of the speakers.

Toastmasters should stop you running late and be able to spot potential problems and deal with them discreetly. It can also be useful to have a third party with a sense of authority if you're worried about family rows on the day. Many hotels and some of the new wedding venues will supply someone to act as a master of ceremonies, or you might just leave the job to the best man or woman.

DECORATIONS

You don't need a team of professional stylists to make your wedding reception look stunning. Consider where you can introduce colours in keeping with the rest of the wedding – marquee linings, the backs of chairs, menus, place settings, napkins and napkin holders. Use left-over scraps from the bridesmaids' dresses; coloured paper; ribbons (wind two colours round the poles of a marquee); and gold and silver marker pens.

Flowers and balloons (see Stockists, pages 284 and 280) also make a reasonably cheap way of cheering up a room, but remember not to place them where they will obscure someone's view of the speeches or make talking to other guests difficult.

CASE STUDIES

- *Tim, 46, and Helen, 41, held their reception in a rather bleak church hall in South Wales. They bought lengths of muslin and draped it from rafters and suspended brightly coloured papier-mâché balls from the ceiling. Helen drew the outline of a cherub which they enlarged and photocopied, sticking the shapes on to card which they painted pink and then attached to the muslin. By the time they had finished, guests felt as though they were entering a heavenly dining-room rather than a draughty church hall.*
- *Ian, 30, and Sally, 32, married in October in a village near Reading and used autumn as a colour theme for the entire day. Sally made her own bouquet and chose predominantly deep reds and browns: chilli peppers, red roses and anemones. The marquee in their back garden was decorated with foliage which friends had collected. Sally made the tablecloths out of maroon-coloured material and dyed muslin in a matching dark purple for the napkins. Guests' names were written on paper which was stuck to individual laurel leaves spray-painted gold as place settings.*

BONBONNIÈRES AND FAVOURS

The idea of giving your guests a small trinket to remember the day by has been around for hundreds of years. In Britain guests could expect to receive favours in the shape of gloves, scarves, garters or ribbons at well-to-do weddings. In Italy it has long been the tradition to present a bonbonnière – five sugared almonds wrapped in thin material and sometimes accompanied by a small present. The five nuts stand for health, wealth, prosperity, happiness and long life.

Both favours and bonbonnières have become popular in this country. In Scotland, in particular, favours such as tiny silver horseshoes, top hats, sprigs of lucky heather or a bride's shoes can be bought in traditional newsagents and stationers. Thorntons Chocolates also sells confectionery brides and bridegrooms in their 'Celebration' range.

Use the bonbonnières or favours to decorate table settings, or as a way of saying a special thank-you to friends (usually women), aunts and grandmothers by distributing them at the end of the meal. If you think this might lead to jealousies, you can always restrict them to children.

MONEYSAVER

Collect five sugared almonds or other sweets and place them in the centre of a fabric such as netting or organza. Gather up with a ribbon to form a little bag. Try to use good-quality almonds (the cheaper kind can damage teeth) and avoid sweets that will melt.

SEATING

Deciding who sits next to whom can be one of the most satisfying parts of arranging a wedding – your chance finally to bring together two people you'd always suspected would get on well but who live at different ends of the country; or even an opportunity for a discreet piece of matchmaking.

You may have a rough idea in your head of who should sit where, but it is not until you commit your thoughts to paper that any potential difficulties will become evident, and because you're dealing with a large number of tables, moving one difficult guest can threaten to push the whole delicate balance out of kilter.

If you choose long tables at right angles to the top table, each guest will have five people they can easily speak to (one on each side and three opposite). Round tables with six settings each will provide the same opportunity. Try to arrange the tables so that as many people as possible have a good view of the top table.

Traditionally, couples sit next to or opposite one another, but if you know both are outgoing and won't mind being split up you could sit them on different tables. Men and women usually alternate, but you needn't feel hidebound by this convention.

If you really can't face deciding where everyone can sit, you could always leave it up to the guests to sit where they want (except perhaps for the top table) or dispense with tables altogether and have a buffet reception (see pros and cons of a buffet page 152, 'The main food choices', Chapter 12). Don't forget to provide a few chairs for elderly guests, or parents with babies.

STRESSBUSTER

Don't be tempted to leave the seating plan until the last minute as it can quickly turn into a very time-consuming source of tension.

CREATIVE WAYS OF BEING SEATED

A seating plan should be placed where it's easy to see (you may need to hire or borrow an easel or pinboard). Either list the guests in alphabetical order and place a table letter or number next to their names, or group guests' names under the headings relating to their table.

If you want to turn the seating plan into a memento of the day, you could put a drawing or photo of each guest under the table heading and on the place setting (ask them to send in a photo when they accept your invitation).

One way of helping to keep tabs on the various connections between guests is to give each table a title (it's up to you whether you go public with them).

- One couple described the tables (in private) as: the nice-but-shy table; the 'family table' (couples with their young children); the 'table from hell' (rather supercilious vicar and parents' friends); the 'creative table' (one out-of-work actor, an artist, and two designers); 'meeja table' (journalists, a record producer and two publishers); and the 'lurv table' (an engaged couple, two people who had only recently become a pair, and an unattached woman who had been promised a seat next to the wedding's only single man).
- Another couple named each table after a significant place in their lives – the SW6 table (when they were both living in Fulham, South London); the 'Bruges' table (after the time they were working abroad); the 'Sheffield' table (they met at university). The seating plan was carefully arranged so that everyone on a particular table had a connection with each place.

THE TOP TABLE AND OTHER SPECIAL GUESTS

Traditionally, the top table should be arranged so that the bride and bridegroom are in the middle with the groom on the bride's right. The bride's mother sits on the groom's right with his father on her other side. The father of the bride sits on the other side of the bride, next to the groom's mother. Chief bridesmaid and the best man usually sit at either end of the table – normally with the best man on the right side (as seen by the guests):

1. Chief bridesmaid; 2. Groom's father; 3. Bride's mother; 4. Groom; 5. Bride; 6. Bride's father; 7. Groom's mother; 8. Best man.

STRESSBUSTER

This formula, of course, is perfect only for the most conventional families and the most conventional weddings. Rather than risk offending anyone, you may decide to have a longer than normal top table. If you find you are left with too many people of one sex, or you want to put some distance between sparring relatives, you can always draft in reinforcements. The minister and spouse, a lone uncle, grandparent, or godparent can swell numbers and defuse tensions.

SPECIAL CASES

People with hearing difficulties or who can't see very well should sit near the top table. Partners of anyone on the top table, or parents of bridesmaids or pageboys, should also be close at hand.

- **Separated or divorced parents**: Discuss with them where they (and any new partners) will sit. Much will depend on who is hosting the day and the warmth of feeling between separated parents. If one of them has a new partner you will have to decide where they should sit – if the relationship is accepted by the family you could find room for them on the top table, if not you may have to discuss finding another seat for them or even asking them not to come. A stand-up reception is one way of avoiding the issue.
- **Parents whose spouses have died**: Your wedding will be a particularly difficult time for a parent in this position. Not only will they be battling with sad memories, but they may dread being in the limelight without their spouse by their side. Ask them where they would like to sit, and if you feel they need extra support, suggest seating someone they are close to, such as a brother, son or friend, next to or near them.
- **Children**: You may want to have a special children's table and even serve separate party food – pizza, for example – and have a child-minder or entertainer in charge of them. Some bridesmaids and pageboys will feel marooned if they are left on the high table without their parents; others will enjoy the kudos, and some will put up with it for only so long. Much will depend on personality and age.

KEEPING CHILDREN HAPPY

By inviting children you've already decided that your wedding is going to have a degree of informality. But if you want harmony too, consider:

- **A special entertainer**: magician, clown, puppeteers or juggler.
- **Inflatable**: the sight of a brightly coloured castle is guaranteed to put children in a good mood after they've sat through a wedding ceremony. Arrange a rota of adults to supervise, or ask the person hiring the inflatable.
- **Crèche**: either hire the services of a child-minder or specialist firm such as Crechendo (see Stockists, page 281), or ask guests. Face paints, colouring books, story-telling and videos make a good diversion.

TEN SUGGESTED QUIZ QUESTIONS

If you have a group of under-elevens coming, you could send each one a set of quiz questions. Paste them on a piece of card decorated with pictures of brides and bridegrooms cut from magazines and enclosed with the official invitations.

The questions could be read out at the beginning of the speeches and the answers given at the end. It's probably safest to make sure everyone wins, and if there aren't too many children you could give them a small prize each such as a chocolate (Thorntons Chocolates makes chocolate brides and grooms), balloon or party bag (available from stationers).

Quiz questions

1. Who's a groom without a horse?

2. Who's got something old, something new, something borrowed, something blue?

3. What are they?

4. Who's the best man/woman?

5. How many people are wearing flowers in their buttonholes?

6. Do you know the names of any of the flowers in the bride's bouquet?

7. Can you find some confetti?

8. Who's wearing a brand-new ring?

9. Can you find a champagne cork?

10. What's white and has three tiers but doesn't look sad?

STRESSBUSTER

Children tend to misbehave when they've been told to sit still. Take the pressure off both parents and children by asking the first speaker to announce that children should feel free to roam around.

FIREWORKS

A firework display can be a good way of marking a change in pace at the reception: to show that the couple is ready to leave or that the formal part of the celebration is over and the dancing is about to begin. You can either buy a pack of fireworks and arrange for a guest to set them off, or you can call in the professionals like the Firework Company (see Stockists, page 284) who will supply both the product and the 'firer'.

The advantages of using a firer is that you don't have to worry so much about safety and whether the guest lighting the fireworks is sober. A professional company should have sufficient insurance to cover damage to buildings and people (although some hotels have their own cover). You should also tell local police that you're planning a display and let the rescue services know if your reception is near the coast.

PUTTING ON THE STYLE

Some firework displays are arranged as a surprise – either by the bride or groom, or by the couple as a thank-you to their parents. You can buy simple firewriting packs which will display your initials and a heart using mini-flares, but if you want something a bit more sophisticated you'll probably need professional assistance. One couple, for example, asked for their initials and two entwined seahorses (creatures which mate for life).

For the more sophisticated displays you'll need a space about the size of a football pitch. Most displays last about five to ten minutes.

SPEECHES

(See also page 132, 'The speech')

The speeches are normally made after the last course of the meal and before the cake-cutting (although some couples prefer to cut the cake first). Often the toastmaster or best man or woman introduces each speaker, but some people prefer not to be introduced.

Traditionally, the order of speeches is:

1. The giver-away (usually the bride's father). This is an ideal opportunity to welcome guests, particularly if they have travelled a long way. The father also normally tells a story about his daughter's childhood (but nothing too embarrassing) and says how happy he is at her choice of husband. If his wife doesn't plan to say anything, he should make it clear that he is speaking for both of them and may also say something about their own marriage. More than anyone else, the father of the bride has a licence for sentimentality but should be careful not to abuse it. Finally, he should toast the health of the bride and groom by saying something like, 'I ask you to rise and drink the health of —', or simply by raising his glass and saying 'To — and —'.
2. The groom starts by thanking the previous speaker. Usually he thanks the best man and may even want to give him a present publicly (although this is often done in private beforehand). He will also thank the bridesmaids and give them presents (or ask the bride to hand them over). The groom thanks his new in-laws and his own family for their support. He usually tells a story about the bride – perhaps about the way they met. Finally, he proposes a toast to the bridesmaids saying either, 'To the bridesmaids', or 'to — and —' (using their first names).
3. The best man or woman thanks the groom on behalf of the bridesmaids, reads any telegrams and messages and announces the cutting of the cake. The tone of their speech should be more light-hearted than the others, but never cynical. They may also propose a toast to absent friends and, at a Jewish wedding, may propose a toast to Her Majesty the Queen or the President of Israel.

OTHER SPEAKERS

- **The bride**: More and more women are deciding they would like to make a speech – partly because they don't see why they should duck a task that their husband has little chance of avoiding and partly because they don't feel comfortable sitting demurely at the top table. But you shouldn't feel pressurized into making a speech if it's going to ruin your enjoyment of the whole day. As a token effort you might do something jointly with your husband – one couple read out the football scores of the teams they knew their guests supported.

- **The mother**: Some mothers are keen to make a speech, especially if their husband has died and they don't want to hand over the responsibility to an uncle or family friends.
- **Guests**: If the atmosphere is right some guests will feel the compunction to join in, although the best man or woman should always be on hand to leap in by announcing the cutting of the cake or the start of the disco if anyone becomes too garrulous or even embarrassing. Some couples have even asked someone from each table to say something about them but this only works if you know you have chosen people who enjoy public speaking.

EXTRA TOASTS

Departure from the traditional order of speakers means you will soon run out of toasts. The couple can be toasted again, or a theme of one of the speeches reiterated:

- The name of the city or place – 'To Dublin', 'To Scotland'
- 'To friendship'
- 'To impulse'
- 'To serendipity'

OTHER TRADITIONS

Amongst traditional Jews there is ritual handwashing and prayers before a blessing of the bread (a single large challah can be made by most Jewish bakers). The host, usually the bride's father, welcomes his guests at the start of the meal. Speeches follow the format outlined above and the celebrations end with the seven Marriage Blessings.

At Italian weddings guests tap cutlery against crockery at intervals during the meal as a way of demanding the couple stand and kiss each other. Doves are often released as a symbol of love.

Guests at Danish weddings take a lighted candle from their place setting to present to the bride and bridegroom at the top table after the meal. This gives everyone a chance to speak to the couple, who by the time the last candle is presented are surrounded by candlelight.

ENTERTAINMENT

Music is an ideal way of subtly changing the tempo of the reception. A pianist, string quartet or harpist gently playing in the background as guests arrive will help people relax. A steel or jazz band should put everyone in the mood for dancing.

- Try to hear the band before booking – either live or on tape.
- Draw up a list of favourite tunes for a disco.
- Plan when the band will take their break – for example when you serve tea and cake, or during the 'going away'.
- Make sure the band has enough to eat and drink.
- If you have a ceilidh or barn dance, check there's enough room and the floor's not slippery. Ask the band leader to act as caller.

WHERE TO FIND MUSICIANS

Local amateurs can be just as good, and often more enthusiastic, than professionals. You may not have to go far for quality, either:

- Universities, colleges and training hospitals often have student jazz bands and string quartets who, although talented, are cheaper than professionals.

- Centres catering for a certain community – Irish, West Indian or Polish, for example – will usually recommend musicians and other performers.

- Organizations with special links can sometimes provide entertainers. One bridegroom, for example, approached a Scottish bank based in London and found their courier was a keen bagpiper.

MONEYSAVER

It's cheaper to hire one musical group rather than several different performers.

DANCING

The bride and bridegroom usually take to the dance-floor first – perhaps to the strains of their favourite song. Parents often follow and then the members of the bridal party dance with each other – the best man with the chief bridesmaid, for example.

At some French and Italian weddings dancing takes place between each course of the meal. During the Greek 'money dance' guests pin banknotes and cheques to the couple's clothes. In some cases the amount more than covers the cost of the reception.

AUDIENCE PARTICIPATION

If you've got extrovert and talented friends ask them to 'do a turn'.

- A friend of one couple who married in Scotland dressed up in a kilt, beard and bonnet as a long-lost uncle and recited a poem in the style of Rabbie Burns about the couple.
- At a wedding in Sheffield the best man had arranged for four of the couple's closest friends to compose verses to fit the tune of 'Waltzing Matilda' about them. Scrolls with the words were handed out at the reception and sung by the guests.
- Guests at a wedding in Cardiff were given Blues Brothers-style dark glasses to wear when the dancing started. Somehow it helped people put their inhibitions behind them.

FOND FAREWELLS

Leaving the best party you're ever likely to attend and which you've spent months planning can be a wrench. There will probably also be friends and family you haven't seen for a long time or who've travelled a long way to come to the wedding.

Make sure you circulate during the reception and give yourself plenty of time to talk to people you don't see very often. If you are not going away on your honeymoon immediately, you could arrange to have brunch the next day with guests you particularly want to spend some time with. One couple even decided to hold the reception the night before their wedding and took a small party of their immediate family to lunch at a hotel after the service.

If you decide to stay until the very end you'll miss out on the drama of going away and the reception may fall a little flat. Many of the guests may also feel uneasy about leaving while you're still there, which can be a problem if they have young children or are elderly.

Whenever you decide to leave, make sure the best man or woman knows and can tell the guests to gather round for a send-off. It's probably best to say goodbye to your parents before the announcement that you are leaving as this can be quite emotional and time-consuming, and guests will appreciate not having to wait too long, perhaps outside in the cold.

By tradition, the bride throws her bouquet just before going away, and whoever catches it will be next to marry. This was originally done at random, with the bride's back to her guests – nowadays, the bride prefers to aim the bouquet at a special friend she hopes will marry soon. It is advisable to give some thought to where the bouquet might land – is there someone who would be horrified to catch it or mortified to miss it? Either inquire beforehand or ask someone else to sound them out. If you're planning to preserve the bouquet don't be too violent with it, and ask whoever catches it to look after it for you.

CHECKLIST FOR GOING AWAY

- Say goodbye and thank you to parents and key people.
- Double-check you have passports and travel documents.
- Hand over house keys to someone who can deliver your presents.
- Check you have your favourite cosmetics with you (these may be in the care of the best woman or your mother) and your luggage is in the going-away car.
- If you're marrying in Scotland remember to hand over your marriage schedule to someone responsible who can return it to the registrar within the next three days for the marriage to be registered.
- Tell your best man or woman where you will be staying – at least for the first night.

PART SIX

WHEN IT'S ALL OVER

19

Honeymoon and Beyond

THE HONEYMOON

The word to describe the holiday period after the wedding is thought to come from the German tradition of drinking honey for thirty days – or one moon – after the ceremony. Today the honeymoon represents a welcome rest after what may have been months of planning. Traditionally the bridegroom paid for the honeymoon, but today most couples split the cost.

BALI OR BOURNEMOUTH

For some couples the honeymoon has to be every bit as luxurious as their wedding day: first-class hotels and travel, and an exotic destination. Others simply want a chance to unwind and enjoy each other's company without distractions.

Ironically, many people find their honeymoon very stressful. It may be the first chance they've had to spend time alone together for weeks, and readjusting to each other's habits isn't always easy. The realization that you're married can also feel a bit daunting and make you treat each other with the sort of formality usually reserved for strangers.

REASONS TO STAY HOME

No worries over: visas, foreign currency, travellers' cheques, inoculations, catching a plane, language barriers, tummy bugs (very unromantic).

Make it memorable by: going somewhere completely new to both of you (a Scottish island or remote corner of Ireland, for example); staying somewhere different (a luxury hotel – if only for one night; a folly or a barge); or pampering yourself with a treatment in a health spa (available in several country house hotels) or sauna.

REASONS TO LEAVE THE COUNTRY

A once-in-a-lifetime holiday will always be linked in your mind to your wedding day; you will probably be able to put the worries of the wedding behind you faster; there'll be less temptation to ring home.

Make the going easy by: spending your first night near the reception venue; breaking your journey rather than attempting a long-haul flight; avoiding an over-ambitious itinerary.

PLANNING A SURPRISE

- Establish ground-rules – climate; length of flight; accommodation (top-class hotel or two-man tent).
- Avoid somewhere one of you has been before – especially with a former lover.
- Think hard about couples-only resorts – you may not want to share your honeymoon with other star-struck lovers.
- Make sure your partner has suitable clothing.

MONEYSAVER

Upmarket hotels sometimes offer packages with similar resorts which can save money.

Unless you're feeling shy, don't keep your honeymoon a secret. Everyone loves a honeymooning couple and you might find your room upgraded or a free bottle on your table at dinner.

THE HONEYMOON NIGHT

Hundreds of years ago newly married couples were put to bed by crowds of wellwishers who would later demand a bloodied sheet as proof that the bridegroom had done his duty and as a way of establishing the bride's purity.

In Ireland, a laying hen was tied to the bedpost in the hope that the bird's fertility would be catching. Alternatively, the couple would be made to eat an egg with a double yolk. The Scottish custom was for a woman with milk in her breasts to prepare the marital bed.

The only tradition now attached to the honeymoon is that this will be one of the most passionate nights of your lives. But, if anecdotal evidence is anything to go by, passion may be the very last thing on your mind. There will be too much to talk about and your memory will be replaying a soundtrack of the entire day's proceedings in your ears.

Countless couples have found they were too distracted, too tired, too drunk or too reluctant to leave their guests. But if your fervour turns out to be about as fiery as damp confetti, stoke it up with the following:

- Make an effort to switch the mood from manic to mellow. Pack a tape of romantic music and some scented candles.
- Give each other a massage and take a relaxing bath (transform an impersonal bathroom with floating candles).
- If sex on your honeymoon night seems less like a voyage of discovery and more like a familiar shuttle route, throw in an element of surprise: try something new, somewhere different, or make imaginative use of the complimentary chocolates on your pillow.

Should these tactics fail, remember there is always the following morning – or the rest of the honeymoon.

CASE STUDY

Charles, 27, a banker, and Charlotte, 26, a primary school teacher, had been living together for three years and were determined to make their honeymoon night special. They decided to abstain from sex for the month before the wedding and – despite being sorely tempted – managed to approach the night with renewed vigour.

WHO'S BOSS?

You'll probably remember very clearly the first time you refer to your partner as husband or wife, or the first time you manage to say either without squirming. According to superstition, this is just one of a list of significant moments in your first hours of married life.

Scottish tradition says that whoever falls asleep first on the wedding night will die first, and whoever gets up in the morning will be the dominant partner in the marriage. Another superstition suggests that whoever is first to spend money as a married person will also rule the roost.

WAS THAT IT?

Coming home from honeymoon can seem a bit flat. It needn't. Ask your close family and friends round for a debriefing meal, or treat them to the premiere of your wedding video.

You may not want to carry your bride over the threshold, but if you don't, remember that the doorstep is the favourite place for those evil spirits that you have so far managed to see off with the help of your stag and hen nights, veil and decoy bridesmaids (see page 136, 'The role of the bridesmaids and pageboys'). In parts of Greece seeds of a pomegranate are scattered round the home in an attempt to induce fertility.

REASONS TO BE CHEERFUL

- Weekends are your own again.
- Family and friends no longer need organizing.
- Photos and videos will make you laugh for months.
- Wedding presents will transform your home and there are probably more to come.
- You can start planning your first anniversary.

COMING-HOME DUTIES

- Check with your best man or woman to see whether you owe them any money. They may have paid the band, the priest's £30 taxi journey to the reception, or the church fees.
- Write any remaining thank-you notes for presents or to anyone who helped out (for example, by making the cake or decorating the reception).
- Send out cake and photos to anyone who couldn't come.
- Tell the appropriate people if you are changing your name (see below).

WHAT'S IN A NAME?

The decision about whether you change your name or not will rest on several factors. You may be very fond of your maiden name and its association with your family, or you may have a surname that is difficult to pronounce or that you feel sits clumsily with your first name. Your husband may have an exotic name that you have always coveted, or he may want to change his name to yours by deed poll.

Reputations are important in most professions, but some jobs place more store on a name than others. Actors, journalists, self-employed people and artists all rely on their names and, while changing titles is not impossible, it doesn't always make the best marketing sense. On the other hand, if your marriage coincides with a new stage in your career – perhaps you're a caterer and you want to expand into corporate events rather than concentrating on birthdays, weddings and christenings – a new name can be a useful way of marking your change in direction.

For some women, opting for a new name is the final act of commitment to their relationship: although they are anxious to retain their own identity they also want to make a statement that they have thrown in their lot with their partner. They also argue that hanging on to your maiden name is a hollow feminist stand since you are merely retaining your father's name in preference to your husband's.

THE COMPROMISE

Some couples decide that they will each use both names: hyphenating their surnames or using them both (unhyphenated); making a completely new word out of the two; or adopting a separate name altogether. If you choose any of the above remember to let officials know in writing (see overleaf).

Others use different names for different occasions. You might use your maiden name at work and your married name in your private life as a way of marking a demarcation between your two lives. A second name can also be useful on occasions when you want to protect your anonymity, but it's safest to be consistent when dealing with large organizations such as financial institutions or the Inland Revenue.

Many couples find that the arrival of children helps to crystallize their thoughts on the matter. You might give one child one surname and the second (if there is one) the other, or let them choose when they are older. Or you may feel that children with different surnames will prove divisive (although family members with different surnames are common now).

LETTING PEOPLE KNOW

(see also page 6, 'Breaking the news')

If you decide to retain your maiden name, be prepared constantly to correct people who assume you are 'Mrs', or to recognize the occasions when it is simply not worth the effort to put people right.

The following should be told if you're changing your name:

Accountant
Bank
Building society
Clubs
Council (for council tax purposes)
Credit card companies
Dentist
Department of Health
Department of Social Security
Doctor/Family Planning Clinic
DVLC
Electoral roll
Employer
Insurance: household and car
Mail order firms
National Insurance
Passport Office (in time for your honeymoon if going abroad)
Policies: endowment and life
Pension scheme
Premium bonds
Savings: other accounts
Shares: company registrars
TV licence

CASE STUDY

Janet, 32, a painter, decided to change her name as a sign of solidarity with her husband. In the information on travel and accommodation that she sent out with the invitations she included a line saying: 'Much to her own surprise Janet Smith is changing her name to Janet Bryce'.

BEING GROWN-UP

- **Make a will**: Any existing will is revoked on marriage. If you die without a will your spouse will receive your personal possessions worth up to £200,000 (or £125,000 if you have children): anything else is shared by your spouse, children or other relatives if you don't have children. A will is a chance to make sure your money goes where you want it to and, especially if you are a high earner, to keep the taxman's share to a minimum. It also allows you arrange guardians for your children.
- **Homes**: A property bought together as joint owners will become the survivor's if one of you dies. Consider other arrangements if you want to limit inheritance tax.
- **Life insurance**: Make sure you are properly covered, taking into account children, mortgage and debts.
- **Tax**: Married couples are entitled to tax relief and should claim it by contacting the Inland Revenue. It can be split between the two of you or given to the highest earner.
- **Investments**: If one of you is in the higher tax bracket, make sure interest and share dividends from joint investments are paid to the lower earner by transferring investments into their name. No tax is paid on capital gains transferred between spouses.
- **Endowment policies**: Think carefully before cashing in any existing policies which usually offer a low surrender value. Instead, consider using them as part of a new loan or as a way of saving.

THE JOINT ACCOUNT DEBATE

Some people view a joint account in the same way as changing their name – as a way of showing their commitment to a relationship. Others see a separate account as a mark of their independence.

The downside of sharing a bank, building society or credit card account is that you are jointly liable for debts and overdrafts – which may become an issue if one of you is particularly profligate. Arranging a loan can also be difficult if one of you is self-employed or has had a poor credit record in the past. It can also be difficult to keep track of your balance if two people are dipping into an account.

A joint account is an advantage if one of you dies since the other will have immediate access to it, rather than waiting for the red tape to be sorted out.

Many couples decide to compromise by having both types of account and using the joint one for paying bills. This can also make buying presents for each other easier since they don't need to be paid for out of the common fund. Alternatively, you might agree to buy presents out of money you earn from over-time or extra freelance work.

THE NEXT FIFTY YEARS

An anniversary can be an excuse to return to the hotel where you spent your honeymoon night, or simply to wear something like a piece of jewellery that you bought for your wedding day.

The longer you're married, the greater the novelty in trying to re-create part of the wedding day. A reunion with your best man or woman might seem over-dramatic now, but in a few years' time they may be living abroad (or you may be). Some people even have a religious ceremony of rededication, others restage the reception menu.

In America couples are sometimes given a white 'memory candle' which, when lit, gives off the smell of lily of the valley. The candle is first used at the wedding and on every anniversary. As it will burn for over 300 hours it should still be going strong for their golden wedding anniversary.

CASE STUDY

A Brazilian plastic surgeon spent £2 million on a party to celebrate his twentieth wedding anniversary. Three thousand guests tucked into 1,000 kilos/120 cwt of caviare and 10,000 bottles of champagne. French actress Catherine Deneuve made a guest appearance and was serenaded by a 100-piece orchestra.

ANNIVERSARIES

One theory behind the traditional anniversary gifts is that they are chosen depending on when various wedding gifts will become worn out. The gifts vary, but the most common list is:

First – cotton
Second – paper
Third – leather or straw
Fourth – silk or flowers

Fifth – wood
Sixth – iron or sugar
Seventh – wool or copper
Eighth – bronze
Ninth – pottery
Tenth – tin
Eleventh – steel
Twelfth – silk and fine linen
Thirteenth – lace
Fourteenth – ivory
Fifteenth – crystal
Twentieth – china
Twenty-fifth – silver
Thirtieth – pearl
Thirty-fifth – coral
Fortieth – ruby
Forty-fifth – sapphire
Fiftieth – golden
Fifty-fifth – emerald
Sixtieth or seventy-fifth – diamond

SO WHAT'S DIFFERENT?

Even if your wedding leaves you feeling unchanged – apart from the memory of a good party – others may not see you in the same way.

You may never have shown even the slightest interest in children, but some people will assume that the main reason you got married was so you could start reproducing. Expect to be asked if there is any 'nappy news' or if you refuse a third glass of wine, don't be alarmed if people take this as a cue that you're desperate to get pregnant. Some friends will decide you have a natural bond with other newly-weds and will arrange special dinner parties.

Although it probably doesn't pay to admit it, there is something comforting about being married. Your relationship may be no better or worse than that of an unmarried couple, but at least someone's been prepared to stand up and make a public commitment to you. You've also become part of a worldwide club that spans thousands of years and crosses countless cultures.

APPENDICES

WEDDING COUNTDOWN: FOR THE BRIDE AND BRIDEGROOM

See also countdowns for beauty and hair treatments (Chapter 8) and for best man or women and ushers (Chapter 10).

*In the lists that follow, these are optional.

AS SOON AS POSSIBLE

Announce engagement in newspaper* and tell family and friends.
Arrange to see minister, priest or rabbi.
Start looking at register offices or licensed buildings and make a provisional booking.
Work out a budget and plan savings.
Choose caterer.
Start looking for entertainment for reception.
Book photographer and video operator, if required.
Ask best man or woman, pageboys, bridesmaids and ushers.
Start looking for dress and attendants' outfits, or find a dressmaker (see page 71, 'Having a dress made'.
Book honeymoon (especially if you want to go somewhere popular).
Book first night.
Choose wedding cake supplier, if they are in demand.
Buy engagement ring*.
Start looking for a hairdresser, if you are getting married away from home.
Arrange for families to meet*.
Hold engagement party*.
Visit wedding fairs.
Take out wedding insurance*.

THREE TO FOUR MONTHS BEFORE

Book register office if you plan a civil wedding (you can't do this more than three months in advance).
Choose wedding rings.
Organize gift list.
Discuss with minister possible music and readings.
Book choir and bellringers*.
Order wedding stationery (see page 24, 'Stationery checklist').
Hire cake stand and special knife if they are not available at reception venue.
Discuss menu and drinks with reception venue and obtain written confirmation of both.
Order transport.
Buy trousseau (going-away outfit and honeymoon clothes).
Tell officials if you intend to change your name (a new passport can take six weeks).
Discuss flowers with florist (see page 176, 'Flowers checklist').
Make sure you have vaccinations and visas for honeymoon where necessary.
Ask friends to perform important roles: reading at the ceremony; giving you away, etc.
Buy presents for each other*.

A MONTH TO SIX WEEKS BEFORE

Send out invitations six weeks before and keep a note of replies.
Buy presents for attendants.
Make sure you have the wedding ring(s) or, if they're being made, that they will be ready in time.
Send thank-you letters as presents arrive.
Give caterers final numbers in writing.
Draw up seating plan and write out place cards.
Have a trial run of your make-up and hairstyle (wearing the veil, hat and headdress if possible). Time how long it takes.
Have final fitting for outfit, wearing your underwear, shoes and veil/hat/headdress.
Time journey from home to wedding venue.
Order traveller's cheques and foreign money for honeymoon*.

Check order of service sheets.
'Wear in' your shoes at home.
Plan hen party and stag night.
Discuss order of shots with photographer.
If you're moving, arrange for mail to be redirected and consider taking telephone number with you.
Write speech*.

A WEEK TO TEN DAYS BEFORE

Arrange for rehearsal and make sure the attendants and giver-away can be there. Check with florists, caterers and reception venue that they are clear about what you want.
Collect any hired clothes.
Have hen party and stag night.
Small bridesmaids and pageboys should have final fitting.
Finalize and time speech*.
Time how long it takes to put your dress or outfit on. Decide who will help you dress.

TWO DAYS BEFORE

Pack honeymoon suitcases.
Give the order of service sheets to the best man.

THE DAY BEFORE

Make sure you have some fresh air.
Arrange for your honeymoon luggage to be sent to the reception.
Make sure all your clothes are pressed.
Arrange your clothes and make-up in one place, but out of the reach of children and animals.
Go to bed at a reasonable time.
Assemble 'kit for coping' for day (see page 105).
Arrange rota for bathroom so that you have priority and enough hot water.
Wash hair if you intend to wear it up.

ON THE MORNING

Have leisurely breakfast.
Bath or shower.
Visit hairdresser's or have them come to you; or do your hair yourself.
Put on underwear.
Apply nail varnish.
Put on make-up, or have it done for you while your nails dry.
Step into dress if possible.

AFTERWARDS

Send out cake boxes.
Write thank-you letters.
Make sure everyone has been paid.
Check you don't owe the attendants any money.
Send photos to anyone who couldn't come, or to people who have played a special role in the day.

ROMANTIC WEDDING VENUES IN ENGLAND

NT = NATIONAL TRUST PROPERTY

SOUTH AND SOUTH EAST

1. **Clandon Park**: 1730s Palladian house built by Venetian architect with two-storeyed marble hall and stunning garden. Contact: Property Manager, David Brock-Doyle, Clandon Park, West Clandon, Guildford, Surrey GU4 7RQ. Tel: 01483 222 482. NT

2. **Boughton Monchelsea Place**: Small Elizabethan manor house with views across the Kent Weald. Boughton Monchelsea Place, Boughton Monchelsea, near Maidstone, Kent ME17 4BU. Tel: 01622 743120

3. **Mottisfont Abbey**: Originally a twelfth-century Augustinian priory, now a house set in old-fashioned gardens with river running through. Mottisfont Abbey and Garden, Mottisfont, near Romsey, Hants. SO51 0LP. Tel: 01794 340757. NT

4. **Rhinefield House Hotel**: Victorian compilation of architectural styles ranging from Tudor to ancient Greek and Roman. Rhinefield House Hotel, Rhinefield Road, Brockenhurst, The New Forest, Hants. SO42 7QB. Tel: 01590 622922

5. **Groombridge Place**: Seventeenth-century country house whose gardens were used in the film *The Draughtsman's Contract*. Groombridge Place Gardens, Groombridge, Near Tunbridge Wells, Kent TN3 9QG. Tel: 01892 861444. Fax: 01892 863996

6. **Finchcocks Museum of Music**: Early Georgian manor house that now houses a collection of historical keyboard instruments. Finchcocks Museum of Music, Goudhurst, Kent TN17 1HH. Tel: 01580 211702. Fax: 01580 211007

7. **Tenterden Town Hall**: Eighteenth-century building with sweeping staircase. Tenterden Town Council, Town Hall, 24 High Street, Tenterden, Kent TN30 6AN. Tel: 01580 762271. Fax: 01580 765647

8. **HMS *Warrior***: Built in 1860, one of the first iron-hulled battleships and still furnished with Victorian fittings. HMS *Warrior* 1860, Victory Gate, HM Naval Base, Portsmouth, Hants. PO1 3QX. Tel: 01705 291379. Fax: 01705 821283

9. **Herstmonceaux Castle**: Imposing fifteenth-century brick castle surrounded by moat. Herstmonceaux Castle, Hailsham, East Sussex BN27 1RP. Tel: 01323 834479. Fax: 01323 834499

10. **The Royal Pavilion**: Prince Regent's exotic seaside retreat with onion-domed turrets. The Royal Pavilion, Brighton, East Sussex BN1 1EE. Tel: 01273 603005

EAST ANGLIA

1. **Marygreen Manor Hotel**: Original Tudor building and hunting lodge once owned by Catherine of Aragon. Marygreen Manor Hotel, London Road, Brentwood, Essex CM14 4NR. Tel: 01277 225252.

2. **Leez Priory**: Tudor manor house in grassy hollow with range of wedding rooms including tower. Leez Priory, Hartford End, Great Leighs, Chelmsford, Essex CM3 1JP. Tel: 01245 362555

3. **Lynford Hall**: Eighteenth-century mansion house resembling French château which once entertained diplomats and political families such as the Kennedys. Lynford Hall, Lynford, Thetford, Norfolk IP26 5HW. Tel: 01842 878351. Fax: 01842 878252

4. **Preston Priory Barn**: Traditional timber-framed barn on working farm. Preston Priory Barn, Preston St Mary, Near Lavenham, Sudbury, Suffolk CO10 9LT. Tel: 01787 247251

5. **Layer Marney Tower**: Grand brick Tudor building surrounded by formal gardens. Layer Marney Tower, Near Colchester, Essex C05 9US. Tel/Fax: 01206 330784

6. **Maison Talbooth Hotel**: Country house hotel in vale painted by John Constable. Maison Talbooth Hotel, Stratford Hotel, Dedham, Colchester, Essex C07 6HN. Tel: 01206 322367

7. **The Fennes Estate**: Homely late-Georgian house in mature gardens. The Fennes Country Estate, Fennes Road, Bocking, Braintree, Essex CM7 5PL. Tel: 01376 324555. Fax: 01376 551209

8. **Hintlesham Hall**: Sixteenth-century manor house in 150 acres of park and golf course. Hintlesham Hall, George Street, Hintlesham, Ipswich, Suffolk IP8 3NS. Tel: 01473 652268

9. **The Guildhall**: Magnificent medieval building in bustling town. The Guildhall, Hadleigh, Ipswich, Suffolk IP7 5DT. Tel: 01473 823884

10. **The Shire Hall**: Ornate 400-year-old former magistrates' rooms. The Shire Hall, Market Hill, Woodbridge, Suffolk IP12 4LU. Tel: 01394 383599

SOUTH WEST

1. **Pump Room & Roman Baths**: Sumptuous Regency splendour housing spa water fountain. The Pump Room and Roman Baths, Stall Street, Bath, Avon BA1 1LZ. Tel: 01225 477000

2. **SS *Great Britain***: Iron ship designed in 1840 by Isambard Kingdom Brunel as a transatlantic passenger liner. SS *Great Britain*, Great Western Dock, Gas Ferry Road, Bristol, Avon BS1 6TY. Tel: 01179 225737

3. **Polhawn Fort**: Built on a peninsula with stunning cliff-top views. Polhawn Fort, Military Road, Rame, Torpoint, Cornwall PL10 1LL. Tel: 01752 822864.

4. **Curdon Mill**: Converted water mill set amid wooded hills. Curdon Mill, Lower Vellow, Williton, Som. TA4 4LS. Tel: 01984 656522

5. **Langtry Manor Hotel**: Former home of Edward VII's mistress Lillie Langtry and scene of secret trysts. Langtry Manor Hotel, 26 Derby Road, East Cliff, Bournemouth, Dorset BH1 3QB. Tel: 01202 553887

6. **Thornbury Castle**: Tudor castle turned country house hotel with spiral stone staircases and four-poster beds. Thornbury Castle Hotel, Castle Street, Thornbury, near Bristol, Avon BS12 1HH. Tel: 01454 281182

7. **Ashton Court Mansion**: Sixteenth-century mansion set in parkland. Ashton Court Mansion, Ashton Court Estate, Long Ashton, Bristol, Avon BS18 9JN Tel: 0117 963 3438. Fax: 0117 953 0650

8. **Tiverton Castle**: Medieval town castle originally originally owned by the Earls of Devon. Tiverton Castle, Park Hill, Tiverton, Devon EX16 6RP. Tel: 01884 253200

9. **Burgh Island Hotel**: Stylish Art Deco island retreat once a favourite haunt of Noël Coward, Agatha Christie and Edward

and Mrs Simpson. Burgh Island, Bigbury-on-sea, Devon TQ7 4BG. Tel: 01548 810514. Fax: 01548 810243

10. **Powderham Castle**: Medieval castle lavishly decorated – the home of the Courtenay family for over 600 years. Powderham Castle, Exeter, Devon EX6 8JQ. Tel: 01626 890243

MIDLANDS

1. **Berrington Hall**: Late eighteenth-century neo-classical house set in park landscaped by Capability Brown. Contact: Property Manager, Berrington Hall, near Leominster, Hereford & Worcester HR6 0DW. Tel: 01568 615721. NT

2. **Hanbury Hall**: William and Mary-style red brick house with painted ceilings and staircase. Contact: Peter Blades, Hanbury Hall, School Road, Hanbury, Droitwich, Hereford & Worcester WR9 7EA. Tel: 01527 821214. NT

3. **Kedleston Hall**: Palladian mansion with one of the most complete set of Robert Adam's interiors in England, set in classical park landscape. Contact: Chris Hagon, Kedleston Hall, Derby DE22 5JH. Tel: 01332 842191. NT

4. **Pittville Pump Room**: Elegant Regency setting with ornate ballroom, in parkland. Contact: Chris Aldred, Pittville Pump Room Manager, Pittville Pump Room, East Approach Drive, Pittville Park, Cheltenham, Glos. GL52 3JE. Tel:01242 523852. Fax: 01242 526563

5. **Combermere Abbey**: Mixture of medieval, sixteenth-century and Gothic architectural styles in grounds which include a lake. Combermere Abbey, Whitchurch, Shropshire SY13 4AJ. Tel: 01948 871637. Fax: 01948 871293

6. **Oakham Castle**: Twelfth-century building now used as a museum. Rutland County Museum, Catmos Street, Oakham, Leics. LE15 6HW. Tel: 01572 723654

7. **Newstead Abbey**: Once an Augustinian priory but better known for the wild dinner parties Lord Byron enjoyed among his pets including a wolf and bear. Newstead Abbey, Newstead Abbey Park, Linby, Notts. NG15 8GE. Tel: 01623 793557

8. **Shrewsbury Castle**: Medieval building with later additions by Thomas Telford. Shrewsbury & Atcham Borough Council, Culture & Tourism Division, The Music Hall, The Square, Shrewsbury, Shropshire SY1 1LH. Tel: 01743 361921. Fax: 01743 358780

9. **Delbury Hall**: Privately owned Georgian house looking on to lake. Delbury Hall, Diddlebury, Craven Arms, Shropshire SY7 9DH. Tel: 01584 841267. Fax: 01584 841441.

10. **Clearwell Castle**: Eighteenth-century castle built in Neo-Gothic style and standing in well-kept formal gardens. Clearwell Castle, Clearwell, Glos. GL16 8LQ. Tel: 01594 832320. Fax: 01594 835523

NORTH EAST

1. **Cragside House**: Victorian mansion which claims to be the first house in the world to be lit by hydro-electricity, surrounded by 405 hectares of beautiful gardens. Rosemary Gillet, Cragside, Rothbury, Morpeth, Northumb. NE65 7PX. Tel: 01669 620333. NT

2. **Beningbrough Hall**: Georgian building with cantilevered staircase set in grounds which include walled garden with pear tree arch and pond. Contact: Assistant Property Manager, Denise Edwards, Beningbrough Hall, Shipton-by-Beningbrough, North Yorkshire YO6 1DD. Tel: 01904 470666. NT

3. **Slaley Hall**: Edwardian mansion set in 1,000-acre estate with luxury facilities such as 23-metre/76-foot swimming pool. Slaley Hall Hotel, Slaley, near Hexham, Northumb. NE47 0BY. Tel: 01434 673350. Fax 01434 673962

4. **Washington Old Hall**: Manor house and ancestral home of USA's first president substantially rebuilt in seventeenth century and set in formal gardens. Washington Old Hall, The Avenue, Washington Village, District 4, Tyne and Wear NE38 7LE. Tel: 0191 416 6879. NT

5. **Shotton Hall**: Eighteenth-century country house with magnificent master staircase. Shotton Hall, Peterlee, Dur. SR8 2PH. Tel: 0191 5862491

6. **Allerton Park and Castle**: Recently restored Gothic country house with high-ceilinged, oak-panelled Great Hall. Allerton Park and Castle, nr Knaresborough, North Yorks. HG5 0SE. Tel: 01423 331123. Fax: 01423 331125

7. **Ripley Castle**: Sumptuous castellated building set in grounds designed by Capability Brown. Ripley Castle Estate Office, Ripley, nr Harrogate, North Yorks. HG3 3AY. Tel: 01423 770152. Fax: 01423 771745

8. **Merchant Taylors' Hall**: Grand medieval venue beneath the city walls with imposing Great Hall. Merchant Taylors' Hall, Aldwark, North Yorks. YO1 2BX. Tel: 01904 624889.

9. **Merchant Adventurers' Hall**: Timber-framed, richly furnished, fourteenth-century building. Merchant Adventurers' Hall, The Company of Merchant Adventurers of the City of York, Fossgate, York, North Yorks. YO1 2XD. Tel: 01904 654818

10. **Langley Castle Hotel**: Fourteenth-century fortified castle and luxury hotel. Langley Castle Hotel, Langley-on-Tyne, Hexham, Northumb. NE47 5LU. Tel: 01434 688888

NORTH WEST

1. **Tullie House Museum**: Converted Jacobean town house with wedding room in tiered Victorian Function Suite. Tullie House Museum and Art Gallery, Castle Street, Carlisle, Cumbria CA3 8TP. Tel: 01228 34781.

2. **Naworth Castle**: Seat of the Earl and Countess of Carlisle. Weddings take place in the Great Hall. Naworth Castle, Brampton, Carlisle, Cumbria CA8 2HE. Tel: 0169 773229. Fax: 0169 773679

3. **Tabley House**: Palladian country house containing Regency furniture. The Tabley House Collection Trust, Tabley House, nr Knutsford, Ches. WA16 0HB. Tel: 01565 750151. Fax: 01565 653230

4. **Walton Hall**: Elizabethan-style mansion built in the 1830s and with a clocktower added in the 1870s. Walton Hall, Walton Hall Gardens, Walton Lea Road, Higher Walton, Warrington, Lancs. WA4 6SN. Tel: 01925 263797. Fax: 01925 861868.

5. **Arley Hall and Gardens**: Original Tudor house lovingly rebuilt by Victorians in Elizabethan style and now with award-winning gardens. Arley Hall and Gardens, Near Northwich, Ches. CW9 6NA. Tel: 01565 777353. Fax: 01565 777465

6. **Peckforton Castle**: Nineteenth-century castle with drawbridge and built on wooded hilltop. Peckforton Castle, Stone House Lane, Peckforton, Tarporley, Ches. CW6 9TN. Tel: 01829 260930. Fax: 01829 261230

7. **Bramall Hall**: Black and white timber-framed Tudor manor house set in parkland. Bramall Hall, Bramhall Park, Bramhall, Stockport, Ches. SK7 3NX. Tel: 0161 4853708

8. **Finney Green Cottage**: Sixteenth-century timber-framed cottage with slate roof and wishing well in the garden. Finney

Green Cottage, 134 Manchester Road, Wilmslow, Ches. SK9 2JW. Tel: 01625 533343

9. **Tatton Park**: Stately home filled with marble and trophies from the empire and set in parkland where deer graze. Tatton Park, Knutsford, Ches. WA16 6QN. Tel: 01565 654822

10. **Armathwaite Hall**: Seventeenth-century country house hotel on the shores of Bassenthwaite Lake. Armathwaite Hall, Bassenthwaite Lake, Keswick, Cumbria CA12 4RE. Tel: 017687 76551

LONDON

1. **Sutton House**: Tudor red brick house with original linenfold panelling and seventeenth-century wall paintings. Contact: Carol Mills, Sutton House, 2 & 4 Homerton High Street, Hackney, London E9 6JQ. Tel: 0181 986 2264. NT

2. **Burgh House**: Queen Anne building in the heart of Hampstead but set back from the road. Burgh House Trust, New End Square, Hampstead, London NW3 1LT. Tel: 0171 431 0144

3. **Cannizaro House**: Georgian country house hotel near Wimbledon Common where Oscar Wilde and Henry James once took tea. Cannizaro House, West Side, Wimbledon Common, London SW19 4UE. Tel: 0181 879 1464

4. **The Ritz**: The height of sophistication in the heart of the capital. The Ritz, 150 Piccadilly, London W1V 9DG. Tel: 0171 493 8181

5. **Langham Hilton**: Restored Victorian luxury hotel – an oasis in the middle of London. The Langham Hilton, 1 Portland Place, Regent Street, London W1N 4JA. Tel: 0171 636 1000. Fax: 0171 323 2340

6. **Battersea Pump House**: Light and airy Victorian brick building by the Thames also makes a dramatic night-time reception venue. The Pump House Gallery, Battersea Park, Albert Bridge Road, London SW11 4NJ. Tel: 0171 350 0523

7. **Templeton House**: Eighteenth-century building on the edge of Richmond Park and once the home of Winston Churchill. Templeton House, 118 Priory Lane, Roehampton, London SW15 5JW. Tel: 0181 878 1672

8. **Trafalgar Tavern**: Elegant naval pub and restaurant with views over the Thames. The Trafalgar Tavern, Park Row, Greenwich, London SE10 9NW. Tel: 0181 858 2437

9. **Ham House**: Stuart house on the banks of the Thames, once at the heart of court life and still surrounded by beautiful gardens. Ham House, Ham Street, Richmond, Surrey TW10 7RS. Tel: 0181 940 1950. Fax: 0181 332 6903. NT

10. **London Zoo**: Weddings take place out of view of the animals but guests can visit the occupants afterwards. Zoo Hospitality, Zoological Gardens, Regent's Park, The Outer Circle, London NW1 4RY. Tel: 0171 586 3339

AROUND LONDON

1. **The Old Palace**: Queen Elizabeth I's banqueting hall situated in the grounds of Hatfield House. The Old Palace, Hatfield Park, Hatfield, Herts. AL9 5NE. Tel: 01707 262055. Fax: 01707 260898

2. **Offley Place**: Large country house with elegant staircase and extensive grounds. Offley Place, Kings Walden Road, Great Offley, Near Hitchin, Herts. SG5 3DS. Tel: 01462 768787. Fax: 01462 768724

3. **Highclere Castle**: Grand Georgian house with Jacobean façade and Italianate central tower. Highclere Castle, Newbury, Berks. RG20 9RN. Tel: 01635 253210. Fax: 01635 810193.

4. **Missenden Abbey**: Recently renovated building set in acres of parkland. Missenden

Abbey, Great Missenden, Bucks. HP16 0BD. Tel: 01494 866811. Fax: 01494 471585

5. **Knebworth Park**: Victorian Gothic fantasy with original Jacobean banqueting hall. Knebworth Park, Knebworth, Herts. SG3 6PY. Tel: 01438 813825. Fax: 01438 813003

6. **Monkey Island Hotel**: Peaceful island setting on the Thames. Monkey Island Hotel, Old Mill Lane, Bray-on-Thames, Maidenhead, Berks. SL6 2EE. Tel: 01628 23400

7. **The Priory**: Tranquil building dating back to the fourteenth century with grounds leading down to the river. The Priory, High Street, Ware, Herts. SG12 9AL. Tel 01920 460316. Fax 01920 484056

8. **Oakley Court Hotel**: Imposing luxury hotel on the banks of the Thames and once used for the location for *St Trinians*. Oakley Court Hotel, Windsor Road, Water Oakley, Windsor, Berks. SL4 5UR. Tel: 01753 609988

9. **Bassetsbury Manor**: Seventeenth-century house set in grounds that include a weir and water mill. Contact: Halls Manager, Wycombe District Council, Queen Victoria Road, High Wycombe, Bucks. HP11 1BB. Tel: 01494 421889. Fax: 01494 421808

10. **Woburn Abbey**: Wedding ceremonies take place in the sculpture gallery of this massive stately home. Woburn Abbey, Woburn, Beds. MK43 0TP. Tel: 01525 290666. Fax: 01525 290271

ROMANTIC WEDDING VENUES IN SCOTLAND

HS = HISTORIC SCOTLAND
NTS = NATIONAL TRUST FOR SCOTLAND

BORDERS AND SCOTTISH LOWLANDS

1. **Traquair House**: Scotland's oldest inhabited house, with maze, secret stairs and its own brewery. Contact: Catherine Maxwell-Stuart, Traquair House, Innerleithen, Peeblesshire EH44 6PW Tel: 01896 830323. Fax: 01896 830639

2. **Dryburgh Abbey**: Remarkably intact ruins and burial place of Sir Walter Scott and Field Marshal Earl Haig, five miles east of Melrose. HS

3. **Carter Bar**: Border crossing point in the Cheviot Hills near a sixteenth-century battleground offers superb views of surrounding countryside. Contact: Roxburgh District Council. Tel: 01450 375991

4. **Caerlaverock Castle**: Dramatic and surprising triangular castle surrounded by moat south-east of Dumfries. HS

5. **Duns Castle**: Fourteenth-century building offering upmarket accommodation. Contact: Mrs Aline Hay, Duns Castle, Berwickshire TD11 3NW. Tel: 01361 883211. Fax: 01361 882015

6. **Floors Castle**: Home of the Duke of Roxburghe, with grand carved stonework,

lead cupolas and views of the River Tweed and Cheviot Hills. Contact: Roxburghe Estates Office, Kelso, Roxburghshire TD5 7SF. Tel: 01573 223333

7. **Grey Mare's Tail**: Beautiful waterfall near Moffat in Dumfriesshire. Contact: NTS

8. **Knockinaam Lodge**: Secluded mid-nineteenth-century house renowned for its cuisine and set in rugged hillside with lawns leading down to its own beach. Contact: Pauline Ashworth or Michael Bricker, Knockinaam Lodge, Portpatrick, Wigtownshire DG9 9AD. Tel: 01776 810435

9. **Comlongdon Castle Hotel**: Fifteen-century building with haunted keep at Clarencefield, Dumfriesshire. Contact: Scotts Castle Holidays (see page 266)

10. **Kirroughtree**: Eighteenth-century mansion with Rococo furnishings and oak-panelled lounge surrounded by hills. Kirroughtree Hotel, Newton Stewart, Wigtownshire DG8 6AN. Tel: 01671 402141. Fax: 01671 402425

CENTRAL AND EASTERN SCOTLAND

1. **Balgonie Castle**: Fourteenth-century tower house with candlelit chapel and great hall attracts couples from around the world. Contact: The Laird of Balgonie, Balgonie Castle, by Markinch, Fife KY7 6HQ. Tel: 01592 750119

2. **Stirling Castle**: One of Scotland's grandest castles and favourite residence of monarchs. Contact: HS

3. **Culcreuch Castle Hotel**: Ancient castle set in 1,600 acres of hills, moors, lochs, burns and woods near Stirling. Contact: Scotts Castle Holidays (see page 266)

4. **Aberdour Castle**: Fourteenth-century castle with gallery, spectacular views over the Firth of Forth and walled garden. HS

5. **Inchcolm Abbey**: The 'Iona of the East', the twelfth-century abbey can be reached by ferry and grey seals can be spotted off the island. Contact: HS. Ferry company on 0131 554 6881, sailings: Easter Saturday–31 June weekends only, July–August daily sailings, September weekends only. *The Maid of the Forth* also sails there. Tel: 01383 823332

6. **Pride of the Union**: Canal boat that cruises along the Almond Aqueduct will host ceremony and reception. Contact: The Edinburgh Canal Centre, 27 Baird Road, Ratho, Midlothian EH28 8RA. Tel: 0131 333 1320. Fax: 0131 333 3480

7. **Linlithgow Castle**: Birthplace of Mary Queen of Scots, by the side of a loch, now without a roof. HS

8. **Edinburgh Castle**: Built on an extinct volcano, the partly Norman castle has panoramic views of the city. HS.

9. **Borthwick Castle Hotel**: Medieval twin-tower keep, once the refuge of Mary Queen of Scots and the Earl of Bothwell. Contact: General Manager, Ms Christine Calloway, Borthwick Castle Hotel, North Middleton, Midlothian EH25 4QY. Tel 01875 820514

10. **Dalhousie Castle**: Luxury hotel including dungeon restaurant and rooms with four-poster beds. Contact: General Manager, Mr Neville Petts, Dalhousie Castle Hotel, Bonyrigg, Midlothian EH19 3JB. Tel: 01875 820153

GRAMPIAN

1. **Muchalls Castle**: Seventeenth-century fortified house overlooking the sea with magnificent plaster ceilings, canopied beds and turret bedrooms. Contact: Muchalls Castle, Stonehaven, Kincardineshire AB3 2RS. Tel: 0569 31170. Fax: 0569 31480. Unsuitable for children under 12

2. **Leslie Castle**: The original seat of the Leslie clan, this turreted fairy-tale castle comes complete with baronial hall for small receptions. Contact: Mr D. Leslie, Leslie Castle, Leslie, by Insch, Aberdeenshire AB53 7TD. Tel: 01464 820869. Fax: 01464 821076

3. **Delgatie Castle**: Dates from the eleventh century. Its painted ceilings depict strange animals with human heads representing previous inhabitants. Contact: Mrs Johnson, Delgatie Castle, Turriff, Aberdeenshire AB53 7TD. Tel: 01888 562750

4. **Meldrum House**: Comfortable stone baronial house richly decorated with antiques and ancestral portraits and surrounded by 15 acres of landscaped parklands. Contact: Meldrum House, Oldmeldrum, Aberdeenshire AB1 0AE. Tel: 0651 872294. Fax: 0651 872464

5. **Kildrummy Castle Hotel**: Country mansion overlooking ruined thirteen-century castle. Kildrummy Castle Hotel, Kildrummy, by Alford, Aberdeenshire AB33 8RA. Tel: 019755 71288. Fax: 019755 71345

6. **Thainstone House**: Classical-style hotel and country club redesigned in nineteenth century by Aberdeen's architect Archibald Simpson. Contact: Thainstone House Hotel and Country Club, Inverurie, Aberdeenshire AB51 5NT. Tel: 01467 621643. Fax: 01467 625084

7. **Spynie Palace**: Residence of bishops of Moray from fourteenth century to 1686, with massive stone tower overlooking Spynie Loch. Contact: Liz McLean, Spynie Palace, Elgin, Moray. Tel: 01343 546358. HS

8. **Fasque House**: Stately home owned and run by the Gladstone family (descendants of the prime minister). Contact: Mrs Gladstone, Fasque House, Fettercairn, Kincardineshire Tel: 01561 340201

9. **Kincardine House**: Mansion on a hillside overlooking Royal Deeside. Contact: Kincardine House, Kincardine O'Neil, Aboyne AB34 5AE. Tel: 03398 84225. Fax: 03398 84394

10. **Castle of Park**: Thirteenth-century baronial castle overlooking 60 acres of naturally landscaped gardens near Cornhill, Banffshire. Contact: Scotts Castle Holidays (see page 266)

HIGHLANDS

1. **Inverlochy Castle**: Grand Victorian mansion. Inverlochy Castle Hotel, Torlundy, Fort William, Inverness-shire PH33 6SN. Tel: 01397 702177

2. **Top of Ben Nevis**: Britain's highest mountain at 4,406 metres/1,343 feet. Tourist Board says no official permission required from landowner

3. **Castle Tioram**: Ancient seat of the Macdonalds of Clanranald, now lochside ruin on rocky outcrop. Access by causeway, beware of advancing tides. Castle Tioram, north of Acharacle, west Scotland

4. **Neptune's Staircase**: Lock system on Caledonian Canal, Banavie, Fort William, Lochaber. Contact: British Waterways Board. Tel: 01463 233140

5. **White Sands of Morar**: Beautiful stretch of beach on west coast. By Morar

6. **Glengarry Castle Hotel**: Victorian turreted building close to Loch Ness, Invergarry, Inverness-shire PH35 4HW. Tel: 018093 254

7. **Jacobite cruises**: To and from Tomnahurich Bridge, Inverness. Contact: Jacobite Cruises, Tomnahurich Bridge, Glenurquahart Road, Inverness, Inverness-shire. IV3 5TD. Tel: 01463 233999

8. **Balfour Castle**: Remote Victorian castle on Shapinsay on the Orkney Islands with panoramic views. Contact: Scotts Castle Holidays (see page 266).

9. **Fort Augustus Abbey**: On shores of Loch Ness. Contact: Fort Augustus Abbey, Inverness-shire PH32 4BD. Tel: 01320 366233. Fax: 01320 366228

10. **Tulloch Castle Hotel**: Rumoured to have been visited by Macbeth, stands in beautiful grounds in the north-east. Contact: Scotts Castle Holidays (see page 266)

SOUTH-WEST SCOTLAND (INCLUDING GLASGOW)

1. **Culzean Castle and Country Park**: Robert Adam's spectacular castle in 560 acres with views of Arran and the Mull of Kintyre. Contact: Administrator's Office. Tel: 01655 760274. Fax: 01655 760615, or NTS

2. **Hutchesons' Hall**: Elegant, early-nineteenth-century building in the centre of Glasgow with impressive staircase and Grand Hall. NTS

3. **Greenbank House**: Eighteenth-century merchant's home on the outskirts of Glasgow, set in 16 acres of land including a walled garden. NTS

4. ***Silver Marlin***: Cruises along Loch Lomond. Contact: Sweeneys Cruises, Riverside, Balloch, Dunbartonshire G83 8LE. Tel: 0389 52376

5. **SS *Sir Walter Scott***: Cruises along Loch Katrine in the heart of Rob Roy country. Contact: Strathclyde Water Department, 419 Balmore Road, Glasgow. Tel: 041 355 5333

6. **Blairquhan Castle**: Secluded private mansion house in beautiful gardens reached by three-mile drive, 'The Long Approach', along River Girvan. Blairquhan Castle, Straiton, Maybole, Ayrshire KA19 7LZ. Tel: 01655 770239. Fax: 01655 770278

7. **Dean Castle**: Fourteenth-century fortified keep with dungeon and fifteenth-century palace set in 200 acres of woodland. Dean Castle, Kilmarnock, Ayrshire. Tel: 01563 533702/534580

8. **Kelburn Castle**: Home of the Earls of Glasgow since 1703, situated in magnificent gardens with spectacular views of Kelburn Glen. Catering, but no accommodation. Kelburn Castle, Fairlie, nr Largs, Ayrshire. Tel: 01475 56865. Fax: 01475 568121

9. **Montgreenan Mansion House Hotel**: Tranquil family home built in 1817, set in gardens and countryside. Montgreenan Mansion House Hotel, Montgreenan Estate, nr Kilwinning, Ayrshire KA13 7QS. Tel: 01294 557733. Fax: 01294 850397

10. **Chatelherault**: Eighteenth-century hunting lodge of the Dukes of Hamilton, once described as the 'finest dog kennels in the world'. Chatelherault, Ferniegair, Hamilton, South Lanarkshire ML3 7UE. Tel: 01698 426213. Fax: 01698 421532

TAYSIDE

1. **Glamis Castle**: Turreted setting for *Macbeth*, and childhood home of the Queen Mother. Contact: Castle Administrator, Estates Office, Glamis, Angus DD8 1RJ. Tel: 01307 840242/393. Fax: 01307 840257

2. **Camperdown Country Park**: Neo-classical mansion house set in beautiful parkland. Contact: The City of Dundee District Council, Leisure and Recreation Department, Olympia, Earl Grey Place, Dundee DD1 4DF. Tel: 01382 434624

3. **HMS *Unicorn***: Wooden vessel claiming to be oldest British-built ship afloat anywhere in the world. Contact: Development Manager, *Unicorn* Preservation Society, The Frigate *Unicorn*, Victoria Dock, Dundee DD1 3JA. Tel: 01382 200900

4. **Castle Menzies**: Sixteenth-century fortified tower house and seat of the chiefs of the Clan Menzies for over 400 years. Con-

tact: Castle Menzies, Weem, Aberfeldy, Perthshire PH15 2JD. Tel: 01887 820982

5. **Glenturret Distillery**: Oldest malt whisky distillery in Scotland. Glenturret Distillery, The Hosh, Crieff, Perthshire PH7 4HA. Tel: 01764 656565

6. **Ben Vorlich**: 1982-metre/3,224-foot summit above Loch Earn with panoramic views. Contact: Crieff Tourist Information Centre, 33 High Street, Crieff, Perthshire PH7 3HU. Tel: 01764 652578. Fax: 01764 655542

7. **Riverside grotto and riverbank**: Surrounded by larch trees on the Tay. Contact: Stakis Dunkeld House, Dunkeld, Perthshire PH8 0HX. Tel: 01350 727 771. Fax: 01350 728924

8. **Lochleven Castle**: Mary Queen of Scots was imprisoned on this wooded island. HS

9. **Huntingtower Castle**: Medieval castle near Perth with fine early painted ceilings. HS

10. **Blair Castle**: White turreted castle, seat of Dukes of Atholl. Contact: Blair Castle, Blair Atholl, Pitlochry, Perthshire. Tel: 01796 481207

USEFUL SCOTTISH ADDRESSES

Britannia, 60-foot cutter. Contact: Isle of Skye Tourist Board, TIC, Portree, Isle of Skye IV51 9BZ. Tel: 0478 612137

Available for charter:
Cruise ship MV *Hebridean Princess*, Hebridean Island Cruises Ltd, Acorn Park, Skipton, North Yorks. Tel: 01756 701338

Royal Scotsman, luxury train. Abercrombie and Kent Travel, Sloane Square House, Holbein Place, London. Tel: 0171 730 9600

Scotts Castle Holidays: Castlecliff, 25 Johnston Terrace, Edinburgh EH1 2NH. Tel: 0131 226 7615. Fax: 0131 220 4717

Historic Scotland: Apply in writing (with details of requirements) to: Nick G. Finnigan, Events Manager, Historic Scotland, Longmore House, Salisbury Place, Edinburgh EH9 1SH

The National Trust for Scotland: 5 Charlotte Square, Edinburgh EH2 4DU. Tel: 0131 226 5922. Fax: 0131 243 9302

ROMANTIC WEDDING VENUES IN WALES

1. **Dan-Yr-Ogof Caves**: The 42-metre/140-foot wide and 18-metre/60-foot high Cathedral Cave is 90 metres/300 feet underground in the Brecon Beacons National Park, lit by candles and contains several waterfalls. Contact: Sarah Price, Dan-Yr-Ogof Caves, Abercraf, Glyntawe, Upper Swansea Valley, Swansea, Wales SA9 1GJ. Tel: 01639 730284.

2. **Powis Castle**: Imposing medieval castle with seventeenth-century garden terraces. Contact: Administrator, Major Neville Williams, Powis Castle and Gardens, Welshpool, Powys SY21 8RF. Tel: 01938 554338. NT

3. **Caerphilly Castle**: Sprawling medieval castle set among hills. Caerphilly Castle,

Mid Glamorgan CF8 1JL, or Cadw: Welsh Historic Monuments, Brunel House, 2 Fitzalan Road, Cardiff CF2 1UY. Tel: 01222 500200

4. **Margam Park Orangery**: Eighteenth-century building overlooking fountains and ornamental gardens, and close to abbey and castle remains. Margam Country Park, Margam, Port Talbot, West Glamorgan SA13 2TJ. Tel: 01639 881635. Fax: 01639 895897

5. **Canolfan Pentre Ifan**: 500-year-old Tudor stone gatehouse set in Pembrokeshire Coast National Park. Canolfan Pentre Ifan, Felindre Farchog, Crymych, Dyfed SA41 3XE. Tel: 01239 820317

6. **Cardiff Castle**: Ancient fortification richly decorated by Victorian owners. Cardiff Castle, Castle Road, Cardiff, South Glamorgan CF1 2RB. Tel: 01222 878100

7. **Lake Country House Hotel**: Originally built as a spa hotel and now set in parkland that includes a lake. Lake Country House Hotel, Llangammarch Wells, Powys LD4 4BS. Tel: 01591 620202. Fax: 01591 620457

8. **Castell Coch**: Victorian fantasy resembling a Rhineland castle surrounded by forest. Castell Coch, Tongwynlais, Cardiff, South Glamorgan CF4 7JS. Tel: 01222 810101

9. **Ruthin Castle**: Thirteenth-century castle and luxury hotel. Ruthin Castle, Castle Street, Ruthin, Denbighshire LL15 2NU. Tel: 01824 702664

10. **Ynyshir Hall**: Eighteenth-century country house hotel set in beautiful grounds. Ynyshir Hall, Eglwysfach, Machynlleth, Powys SY20 8TA. Tel: 01654 781209. Fax: 01654 781366

ROMANTIC WEDDING VENUES IN NORTHERN IRELAND

(Use the prefix [08] when dialling from the Republic of Ireland.)

1. **Portaferry Hotel**: Waterside village inn overlooking Strangford Lough with its bird sanctuary and designated wildlife area. Contact: John and Marie Herlihy, Portaferry Hotel, The Strand, Portaferry, County Down BT22 1PE. Tel: 012477 28231. Fax: 012477 28999

2. **Tempo Manor**: Victorian house with some four-poster beds, surrounded by lakes and gardens. Contact: John and Sarah Langham, Tempo Manor, Tempo, County Fermanagh. Tel: 01365 541450. Fax: 01365 541202

3. **Blessingbourne**: Victorian mansion with mullioned windows and view of lake and mountains. Contact: Captain and Mrs R. H. Lowry, Blessingbourne, Fivemiletown, County Tyrone. Tel: 01 365 521 221

4. **Tyrella House**: Elegant building near the Mourne Mountains with grasslands that sweep down to a private sandy beach. Contact: David and Sally Corbett, Tyrella House, Downpatrick, County Down. Tel: 01 396 851 422. Fax: 01 396 851 422

5. **Culloden Hotel**: Gothic building overlooking Belfast Lough and County Antrim coastline. Contact: Philip Weston, Bangor Road, Holywood, nr Belfast, County Down. Tel: 01232 425223. Fax: 01232 426777

6. **Magherabuoy House Hotel**: Set on a hill overlooking the Atlantic and close to the Giant's Causeway. Contact: Magherabuoy House Hotel, 41 Magheraboy Road, Portrush, County Antrim. Tel: 01265 823507. Fax: 01265 824687

7. **Beech Hill Country House Hotel**: Eighteenth-century house set in wooded grounds. Beech Hill Country House Hotel, 32 Ardmore Road, Londonderry BT47 3QP. Tel: 01504 49279. Fax: 01504 45366

8. **The Dunadry Inn**: 10-acre riverside hotel built on the site of a former paper mill. The Dunadry Inn, 2 Islandreagh Drive, Dunadry, Country Antrim BT41 2HA. Tel: 01849 432474. Fax: 01849 433389

9. **Streeve Hill**: Eighteenth-century house with brick Palladian façade and interesting gardens. Contact: Peter and June Welsh, Streeve Hill, Limavady, County Londonderry BT49 0HP. Tel: 08 5047 66 563. Fax: 01 5047 68 285

10. **Galgorm Manor**: Nineteenth-century mansion house in 85 acres of wooded estate by River Maine. Galgorm Manor, 136 Fenaghy Road, Ballymena BTU2 1EA County Antrim. Tel: 01266 88100

Note: these venues cannot be used for the marriage ceremony, only for the reception or honeymoon.

ROMANTIC WEDDING VENUES IN THE REPUBLIC OF IRELAND

(Use the prefix [00 353] when dialling from the United Kingdom.)

WEST IRELAND

1. **Knappogue Castle**: This fifteenth-century building with beautiful views and antique furniture and paintings has entertained VIPs like Charles de Gaulle and Ronald Reagan. Contact: Knappogue Castle, Quin, County Clare. Tel: 061 360788

2. **Old Ground Hotel**: Ivy-clad mansion set in peaceful gardens and close to the Atlantic coast. Old Grand Hotel, Ennis, County Clare. Tel: 065 28127 Fax: 065 28112

3. **Delphi Lodge**: Tranquil house surrounded by woods and mountains and overlooking a lake. Contact: Peter and Jane Mantle, Delphi Lodge, Leenane, County Galway. Tel: 095 42211 Fax: 095 42296

4. **St Ernans House Hotel**: Situated on a wooded tidal island connected to the mainland by a causeway, the house was built in 1826 and offers views of the sea. Contact: Brian and Carmel O'Dowd, St Ernans House Hotel, Donegal, County Donegal. Tel: 073 21065. Fax: 073 22098

5. **Currarevagh House**: Victorian manor 100 yards from Lough Corrib in 150 acres of private woodland. Contact: Harry and June Hodgson, Currarevagh House, Oughterard, Connemara, County Galway. Tel: 091 82312/82313

6. **Markree Castle**: Sligo's oldest inhabited house, with decorative plasterwork and Irish oak staircase. Contact: Charles and Mary Cooper, Markree Castle, Colloney, County Sligo. Tel: 071 67800. Fax: 071 67840

7. **Dromoland Castle**: Baronial castle with wood and stone carvings and panellings, renowned for its restaurant. Dromoland Castle, Newmarket-on-Fergus, County Clare. Tel: 061 368144. Fax: 061 363355

8. **Ashford Castle**: Stunning thirteenth-century building set in beautiful grounds. Ashford Castle, Cong, County Mayo. Tel: 092 46003. Fax: 092 46260

9. **Bunratty Castle**: One of the most complete medieval castles in Ireland. Contact: Shannon Castle Banquets and Heritage, Bunratty, County Clare. Tel: 061 360788. Fax: 061 361020

10. **Glenlo Abbey Hotel**: Eighteenth-century residence in 134-acre estate overlooking Lough Corrib. Contact: Glenlo Abbey Hotel, Bushypark, County Galway. Tel: 091 26666. Fax: 091 27800

SOUTH IRELAND

1. **Glin Castle**: White castle resembling a child's fort set on the river Shannon and surrounded by formal gardens contains neo-classical ceilings and unusual double staircase. Contact: Desmond and Olga Fitz-Gerald, Glin Castle, Glin, County Limerick. Tel: 068 34112/34173. Fax: 068 34364

2. **Park Hotel**: Victorian country house hotel surrounded by subtropical gardens. Park Hotel Kenmare, Kenmare, County Kerry. Tel: 064 41200. Fax: 064 41402

3. **Ballyvolane House**: Comfortable eighteenth-century building set in formal gardens. Jeremy and Merrie Green, Ballyvolane House, Castlelyons, County Cork. Tel: 025 36349 Fax: 025 36781

4. **Lismore Castle Gardens**: Home of the Dukes of Devonshire overlooking Blackwater valley, dating back to thirteenth century. Small parties of up to sixteen. Lismore Castle Gardens, Lismore, County Waterford. Tel: 058 54424. Fax: 058 54896

5. **Assolas Country House**: Seventeenth-century building set in sweeping lawns and by river's edge. Contact: Bourke Family, Assolas Country House, Kanturk, County Cork. Tel: 029 50015. Fax 029 50795

6. **Ballylickey Manor House**: Former shooting lodge built 300 years ago stands in award-winning flower gardens overlooking Bantry Bay. Contact: Christian and George Graves, Ballylickey Manor House, Ballylickey, Bantry Bay, County Cork. Tel: 027 50071. Fax: 027 50124

7. **Ballymaloe House**: Large family farmhouse on 400-acre farm. Contact: G. M. and R. I. Allen, Ballymaloe House, Shanagarry, Midleton, County Cork. Tel: 021 652531

8. **Caragh Lodge**: Mid-Victorian house set in gardens of azaleas, camellias and magnolias on the shores of Caragh Lake with views of McGillicuddy Reeks and Carrauntoohil (Ireland's highest mountain). Contact: Mary Gaunt, Caragh Lodge, Caragh Lake, County Kerry. Tel: 066 69115. Fax: 066 69316

9. **Longueville House**: Built in 1720 and with the Blackwater river running through the estate which also has its own vineyard. Contact: The O'Callaghan Family, Longueville House, Mallow, County Cork. Tel: 022 47156. Fax: 022 47459

10. **Adare Manor**: Mysterious grey building with oak stairway decorated with carved ravens, and gallery reputed to be the second longest in Europe. Adare Manor, Adare, County Limerick. Tel: 061 396566. Fax: 061 396124

11. **Gurthalougha House**: A nineteenth-century hunting lodge on the shores of Lough Derg with a cobbled, flower-filled courtyard. Contact: Michael and Bessie Wilkinson, Gurthalougha House, Ballinderry, nr Nenagh, County Tipperary. Tel: 067 22080. Fax: 067 22154

EAST IRELAND (INCLUDING DUBLIN)

1. **Humewood Castle**: Magnificent granite and sandstone Victorian castellated mansion with views of Wicklow Mountains. Humewood Castle, Kiltegan, County Wicklow. Tel: 0508 73215

2. **Castle Leslie**: Victorian castle with stucco work and Italian and Spanish furniture set in parkland with lake. Castle Leslie, Glaslough, County Monaghan. Tel: 047 88109. Fax: 047 88256

3. **Hunter's Hotel**: Old coaching inn along the banks of the Vartry river. Contact: Gelletlie Family, Hunter's Hotel, Rathnew, County Wicklow. Tel: 0404 40106. Fax: 0404 40338

4. **Moyglare Manor**: Half a mile of tree-lined avenue leads to this Georgian house which is accessible for Dublin airport. Contact: Norah Devlin, Moyglare Manor, Moyglare, Maynooth, County Kildare. Tel: 01 6286351. Fax: 01 6285405

5. **Rathsallagh House**: Converted Queen Anne stables in 530 acres of parkland with walled garden and heated indoor swimming pool. Contact: Joe and Kay O'Flynn, Rathsallagh House, Dunlavin, County Wicklow. Tel: 045 403112. Fax: 045 403343

6. **Tinakilly House**: Victorian mansion with elegant antique furnishings and some four-poster beds. Contact: William and Bee Power, Tinakilly Country House Hotel and Restaurant, Rathnew, County Wicklow. Tel: 0404 69274. Fax: 0404 67806

7. **Barberstown Castle**: Built in the thirteenth century, the award-winning hotel is thirty minutes' drive from Dublin airport. Contact: Kenneth and Catherine Healy, Barberstown Castle, Straffan, County Kildare. Tel: 01 6288157. Fax: 01 6277027

8. **Kinnitty Castle**: Cosy hotel with open log fires and candlelit rooms in the Slieve Bloom mountains. Kinnitty Castle, Kinnitty, Birr, County Offaly. Tel: 0509 37318. Fax: 0509 37284

9. **Martinstown House**: 200-year-old elegant home set in 170 acres of wooded land. Contact: Thomas and Meryl Long, Martinstown House, The Curragh, County Kildare. Tel/Fax: 045 441269.

USEFUL IRISH ADDRESSES

1. **Elegant Ireland**: 15 Harcourt Street, Dublin 2. Tel: 01 475 1632/475 1665. Fax: 01 475 1012.

Rents out a range of properties. Some are rented for a minimum of one week, others for a shorter time, and some will accept daily bookings. They range from self-catering to large properties which have their own cook.

2. **The Hidden Ireland**: PO Box 4414, Dublin 4. Tel: 01 6681423. Fax: 01 6686578. Offers accommodation in buildings of architectural interest which are run as family homes and provide a country house party atmosphere. Fax for a booklet containing details of properties.

3. **An Taisce – The National Trust for Ireland**: Tailors Hall, Back Lane, Dublin 8. Tel: 01 454 1786

4. **Irish Heritage Properties**: Hillsbrook, Dargle Valley, Bray, County Wicklow. Tel/Fax: 01 849 1078

5. **Ireland's Blue Book, charming country houses and restaurants**: Ardbraccan Glebe, Navan, County Meath. Tel: 046 23416. Fax: 046 23292

Further Reading

The Oxford Book of Marriage (Oxford University Press) (useful source for readings)

Sharing the Future, Jane Wynne Willson (the British Humanist Association) (a practical guide to non-religious wedding ceremonies)

The New Jewish Wedding, Anita Diamant (Summit Books)

Reform Marriage, a Traditional Approach, Rabbi Rachel Montagu (the Reform Synagogues of Great Britain)

The Two of Us: Affirming, Celebrating and Symbolizing Gay and Lesbian Relationships, Larry J. Uhrig (Alyson Press)

Essential Guide to Lesbian and Gay Weddings, Tess Ayers and Paul Brown (HarperCollins)

Beat PMS Through Diet, Maryon Stewart (Vermilion)

Bloomsbury Encyclopaedia of Aromatherapy, Chrissie Wildwood (Bloomsbury)

Canapés and Frivolities, Anton Edelman and Jane Suthering (Pavilion)

Finger Food and Party Snacks, Linda Fraser (Lorenz Books)

Icing Made Easy, available from Tate & Lyle (see Useful Addresses page 276)

Leith's Book of Cakes, Prue Leith (Bloomsbury)

Leith's Cookery Bible, Prue Leith and Caroline Waldegrave (Bloomsbury)

My Day as a Bridesmaid, Caroline Plaisted (Bloomsbury)

Alfie and Annie Rose Storybook, Shirley Hughes (Bodley Head)

Costume for Births, Marriages and Deaths, P. Cunnington and C. Lucas (A & C Black)

'Queen Victoria's Wedding Dress and Lace', Kay Staniland and Santina M.Levey (*Costume, The Journal of the Costume Society*, 17, 1983)

Hallmarks, available from the Assay Office, Publications Dept, Goldsmiths' Hall, Gutter Lane, London EC2V 8AQ

The Company of Goldsmiths of Dublin (explains Irish hallmarks) issued by the Company of Goldsmiths of Dublin, Assay Office, Dublin Castle, Dublin 2

Useful Addresses

CAKES

British Sugarcraft Guild, Wellington House, Mosseter Place, London SE9 5DP. Tel: 0181 859 6943

Tate & Lyle, Thames Refinery, Silvertown, London E16 2EW. Tel: 0171 626 6525
(Freelance home economist will answer sugar-related queries: booklet *Icing Made Easy* also available)

CONTRACEPTION AND ADVICE ON HEALTHY PREGNANCY

Family Planning Association, 2–12 Pentonville Road, London N1 9FP. Tel: 0171 837 5432

Family Planning Association, Wales, 4 Museum Place, Cardiff CF1 3BG. Tel: 0222 342766

Family Planning Association, Northern Ireland, 113 University Street, Belfast BT7 1HP. Tel: 0232 325488

National Childbirth Trust, Alexander House, Oldham Terrace, London W3 6NH. Tel: 0181 992 8637

Wellbeing, 27 Sussex Place, Regents Park, London NW1 4SP. Tel: 0171 262 5337

DIET/PREMENSTRUAL STRESS

The Women's Nutritional Advisory Service (WNAS) has clinics in London, Lewes and Hove. For a telephone consultation send four loose first-class stamps and an A5 self-addressed envelope to:
PO Box 268, Lewes, East Sussex BN7 2QN

WNAS Overcome PMS Naturally helpline is on 0839 556600. The dietline is on 0839 556601

THE DRESS

Repairing old veils and dresses

The Royal School of Needlework, 12a Hampton Court Palace, East Molesey, Surrey KT8 9AU repair veils. You can visit, or send the veil by post with instructions.

The Textile Conservation Centre at Apartment 22, Hampton Court Palace, East Molesey, Surrey KT8 9AU, offers advice and carries out work. Tel: 0181 977 4943.

Textile Restoration Studio at 2 Talbot Road, Bowdon, Ches. WA14 3JD, will restore old garments and provide mail-order products for storage. Tel: 0161 928 0020.

Write to the Conservation Register of the Museums and Galleries Commission, 16 Queen Anne's Gate, London SW1H 9AA for a list of costume conservators and restorers. Tel: 0171 233 4200

Dressmakers

For a list of dressmakers in your area contact: Butterick Company Limited, New Lane, Havant, Hants. PO9 2ND. Tel: 01705 486221

Drycleaning

Drycleaning Information Bureau. Tel: 0181 863 8658

FLOWERS

National Association of Flower Arrangement Societies (for clubs in your area), 21 Denbigh Street, London SW1V 2HF. Tel: 0171 828 5145

Society of Floristry, 59 Tree Tops, Portskewett, Gwent NP6 4RT. Tel/Fax: 01291 424039

FORMALITIES

General Register Office of England and Wales, St Catherine's House, 10 Kingsway, London WC2B 6JP. Tel: 0171 396 2828

General Register Office for Scotland, New Register House, 3 West Register Street, Edinburgh EH1 3YT. Tel: 0131 334 0380.

General Register Office, Joyce House, 8–11 Lombard Street East, Dublin 2. Tel: (00 353) 01 671 1000

General Register Office of Northern Ireland, 49–55 Chichester Street, Belfast BT1 4HH. Tel: 01232 252000

Register General for Guernsey, The Greffe, Royal Court House, St Peter Port, Guernsey GY1 1PB. Tel: 01481 725277

Superintendent Register for Jersey, States Buildings, 10 Royal Square, St Helier, Jersey JE1 1DD. Tel: 01534 502000

GAY AND LESBIAN CEREMONIES

George Broadhead, Gay and Lesbian Humanist Association, 34 Spring Lane, Kenilworth, War. CV8 2HB. Tel: 01926 58450

Lesbian and Gay Christian Movement, Oxford House, Derbyshire Street, London E2 6HG. Tel: 0171 739 1249
See also 'Mixed faith/religious compromise', page 280.

MUSIC

Irish

Anderstown Traditional and Contemporary Music School. Contact: Thomas McIllroy. Tel: 01232 239303

Belfast Set Dance and Traditional Music Society. Contact: Tom Clarke. Tel: 01232 647608

Irish Language Culturann Arts Centre. Contact: Janet Mulleoir. 216 Falls Road, Belfast BP12 6AH Tel: 01232 239303

Organization for Traditional Irish Music, Song and Dancing, Comhaltas Ceotoiri Eireann, Belgrave Square, Monkstown, County Dublin. Tel: (00 353) 01 280 0295

General

Mechanical Copyright Protection Society Ltd (MCPS), Elgar House, 41 Streatham High Road, London SW16 1ER. Tel: 0181 664 4400. Fax: 0181 769 8792.

Music Publishers' Association, Third Floor, Strandgate, 18/20 York Buildings, London WC2N 6JU. Tel: 0171 839 7779

NON-RELIGIOUS CEREMONIES

British Humanist Association, 13 Prince of Wales Terrace, London W8 5PG. National helpline: 0990 168122

PHOTOGRAPHY

Association of Professional Videomakers, 9 Curzon Road, London N10 2RB. Tel: 0181 365 2400

British Institute of Professional Photography, Fox Talbot House, Amwell End, Ware, Herts. SG12 9HN. Tel: 01920 464011

The Guild of Wedding Photographers UK, 13 Market Street, Altrincham, Ches. WA14 1QS. Tel: 0161 926 9367
Will supply photographers in your area who have reached a certain standard.

Irish Professional Photographers' Association, 5 Knocklyon Road, Templeogue, Dublin 16. Tel: (00 353) 01 4939488

Master Photographers' Association, Hallmark House, 2 Baumont Street, Darlington, Dur. DL1 5SZ. Tel: 01325 356555

Professional Photographers' Association, (Secretary's address), 3 Jinglers Court, Banbridge, County Down, BT32 3YJ, Northern Ireland. Tel: 0182 06 26026

RECEPTION

Guild of Professional Toastmasters, 12 Little Bornes, Dulwich, London SE12 8TE. Tel: 0181 670 5585. Fax: 0181 670 2255

RELIGIONS

Baptist

Baptist Union, Baptist House, 129 The Broadway, Didcot, Oxon. OX11 8XD. Tel: 01235 512077

Buddhist

Buddhist Society, 58 Eccleston Square, London SW1V 1TH. Tel: 0171 834 5858

Church of England

General Synod of the Church of England, Enquiry Centre, Church House, Great Smith Street, London SW1P 3NZ. Tel: 0171 222 9011

Episcopal

Episcopal Church, General Synod, 21 Grosvenor Crescent, Edinburgh EH12 5EE. Tel: 0131 225 6357

Church of Scotland

Church of Scotland, 121 George Street, Edinburgh EH4 2YR. Tel: 0131 225 5722

The Registry Office, Central Avenue, Gretna DG16 5AQ. Tel: 01461 337 648

Greek Orthodox

Greek Archdiocese, 5 Craven Hill, London W2 3EN. Tel: 0171 222 9011

Methodist

The Methodist Church, 1 Central Building, Westminster, London SW1H 9NH. Tel: 0171 222 8010

Jewish

(See also Mixed Faith/Religious Compromise, below)
Jewish Marriage Council, 23 Ravenhurst Avenue, London NW4 4EL. Tel: 0181 203 6311

The Reform Synagogues of Great Britain, 80 East End Road, London N3 2SY. Tel: 0181 349 4731

To arrange a wedding in Israel:
The Israel Movement for Progressive Judaism, 13 King David Street, Jerusalem 94101. Tel: 009722 203448

Calligraphers:
Ruth Brookner. Tel: 0181 959 4848

Muslim

The Muslim Law (Shariah) Council UK, 20–22 Creffield Road, Ealing, London W5 3RP. Tel: 0181 992 6636

Quaker

Quaker Religious Society of Friends, Friends' House, 173–177 Euston Road, London NW1. Tel: 0171 387 3601

Roman Catholic Church

The Catholic Marriage Advisory Council, 1 Blythe Mews, Blythe Road, London W14 0NW. Tel: 0171 371 1341

Roman Catholic Church, 106 Whitehouse Loan, Edinburgh EH9 1BB. Tel: 0131 452 8244.

Sikh

Sikh Missionary Society UK, 10 Featherstone Road, Southall, London UB2 5AA. Tel: 0181 574 1902

United Reform

United Reformed Church, 86 Tavistock Place, London WC1H 9RT. Tel: 0171 916 2020

Mixed faith/religious compromise

Jonathan Blake: Former ordained Church of England minister who now works independently as a freelance helping couples to create their own, tailor-made marriage ceremony in any setting and usually after a register office ceremony. Specializes in inter-faith and single-sex ceremonies and weddings for divorcees and couples who want something more spiritual than a civil ceremony. For a brochure contact:
Whispering Trees, 273 Beechings Way, Gillingham, Kent ME8 7BP. Tel: 01634 262920

Rabbi Guy Hall will perform a blessing between a Jew and non-Jew. Tel: 0181 343 0069

Asian Family Counselling Service, 74 The Avenue, West Ealing, London W13 8LB. Tel: 0181 997 5749

RELAXATION

British Reflexology Association, Monks Orchard, Whitbourne, Hereford & Worcester WR6 5RB. Supplies a list of members nationwide.

Council for Complementary and Alternative Medicine, 179 Gloucester Place, London NW1 6DX. Tel: 0171 724 9103

TATTOOS

For a list of tattooists in your area write to: Association of Professional Tattoo Artists (APTA), 157 Sydney Road, London N10 2NL. Tel: 0181 444 8779.

TRANSPORT

For a hot-air balloon pilot in your area contact: British Balloon and Airship Club, Wellington House, Lower Icknield Way, Longwick, nr Prince's Risborough, Bucks. HP27 9RS. Tel: 01604 870025

VENUES

Redundant churches: Church Commissioners, 1 Millbank, Westminster, London SW1P 3JZ. Tel: 0171 222 7010

WEATHER

Met Office Inquiry Officer. Tel: 01344 854455 for the number for your area.

Call Met Eirean on 01 80 64 217 (within the Irish Republic) or 00 353 18064217 (from the UK).

STOCKISTS

ABROAD

Travel agents specializing in overseas weddings:

Kuoni Travel, Kuoni House, Dorking, Surrey RH5 4AZ. Tel: 01306 740888

Thomson Holidays, Weddings in Paradise. Tel: 0161 911 8338

Virgin. Tel: 01293 617181

The Little White Chapel in Las Vegas. Tel: 001 702 382 5943

Las Vegas Convention and Visitors' Bureau. Tel: 0990 238832

Empire State Building, New York City. Tel: 001 212 736 3100

Overseas Connection. Tel: 001 516 725 9308

The Disney Wedding Specialists. Tel: 0171 605 2846

Norvista (for ice weddings). Tel: 0171 409 7334, or Kiruna Tourist Office, Hjalmar Lundbandsvag 42, 981 85, Kiruna, Sweden.

Crystal Ski Weddings. Tel: 0181 241 5000.

Overseas organizers:
Inspirations. Tel: 01293 820207 (Sri Lanka or Goa); Tel: 01293 822828 (hot air balloon in Kenya)

Weddings Abroad: Tel: 0161 941 1122

ACCESSORIES

Eda Rose Millinery, 'Lalique', Wallingford, Oxon. OX10 8BT. Tel/Fax: 01491 837174

Hassall & Carlow (specializes in made-to-order shoes, gloves, hats, handbags, also mail order) and Tiziano (wedding dress shop), both at: 283 Upper Street, Islington, London N1 2TZ. Tel: 0171 359 4440

BALLOONS

Pioneer Europe, Unit 1b, Goodliffe Park, Standsted Road, Bishop's Stortford, Herts. CM23 5PP. Helpline: 01279 501090 (suggests qualified balloon decorators)

Just Balloons, 127 Wilton Road, Victoria, London SW1 V1JZ Tel: 0171 434 3039

Harlequin Balloons. Tel: 01440 62719

BETS

See 'Gifts', page 285

BRIDAL FAVOURS AND BONBONNIÈRES

Bomboniere Italiane, 8 Lee Road, Perivale, London UB6 7DD. Tel: 0181 248 5100

1st Impressions, 109 Ellenborough Close, Thorley Park, Bishops Stortford, Herts. CM23 4HU. Tel: 01279 758943

Chequers (DIY and made to order, also wedding cake accessories and stationery), 318–320 Portobello Road, London W10 5RU. Tel: 0181 960 3315

BRIDESMAIDS' AND PAGEBOYS' OUTFITS

BHS: Marylebone House, 129–137 Marylebone Road, London NW1 5QD. Tel: 0171 262 3288

For very young attendants

Prettymades. Tel: 01425 279019

Junior Belle. Tel: 0171 254 8111

Linda Tidmarsh. Tel: 01689 838009

Elefant Kiri, 493 Fulham Palace Road, London SW6 6SU. Tel: 0171 610 6830

CAKES

Pat-A-Cake (novelty. and 'flyaway' cakes for weddings abroad), Kate Poulter, 83 Dartmouth Park Road, Dartmouth Park, London NW5 1SL. Tel: 0171 485 0006

Rachel Mount (personalized cakes), Unit G10, Broadway Studios, 28 Tooting High Street, London SW17 0RG. Tel: 0181 672 9333. Fax: 0181 767 3247

British Sugarcraft Guild, Wellington House, Messeter Place, London SE9 5DP. Tel: 0181 859 6943

The Sugarcraft Directory (lists specialists in sugarcraft and cake decorating), available from: Cake Art, Venture Way, Crown Estate, Priorswood, Taunton, Som. TA2 8DE. Tel: 01823 31532

CATERING AGENCIES

Leith's List (cooks trained at Leith's School of Food and Wine). Contact: Alison Cavaliero, Leith's School of Food and Wine, 21 St Albans Grove, London W8 5BP. Tel: 0171 229 0177. Fax: 0171 937 5257

Book-A-Cook. Contact: Vivienne Armitage, Throop House, Throop, Dorchester, Dorset DT2 7JD. Tel: 01929 471505

Noodles. Contact: Mrs Angela Straker, Dupplin Castle, by Perth, Perthshire PH2 0P4. Tel: 01738 440 720

Bunbury Domestic Employment Agency, Foxdale, Bunbury, Tarporley, Ches. CW6 9PE. Tel: 01829 260148

Lovat Cooking, Tom of Lude, Blair Atholl, Perthshire PH18 5TT. Tel: 01796 481 644

CHARITY SHOPS SPECIALIZING IN BRIDALWEAR

Oxfam shops: 'Sweet Charity', 300 Walsgrave Road, Coventry CV2 4BL; 56 Darley Street, Bradford BD1 3HN.

Cancer Research Campaign: 172 Terminus Road, Eastbourne, East Sussex BN21 3BB. Tel: 01232 39703; 125 High Street, Hounslow, London TW3 1QL. Tel: 0181 572 6662; 82 Stanford New Road, Altrincham, Ches. WA14 1BS. Tel: 0161 929 0598; 7 High Street, Southend, Essex SS1 1JE. Tel: 01702 432698

Cancer Research Group, 50 High Street, Newtownards, County Down BT23 3HZ. Tel: 01247 820268

CHILDREN

Crêchendo (supplies crèches and individual entertainers), Crechendo Events Ltd, St Luke's Hall, Adrian Mews, Ifield Road, London SW10 9AE. Tel: 0171 259 2727. Fax: 0171 259 2700

COOKERY COURSES

Leith's School of Food and Wine, 21 St Albans Grove, London W8 5BP. Tel: 0171 229 0177. Fax: 0171 937 5257

Country House Cookery. Contact: Rita Meade, Berry Lodge, Annagh, Miltown Malbay, County Clare, Republic of Ireland. Tel: (00 353) 065 87022

Ballymaloe Cookery School. Contact: D. Alten, Shanagarry, County Cork, Republic of Ireland. Tel: (00 353) 021 646785. Fax: (00353) 021 646909.

COSTUME HIRE

Angels & Bermans, 119 Shaftesbury Avenue, London WC2H 8AE. Tel: 0171 836 5678

THE DRESS

African designs

House of Ronke designs colour schemes for entire bridal party,. specializing in African hand-embroidered fabrics. Tel: 0181 673 7785

Drycleaning and preservation

Concorde of Knightsbridge (will collect from anywhere), 48 Walton Street, London SW3 1RB. Tel: 0171 584 0784

Jeeves of Belgravia, 30–48 Lawrence Road, London N15 4EX. Tel: 0181 809 3232

Dyeing

Chalfont Cleaners and Dyers, 22 Baker Street, London NW1 5RT. Tel: 0171 935 7316

Larger and smaller sizes

Alfred Angelo (sizes 8–28). Alfred Angelo, 25 Presley Way, Crown Hill, Milton Keynes, Bucks. MK8 0ES. Tel: 01908 262626

Bridal Fashions Ltd (sizes 8–22), London Road, Grantham, Lincs. NG31 6HX. Tel: 01476 593311

Pronuptia (sizes 8–28). Tel: 01254 664422

Sallie Bee/Sposa (up to size 30), 1172 Stratford Road, Hall Green, Birmingham BZ8 8AS Tel: 0121 778 6066

Secondhand

Occasions (to hire or buy), 62 High Street, Market Harborough, Leics. LE16 7AF. Tel: 01858 410933

The Wedding Dress Exchange (also buys dresses), Wedding Dress Exchange, 18 Deodar Road, London SW15. Tel: 0171 385 3940

Storage

The Empty Box Company, Coomb Farm Buildings, Balchins Lane, Westcott, Dorking, Surrey RH4 3LE. Tel: 01306 740193

Winter accessories

Wizard of Oz for a full-length hooded cloak. Tel: 0171 938 1025

SoieMême for muffs. Tel: 0171 483 3843

DRESSMAKING

Schools

Alison Victoria School of Sewing, Ravenstone Hall, Ravenstone, Leics. LE67 2AA. Tel: 01530 835668

Janome Sewing School of Excellence, The Janome Centre, Southside, Bredbury, Stockport, Ches. SK6 2SP. Tel: 0161 406 8010

Liberty Sewing School, Regent Street, London W1R 6AH. Tel: 0171 734 1234

Fabrics

MacCulloch and Wallis, 25/26 Dering Street, London W1R 0BH. Tel: 0171 629 0311
Also stock patterns in sizes 10–20.

Simons International Bridal Fabrics, Commercial Works, 55/57 Blackburn Road, Accrington, Lancs. BB5 4PF. Tel: 01254 382029

FIREWORKS

The Firework Co., Gunpowder Plot, Bridge Street, Uffculme, Devon EX15 3AX. Tel: 01884 840504. Fax: 01884 841142

FLOWERS

Treasured Moments, Freepost (HA 4625), Harrow, London HA2 9BR. Tel: 0181 933 4540
Specializes in tropical flower arrangements and Belgian chocolates.

Mary Jane Vaughan, Fast Flowers, 609 Fulham Road, London SW6 5UA. Tel: 0171 381 6422
Modern designs, also environmentally friendly confetti.

Flower Workshop Company. Tel: 01622 812108 or 01732 841380
Stocks fresh, silk and dried flowers.

The Flower House (Paula Pryke flower school), Cynthia Street, London N1 9JF. Tel: 0171 837 7373

Preservation

Ann Plowden. Tel: 01362 860573
Will press flowers or bouquet in frame or album.

Eternally Fresh. Tel: 01932 780498
Will preserve flowers in paperweight.

Pressed for Time, 37 Lower Swanwick Road, Lower Swanwick, Southampton SO3 7DY. Tel: 01489 574668
Pressed and mounted bouquets – nationwide collection.

GIFTS

Gift organizers

Wedding List Services, 127 Queenstown Road, London SW8 3RH. Tel: 0171 978 1118

Wedding List Co., 91 Walton Street, London SW3 2HP. Tel: 0171 584 1222

Gifts

Red Letter Days Ltd, Melville House, 8/12 Woodhouse Road, North Finchley, London N12 0RG. Tel: 0181 343 8822. Fax: 0181 343 9030

Body Part Casts: Creative Replicas. Tel: 0171 371 0032

International Star Registry. Tel: 0171 226 6886

Trees: The Woodland Trust Autumn Park, Grantham, Lincs. NG31 6LL. Tel: 01476 74297

Bets: c/o Graham Sharpe, William Hill, Greenside House, Station Road, Wood Green, London N21 4TP. Tel: 0181 918 3600

HATS

See 'Accessories', page 279

HEADDRESSES AND TIARAS

Jewellery

Bijoux Heart, 2 Boswell Street, Rotherham, South Yorkshire S65 2ED. Tel: 01709 363318 (brochure available)

Basia Zarzycka, 135 Kings Road, London SW3 4PN. Tel: 0171 351 7276

Joanna Thorne, Diva Bridalwear, 48 Hendon Way, Childs Hill, London NW2 2NR. Tel: 0181 458 5679

Headdresses

Warren York International, London Road, Grantham, Lincs. NG31 6HX. Tel: 01476 590255. Fax: 01476 579539

ICE SCULPTURE

Duncan Hamilton. Tel: 0181 944 9787

INSURANCE

Ecclesiastical Direct, Gloucester. Tel: 0800 336622

General Accident, Wedding Insurance Services Ltd, Freepost, Ringwood, Hants. BH24 3BR. Tel: 01202 519645

Cornhill Insurance (arranged by Jackson, Emms & Co. Ltd.), Oxford House, 181 Oxford Road, Reading, Berks. RG1 7UZ. Tel: 01734 575491

Wedding Plan, 82 Upper Saint Giles Street, Norwich NR2 1LT. Tel: 01603 767699

MAKE-UP LESSONS

London Esthetique, 75–77 Margaret Street, London W1N 7HB. Tel: 0171 636 1893. Offers one-day seminars for brides on beauty and make-up, also one-to-one sessions with make-up artists who will also travel to most places to do your make-up on the day.

Glauca Rossi, School of Make-up, 10 Sutherland Road, London W9 2HQ. Tel: 0171 289 7485.

MARQUEES

Alfred Bull & Co. Ltd. (in the South-East, also themed events), Woodbridge Meadows, Guildford, Surrey GU1 1BB. Tel: 01483 575492

MEMORIES

Forever Yours, Multimedia Factory, 35 Bedfordbury, Covent Garden, London WC2N 4DU. Tel: 0171 240 1640

Helen Atkinson (arranges mementoes into picture frames, etc.). Tel: 01223 503503

MENSWEAR

Favourbrook, 19–21 Piccadilly Arcade, Jermyn Street, London SW1Y 6NH. Tel: 0171 491 2337. Fax: 0171 499 9537

Head offices:

Lords Formal Wear, First Floor, Cabot Place East, Canary Wharf, London E14 5QT. Tel: 0171 363 1033. Fax: 0171 363 1034

Moss Bros Group plc, 8 St John's Hill, London SW11 1SA. Tel: 0171 924 1717. Fax: 0171 350 0112

Youngs Formalwear, Pronuptia–Youngs Limited, Unit 9, Hutton Street, Blackburn, Lancs. BB1 3BY. Tel: 01254 664422. Fax: 01254 681206

MUSIC

Belfast Harps, Brookfield Mill, Cramlin Road, Belfast BT14 7EA. Tel: 01232 352555. Contact: Janet Harbinson.

Opus Seven (national), 32 Upper Mall, Hammersmith, London W6 9TA. Tel: 0181 563 7253

Cantare, Shelley House, Newport Road, Burgess Hill, West Sussex RH15 8QG. Tel: 01444 871691

PHOTOGRAPHY

Colab Ltd., Herald Way, Binley, Coventry, West Midlands CB3 1BB. Tel: 01203 440404
Its 'Caring Memories' restoration service is available from good photographic shops and its 'If only . . .' (which can remove or insert people into shots, and deal with details such as closed eyes or poor exposure that spoil photos) direct from the company.

Janey Cunningham. Tel: 01932 562530. Mobile: 0589 176223
Specializes in reportage-style photography.

RELAXATION

Vitalizers, 17 Beechwood Court, Park Road, Chiswick, London W4 3HJ. Tel: 0181 742 2494
Nutritional and lifestyle advice, will draw up aromatherapy treatment for you.

The Institute for Complementary Medicine, PO Box 194, London SE16 1QZ. Tel: 0171 237 5165.

RINGS

For a range of over eighty artists from around the world:
Electrum Gallery, 21 South Molton Street, London W1Y 1DD. Tel: 0171 629 6325
Will post illustrations of work to prospective clients

Adornment, 61a Scotts Lane, Shortlands, Bromley, London, BR2 0LT. Tel: 0181 658 2352. Fax: 0181 663 1601
Personalized ring pillows, bridesmaids' gifts, etc.

SHOES

Bridal Footsteps. Tel: 01473 240483
Gina, 189 Sloane Street, Knightsbridge, London SW1X 9QR Tel: 0171 235 2932
Both will make up shoes in your own material

Dye-Versions, 22 Derry Close, Upton, Wirral, Merseyside L49 0XG. Tel: 0151 677 5756

Matchmaker, 137 Kings Road, Brentwood, Essex CM14 4DR. Tel: 01277 263500
The above will dye shoes and bags to match outfits.

SOMETHING OLD

Auctioneers Phillips, 101 New Bond Street, London W1Y 0AS. Tel: 0171 629 6602. They have regular sales of textiles, lace and costumes.

Cocoa, 7 Queens Circus, Montpellier, Cheltenham, Glos. GL50 1RX. Tel: 0242 233588. The shop will make up dresses to your designs. It also hires out antique dresses, veils, parasols, headdresses and silk flowers.

Catherine Buckley, 302 Westbourne Grove, London W11 2PS. Tel/Fax: 0171 229 8786. By appointment only. Sells and hires out dresses, many of which are twenties-style.

STAG AND HEN NIGHTS

Murder mystery, paintballing, bungee jumping, motor sports, etc.: Acorn Activities, PO Box 120, Hereford & Worcester HR4 8YB. Tel: 01432 830083. Fax: 01432 830110

Tank driving, etc.: Anglian Activity Breaks, Garden House, Framingham Pigot, Norwich, Norfolk. Tel: 01508 492132. Fax: 01508 492888

Tanks etc. Howie Irvine, Cairnton, Lumphanan, Banchory, Deeside AB13 4QP. Tel: 013398 83536

South Down Llama Trekking, Roundhill Cottage, Brighton Road, Newtimber, Hassocks, East Sussex BN6 9BS. Tel: 01273 857422

Cowboy activities: Drumcoura City, Ballinamore, County Leitrim, Republic of Ireland. Tel: (00 353) 078 44676

Dolphinwatch, Carrigaholt, County Clare, Republic of Ireland. Tel: (00 353) 088 584711

Hot seawater, seaweed and steam health baths: Kilcullen's Bath House, Enniscrone, County Sligo, Republic of Ireland. Tel: (00 353) 096 36238

Off Road Driving, Castle Leslie, Glaslough, County Monaghan, Republic of Ireland. Tel: (00 353) 047 88364

STATIONERY

East Coast Design. Tel: 0192 251 5432
Golden suns, moons and stars.

Adrienne Kerr. Tel: 0131 332 5393
Has range of designs including eighteenth-century oval painted card and Charles Mackintosh-inspired cards. Also accepts one-off commissions.

Oliver Collection. Tel: 01209 612 318
Celtic and medieval designs.

One & Only, 10 Barley Mow Passage, Chiswick, London W4 4PH. Tel: 0181 994 6477
Bespoke albums and stationery.

What's In a Name, St Julians, Sevenoaks, Kent TN15 0RX. Tel: 01732 743501
Personalized wedding invitations including bottle labels

Sam Toft. Tel: 01273 694614
Personalized illustrations on cards.

TATTOOS

Self-adhesive tattoos can be purchased direct from Body Art Limited, Unit 11, Summit Centre, Summit Road, Potters Bar, Herts. EN6 3QW. Tel: 0707 665015. Fax: 0707 660200.

The Laser Clinic removes tattoos using laser treatment and has bases in Birmingham, Bristol, London, Manchester, Southampton and Stoke-on-Trent. For information ring 0800 227777.

TRANSPORT

Bells and Two Tones, Sandpits Bungalow, High Street, Shirrell Heath, Hants. SO32 2JN. Tel: 01329 834 234
Hires out open-top fire engines and vintage police cars (mainly in the South-East).

American Classic Hire Company, 358 Harlington Road, Hillingdon, London UB8 3HF. Tel: 01895 421962
Includes 1950s convertibles (Cadillacs, Chevrolets, and Lincolns – including one formerly owned by Roy Orbison)

Carriages Vehicle Agency, 147 Nork Way, Banstead, Surrey SM7 1HR. Tel: 01737 353926
Includes Chitty Chitty Bang Bang, the Batmobile from the original series, the Yellow Rolls-Royce from *Darling Buds of May*.

Cambridge Omnibus and Carriage Hire, 28 St Audreys Close, Histon, Cambs. CB4 4JX. Tel: 01223 237395. Fax: 01223 561789
Old-style bus

Chalfont Carriage Company, Model Farm, Gorelands Lane, Chalfont St Giles, Bucks. Tel: 0494 872304/873929
Range of horse-drawn broughams, omnibuses, landaus and other carriages

Virgin Balloon Flights Ltd, 17 Linhope Street, London NW1 6HT. Tel: 0171 706 1021. Fax: 0171 224 8353

CB Helicopters, Building 447, Biggin Hill Airport, Biggin Hill, Kent TN16 3BN. Tel: 01959 540633

UNDERWEAR

Agent Provocateur, 6 Broadwick Street, London W1Z 1FH. Tel: 0171 439 0229
Stocks original 1950s basques.

Rigby and Peller, 2 Hans Road, London SW3 1RX. Tel: 0171 589 9293

Garters

Barry and Guion, Bridalwear Specialists (Department JG1), 4 Bingle Bank, Bardsey, Leeds, West Yorkshire LS17 9DW

Large and small

Berlei (smaller sizes) available in all major stores

Bust Stop, 31–33 Park Road, Teddington, London TW11 OAB. Tel: 0181 943 9733 for mail order
Lingerie and swimwear for the big-busted.

A to B, 35 Manor Road, Teddington, London TW11 8AA. Tel: 0181 943 9733
For smaller cup sizes.

WEDDING ORGANIZERS

Linda Magistris. Tel: 0171 373 9289

Private Function. Tel: 01235 533684

Garlands, Linda Thurlow, (specialist in non-religious weddings), 10 Allenby Road, Maidenhead, Berks. SL6 5BB. Tel: 01628 26852

Utopia (Lisa Clarke). Tel: 0181 870 6607/0378 147627

INDEX

ACKNOWLEDGEMENTS

I would like to thank the following people for their help in the course of preparing this book:

Phyllis Annesley; Lionel Benjamin, Banqueting Manager, Langham Hilton; John Bentley; Kavita Bhasin and family; Sally Blackwell; Jeffrey Blumenfeld, Director, Jewish Marriage Council; The Body Shop; Clare and Sandy Burnett; Chris Butterworth; Monika Buttling-Smith; Dickins and Jones; Sarah Elliott; Family Planning Association; Society of Florists; Kevin Freeman, Diva Bridalwear; Ian Gee, Partner, The Guild of Wedding Photographers UK; Penny Gee; Sally Goldsby, World Gold Council; Missie Graves and Tatters; Andrew and Donna Hay; Paul Horrell; Kodak; Linda MacDonald, Dressmaking and Promotions Co-ordinator, Butterick Company Limited; Majestic Wine Warehouses; Ann-Janine Murtagh; Muslim Education Trust; Northern Ireland Tourist Office; Office for National Statistics (Press Office); Alison Ottaway, Alfred Bull & Co. Ltd.; Alan Pfaff, General Manager, Moss Bros, Covent Garden; Bridie Pritchard; Gemma Reay; Republic of Ireland Tourist Office; Zoë Rowe; Mrs Penelope Ruddock, Curator, Museum of Costume, Bath; Vidal Sassoon; Scottish Tourist Office; Richard Scrivener; Maryon Stewart and the Women's Nutritional Advisory Service; Joanna Styles; Victoria Wine; Caroline Waldegrave and Puff Fairclough of Leith's School of Food and Wine.